The Challenge of Organizing and Implementing Corporate Social Responsibility

The Challenge of Organizing and Implementing Corporate Social Responsibility

Edited by

Jan Jonker

and

Marco de Witte

First published 2006 by
PALGRAVE MACMILLAN
Houndmills, Basingstoke, Hampshire RG21 6XS and
175 Fifth Avenue, New York, N.Y. 10010
Companies and representatives throughout the world

PALGRAVE MACMILLAN is the global academic imprint of the Palgrave
Macmillan division of St. Martin's Press, LLC and of Palgrave Macmillan Ltd.
Macmillan® is a registered trademark in the United States, United Kingdom
and other countries. Palgrave is a registered trademark in the European
Union and other countries.

ISBN-13: 978–1–4039–4238–8
ISBN-10: 1–4039–4238–2

This book is printed on paper suitable for recycling and made from fully
managed and sustained forest sources.

A catalogue record for this book is available from the British Library.

Library of Congress Cataloging-in-Publication Data
    The challenge of organizing and implementing corporate social
responsibility / edited by Jan Jonker and Marco de Witte.
        p. cm.
    Includes bibliographical references and index.
    ISBN 1–4039–4238–2 (cloth)
        1. Social responsibility of business. 2. Industrial management – Moral and
    ethical aspects. I. Jonker, J. (Jan) II. Witte, Marinus Cornelis de, 1959–
HD60.C442 2006
658.4′08—dc22   2005056615

10 9 8 7 6 5 4 3 2 1
15 14 13 12 11 10 09 08 07 06

Printed and bound in Great Britain by
Antony Rowe Ltd, Chippenham and Eastbourne

Contents

List of Figures and Tables

Figures

Tables

Notes on the Contributors

Subhabrata Bobby Banerjee is Professor of Strategic Management and Director of Research at the International Graduate School of Business, University of South Australia, Adelaide. He has taught at the University of Massachusetts, where he received his PhD, at the University of Wollongong, where he headed the doctoral programme, and at RMIT University, where he was Director of the Doctor of Business Administration programme. His research interests are sustainable development, corporate environmentalism, globalization, postcolonial theories and indigenous ecology. His work has appeared in numerous international journals.

Robert Beckett is a researcher specializing in the communication of ethics and the ethics of communication. He was awarded an MBA by the University of Portsmouth Business School in 1997. Since 2000 he has been a director of the commercial partner to the Institute of Communication Ethics, and in 2001 he became a member of the Institute. Prior to that he worked in the field of UK corporate social responsibility and the international advertising, marketing and design industries.

David Birch has been Professor of Communication and Director of the Corporate Citizenship Research Unit, Deakin University, Melbourne, since 1997. He is General Editor of *The Journal of Corporate Citizenship* and is on the editorial boards of several International journals. He has been involved in research partnerships with leading organizations in Australia. He is a member of the board of the Australian Corporate Citizenship Alliance and Ability Australia Foundation, and a founding member of the Australian Corporate Citizenship Alliance and the newly reformed Social and Ethical Auditing Institute. He has published widely in the fields of communication, media, cultural studies, corporate citizenship, corporate social responsibility, governance and accountability.

Theo de Bruijn holds a Master's degree in technology and society from the Technical University Eindhoven and a PhD in public administration from the University of Twente. He joined the Center for Clean Technology and Environmental Policy (CSTM) in 1989 and specialized in the governance of industrial transformation. He currently coordinates research in this field, as well as publishing and teaching on the interaction between public authorities and industry in environmental affairs, and teaching environmental management in undergraduate and postgraduate courses. He is also the European coordinator of the Greening of Industry Network, a global network for the transition towards sustainable industry.

Jacqueline Cramer worked as an associate professor at the University of Amsterdam in 1976–89 and as a senior researcher at the Centre 'Strategy, Technology and Policy' of TNO in 1989–99. She is currently Director of Cramer Environmental Consultancy and works as a part-time professor of environmental management at the University of Utrecht. She is a member of various national and international advisory boards of governmental, industrial and non-profit organizations.

Robert-Paul Doove has worked as a junior researcher at the Nijmegen School of Management, Radboud University of Nijmegen, and since July 2003 he has been on the team of the 'Silent Leaders' project, which forms part of the Dutch national research programme on CSR. His Master's thesis was on strategic corporate responsibility at multinational business enterprises and in the near future he hopes to start a PhD research project on strategic CSR.

Olaf Fisscher has been at the University of Twente since 1989 and is currently Professor of Organization Studies and Business Ethics and Chair of the Department of Technology and Organization at the School of Business, Public Administration and Technology. He holds a Master's degree in industrial engineering management and obtained his PhD in social sciences at the University of Groningen in 1986. His research focuses on organizing for innovation and organizing for corporate social responsibility. He teaches innovation management, business ethics and quality management and is the coordinator of the Master's innovation management programme.

David Foster works in the Faculty of Business at the University of the Sunshine Coast. Over the last few years he has developed a strong research interest in the nature of management quality in general and stakeholder relationships in particular. He has recently completed his PhD, which focused on the involvement of stakeholders in protected area management in Victoria, Australia. He has held the position of Head of Department of Hospitality, Tourism and Leisure at RMIT University and of Leisure Studies at Phillip Institute.

Math Göbbels is a quality manager and consultant at Biblioservice Gelderland in the Netherlands, a non-profit organization that provides library services to public libraries. He is currently preparing his doctoral dissertation at the School of Management, Radboud University, Nijmegen. His research focuses on the hidden and neglected assumptions that underlie the debate on CSR standards. He has worked as a researcher at Nyenrode University and as a senior consultant in the field of quality management, business excellence and auditing.

André Habisch is Professor of Social Ethics at the Catholic University of Eichstaett-Ingolstadt and Director of the Center for Corporate Citizenship. He is also Visiting Professor at the International Centre for Corporate Social

Responsibility, Nottingham University Business School, and a member of the editorial board of the *Journal for Corporate Citizenship*. He was a member of the German parliamentary commission on the 'Future of Voluntary Engagement' in 1999–2002. He has published widely on social capital, corporate social responsibility, network of civic engagement, local family policy initiatives and cross-sectoral cooperation between business and non-profit organizations.

Angela van der Heijden works as a junior researcher at the University of Utrecht. Her Master's thesis was on the institutional and social context in which corporate foundations donate to charitable causes in Europe and the United States. After her graduation she worked at the Netherlands Architecture Institute. Her current research focuses on the implementation of corporate social responsibility in companies and business chains.

Malcolm Higgs is Director of the School of Leadership, Change and HR and Director of Research at Henley Management College in the UK. Prior to moving to Henley to take up the position of Academic Dean he was a principal partner in Towers Perrin's human resource management practice. This followed eight years' consulting experience with the Hay Group and Arthur Young. He has published widely on the topic of emotional intelligence. He is a member of the British Psychological Society, a Chartered Occupational Psychologist and Chairman of the consulting firm RFLC.

Jan Jonker works at the School of Management, Radboud University, Nijmegen, and has run his own consultancy practice for more than 15 years. His research interest is management and corporate social responsibility, particularly in relation to the development of business strategies. He holds an MSc from Leiden University and a PhD from Nijmegen University. He is the author and coauthor of eight books and has published over a hundred articles. He gives public lectures and presentations in various countries and is a visiting professor in England and France.

Edgar Karssing is a senior trainer and researcher at the Institute for Responsible Business, University of Nyenrode, where he has worked since January 1995. He has participated in several research projects and published extensively on integrity, the management of integrity, moral competence and philosophy. He is currently preparing his PhD thesis on integrity in theory and practice.

Myriam Laberge is a Director of the Collaborative Learning and Innovation Group at Simon Fraser University, Vancouver. As a principal at CoreRelation Consulting Inc. she brings her experience of whole system transformation to the design of multistakeholder conferences and engagement processes. Over the past decade she has helped various private and public sector organizations to build effective networks.

Jeremy Moon is Professor and Director of the International Centre for Corporate Social Responsibility and a Deputy Director of Nottingham University Business School. He has held visiting positions at the European University Institute in Florence, Churchill College at Cambridge University, the Institute for Advanced Studies in Princeton, and the University of Manchester. His research includes the relationship between CSR and public policy and government regulation, CSR in business education and comparative CSR. He is currently cowriting a book on corporations and citizenship and has published many articles in journals.

André Nijhof is an Assistant Professor at the faculty of Business, Public Administration and Technology, University of Twente. The central topic of his research is the interconnectedness between the moral reasoning of individuals and group dynamics and structural conditions in the institutional context. He is involved in several research projects on the development of strategies for corporate social responsibility, especially in the construction, insurance and health care sectors. He has published extensively in both Dutch and international journals.

Marcel Postema has worked as a junior researcher at the Nijmegen School of Management, University of Nijmegen, and as a researcher on the 'Silent Leaders' project, which is part of the Dutch national research programme on CSR. His MA thesis was on strategic corporate responsibility in multinational business enterprises and he is now planning to start a PhD research project on strategic CSR.

Nigel Roome holds the chair in sustainable enterprise and transformation at Erasmus University, Rotterdam and is head of the Erasmus Centre for Studies in Sustainable Development and Management. He previously held academic positions in the UK and chairs in the Netherlands and Canada, and has acted as an academic supervisor. He is coinitiator of the project 'Dutch corporate social responsibility and its European context'.

Michiel Schoemaker is a researcher and consultant. His consulting activities focus on talent management, organizational change and organizational identity. He obtained his PhD in business administration from the University of Nijmegen in 1998. Since 2003 he has been a Professor at the Nijmegen School of Management. His main research interests are new forms of contractual (labour) relations and organizational reanewal. He also teaches organizational theory, organizational behaviour, organizational change and human resource management.

Ann Svendsen is Executive Director of the Collaborative Learning and Innovation Group and an Adjunct Professor at the Centre for Sustainable Community Development, Simon Fraser University, Vancouver. She is also a principal of CoreRelation Consulting Inc., a firm specializing in stakeholder engagement. She is the author of *The Stakeholder Strategy* (1998) and advises companies and government agencies worldwide on stakeholder engagement.

Marco de Witte (1959) is an Associate Professor at the Faculty of Management and Organisation, University of Groningen, The Netherlands and a partner at HGRV Consultants and Managers. In lectures, research and consultancy projects he focuses on the alignment of strategic business positioning, organizational development and the implementation of change.

1

Introduction

Jan Jonker and Marco de Witte[1]

Introduction

The way in which business organizations operate in contemporary society
has become an established field of investigation. There is a growing yet
'fuzzy' societal, organizational and political movement that is often referred
to as corporate social responsibility (CSR). This often emerges at the boundary of the business organization and is expressed in changing relations with
stakeholders and society at large, leading to an array of new activities that
range from philanthropy to debates on social capital and cohesion in
business–community partnerships in, for example, less-developed countries.
The picture emerging from this diversity is rich but rather confusing. At a
fundamental level CSR appears to be a complex and multidimensional organizational phenomenon. The essence is re-evaluating and recalibrating the
relationship between the organization and its wider context. In this respect
CSR can be defined as the extent to which and the way in which an organization is consciously responsible for and accounts for its action and non-
action(s) and the impact of these on its stakeholders.

The ongoing debate indicates that the classic business paradigm is in need
of revision. We consider that the present CSR movement is a first-generation
attempt to discuss and redefine the role and position of business organizations in contemporary society. The core issue is how to organize systematic
and transparent interactions with a growing number of stakeholders and the
issues they represent, but how these concerns can be embedded appropri-
ately in the organization remains unclear. Understanding what it implies to
(re)organize in order systematically to take into account this wider context
and its constituencies is the focus of this volume. We view the contemporary
business organization as operating in a complex context in which a growing
number of stakeholders and issues influence its policies, practices, products
and services, leading to a number of organizational challenges that are not
always recognizable or solvable by means of established business paradigms
and concepts. What seems to be required is a better understanding of the

strategic, tactical and operational translation of CSR into the core of the organization. That is what the term social responsibility refers to. It is hoped that the results of our exploration will prove valuable in terms of the knowledge and experience required to explore and further develop the business case for CSR.

What is a business organization?

The central argument in the CSR debate is that business organizations ought to play a more prominent role in society, given their dominant economic position. There is substance to this argument in that over the past decades – if not from early in the twentieth century – businesses have become the world's dominant economic entities. This has led to a fundamental shift in power between businesses, governments and civil society. Businesses are viewed as the master creation of modern society, a vehicle for human society to gain a creative power hitherto unimagined.

There is little value in discussing the role of business without a clear understanding of the nature of the business organization, and identification of the business aim is crucial to understanding what CSR is all about. Investigating its purpose allows identification of the characteristics that differentiate it from other forms of organized activity.

The business organization is a limited and specific form of deliberately and functionally organized human activity. Its purpose is to make profits by selling goods or services. The requirement to earn a profit is the defining characteristic of the business organization, compared with other forms of organized human activity. In the process of making a profit it has to consider its relationships with a variety of parties, a number of which have a stake in the business and in whose interests the business in turn has a stake.

However, does the business have a duty to society to do more than just make profits? Does the need to be sensitive to the needs of people and the environment, to be a good corporate citizen, mean that it is now part of the aim and strategy of a business to focus more attention on the requirements of its employees, customers, the environment and the local community? According to the classical business paradigm the short answer is 'no'. The business organization exists to provide goods or services in order to make profits. This does not imply that other forms of organization are inferior or do not have the right to exist. It simply means that if a business is not making profits its reason for being is violated. So the question remains of how the process of profit making is organized. How are stakeholders and external issues taken into account? How are relationships between the organization and its wider societal, ecological and political context shaped? Or to put it another way, what is the nature and impact of the interdependency between an organization and its context? Could it be that addressing these issues is what CSR is all about?

Setting the stage for transition

A business organization is by definition configured around three elements: (1) the assessment of environmental developments of actors and factors and the choices that are based on this assessment, (2) a defined business position and (3) appropriate organizational design and development. It is the unique configuration of these elements that lead to a recognizable business proposition. However the business world is changing and conceptions about the business organization and its environment are in turmoil. It is accepted that a business operates in a network of stakeholders who directly or indirectly influence the operations of the business. Traditionally suppliers, shareholders, employees, government organizations and customers are distinguished in that respect. But in the global business environment new stakeholders are entering the scene, including local communities, non-governmental organizations (NGOs), multinational NGOs, social movements and so on. All these stakeholders – old and new – have the right to speak and be heard, to address businesses on legitimate grounds. They are addressing an growing number of new issues, ranging from the use of raw materials to human rights, from investment in the local community to the provenance of consumer goods, from the use of child labour to genetically modified ingredients. Businesses have to make appropriate responses to these issues, either mandatorily or voluntarily, and their answers must be defendable and transparent. These issues can be translated into five managerial Rs: risk, reputation, regulation, responsibility and results, which are reinforced by the media and information and communication technology (ICT). Taken together they put pressure on businesses to act. The question is whether the latter possess the perception (in terms of vision, values and strategies), capability (in terms of competences and skills) and systems (in terms of structure, information and processes) to respond properly. If not, what kind of organizational design would be appropriate for developing these capabilities and systems and how can a sense of awareness be fostered?

Contemporary organizational theory

There are many images of organizations and all are right in their own way. Here we view the organization as a nexus of contracts. The organization seeks to explore and invest in strategic organizational behaviour vis-à-vis stakeholders in order to stay in business. This leads to dynamic relations, partnerships and commitments. The key is to balance and satisfy the needs and expectations of stakeholders in order to make a profit. Managers can therefore be seen as interest balancers. Accordingly a business is perceived as:

- An open, living, deliberately constructed social entity, aiming for profit.
- Capable of identifying its stakeholders and their needs and expectations.

- Competent to address those needs and expectations through strategic processes.
- Able to adopt an appropriate organizational (local) theory and concepts to respond to needs and expectations.
- Able to organize through its culture, structures, information and employees the satisfaction of those needs and expectations.
- Capable of developing appropriate values, competences and skills.
- Capable of establishing effective methods of communicating its choices and organizational processes in respect of actions taken or planned, given that needs and expectations change and conflict.

At the bottom line are the stakeholders. Combined with the four Rs and supported by the media and ICT they have the potential to be a considerable driving force. They can force businesses to rethink and redefine their social and environmental responsibilities without losing sight of their primary economic responsibilities. They can also bring into question the strategies and practices, that lead to the business proposition. In this regard one could view CSR as a business strategy, providing direction and creating and maintaining relationships and structures that enhance performance and continuity. Reorganizing the balance between external and internal drivers in the light of needs and expectations is most probably the most fundamental challenge of CSR.

Although the CSR debate has been promising so far, it still tends to be more about semantics than substance. One could argue that CSR is still in its infancy and that at present we are merely witnessing behaviour that is consistent with a growing awareness of CSR during the process of agenda-setting. Clearly there are calls for operational translation, often referred to as 'developing the business case for CSR'. This implies the translation of general ideas into appropriate business strategies that fit specific businesses in a particular context since the current ones do not adequately address the complex issues at hand. What also seems to be missing is a real theoretical underpinning for the CSR movement. If we add to this the accepted practice of using technical solutions for most organizational problems the picture is rather gloomy. As long as businesses do not perceive CSR as an essential factor in business continuity it will remain a mixture of semantics, avoidance, compliance and social philanthropy, or it might be abandoned. Moreover, given the dominant economic position of businesses in contemporary society the eventual scenario might be even worse.

Business–society discourses

The aim of this book is to provide a better understanding of the changing role of business organizations in a society in transition. The premise is that the drivers of change should be sought within businesses and harnessed to implementation strategies. But, if the primary responsibility of businesses is to make a profit, where does social responsibility come into it? The CSR literature is unclear about the rationale for claiming that businesses have a social responsibility. Since so many issues are affected by business operations, how can businesses differentiate between which are important and which are not? There is a real danger of overloading businesses with expectations they can never meet. In our view responsibility relates to balancing business goals and strategies with the diverse and sometimes conflicting interest of stakeholders. Handling this in an accountable manner is a clear component of the changing role of business.

When trying to understand this changing role we are confronted with three prominent discourses: the economic discourse, the ecological discourse and the social discourse. We shall briefly outline each of these below.

The economic discourse

Obviously we in the Western world live in a capitalist, market-oriented economy, and we have done so for more than two centuries. The origins of this lie in the transformation of commodities (raw materials) into products. The result is an economy based on a one-dimensional interpretation of the word 'profit'. Despite the creation of wealth and wellbeing for some, many others have been excluded. Today we are in the midst of a transition towards an economy based on intangibles, while the transformation of commodities is almost entirely outsourced to countries where labour is still cheap. More and more people and organizations are expressing fundamental doubts. From antiglobalists to Friends of the Earth, each and every one is voicing harsh criticism of the system of which they are a part. At the same time we are witnessing the rise of new economies such as India and China. Despite solemn promises of Europe becoming the most competitive region in the world the plans have yet to leave the drawing board. One could say that we are prisoners of our own creation and have no real alternative, that we are facing a kind of socioeconomic prisoner's dilemma that could eventually lead to a redistribution of commodities, power and access.

The ecological discourse

In the quest for wellbeing the destruction of natural resources was more or less ignored until the 1960s and the publication of the now famous Rome Report when it became evident that mankind was having a devastating impact on the natural environment. More than 40 years later little has changed and we are consuming natural resources at an unprecedented rate. In the United States, it takes 12.2 acres to supply the average person's basic needs; in the Netherlands it is 8.0 acres and in India it is 1.0. The Dutch ecological footprint covers 15 times the area of the Netherlands. India's footprint exceeds its area by only about 35 per cent. Most strikingly, if the entire world lived like the citizens of North America it would take an area three times that of the Earth to support the world's present population. An avalanche of mandatory and voluntary regulations and technological measures have been introduced to curb the abuse of natural resources and the adverse effects of human activities. Notwithstanding all these measures, the ecological impact of organized activity will lead to irreplaceable destruction and generate in turn unprecedented natural, social and economic transformations.

The social discourse

The final discourse is to do with the tissue of society, its institutional fabric. In the past decades the influence of traditional institutions such as churches and school, has considerably weakened and the power of the state has eroded. National governments are losing ground to supranational groupings such as the EU, and as a consequence people no longer quite know where they belong and have become footloose in terms of location and norms. Who is setting the standards and who is safeguarding them? In this social and political vacuum debates on right and wrong, rules and regulations, standards and acceptable deviations from them, and issues that should or should not be addressed are increasingly being held in multi-interest arenas where the participants include representatives of business networks, multinational NGOs and transnational governmental bodies.

One could say that CSR is about satisfying the needs and expectations of all stakeholders in the various discourses, but that is not a simple task. Stakeholders in the various forums have different goals that may not be reconcilable. How can one balance the requirement for a corporate dividend against the interests of a community that is producing green beans in a country far away? If CSR is about creating value for all parties involved, this implies that the interests of economic, ecological and social stakeholders are assessed and balanced against each other, but how can this be done and what is the common denominator under which they can be expressed?

In the act of balancing these interests certain dilemmas tend to shape the rules of the game, such as short term versus long term, close by versus far away, us versus the others, tangible versus intangible, profit versus what? It goes without saying that the economic (market) paradigm predominantly influences choices in the short term, and therefore economic interests take precedence over social or ecological ones. Yet the ultimate promise of the three discourses is eventually to find balance. CSR is an attempt to address these issues through the business organization.

Concepts of CSR

Businesses combine these discourses with CSR in various ways, including the following.

First, semantics and window-dressing are often combined with a modern variation of social philanthropy. The central mantra is 'We are doing good by doing well'. Examples are 'The Shell Price of Sustainable Innovation', and the purchase of Christmas gift packages from less developed countries and products from Max Havelaar. Research shows that a majority of businesses have recently learned to adapt their business language to the vocabulary of CSR, and social philanthropy has always existed. Although there is nothing wrong with all this it does not really go to the heart of CSR.

Second, CSR is treated as an act of compliance, of conforming to rules and regulations and doing what the law requires you to do. However the growing number of corporate scandals makes it clear that complying with the law is not always taken seriously.

Third, CSR entails paying simultaneous attention to the three Ps (people, planet, profit). Many businesses claim to have been doing this for years, albeit not under the heading of CSR. Now they are telling the world about it, and as a result annual reports are replete with information on social and environmental activities. CSR in this respect is all about good housekeeping or stewardship. A crucial question here is, who is dictating the terms and setting the targets for the actions of businesses? Do multinational corporations apply the norms, standards and values of their country of origin, or are they acting just above the compliances level in the countries in which they operate? If they are paying wages 5 per cent above the average, are they doing well in terms of CSR? It is obvious that a strong normative element is entering the discourse here.

Fourth, CSR is treated as a clear-cut business proposition, with businesses building competitive advantage within their supply chain and markets. This approach especially applies to environmentally aware businesses (one could also call them value-led businesses) such as the Body Shop, Max Havelaar, Triodos Bank, Ben & Jerry and Ecostyle. However these are often just niche players in their sector.

Moreover, CSR is integrated into the day-to-day business strategy as an integrated part of everything the business undertakes. With this approach CSR is not a separate problem the business has to take care of but an element of its frame of reference and its strategic, operational and tactical decisions. Two aspects of this approach are noteworthy. First, new stakeholders and new issues are taken into account. What do they mean for our business? What do they imply in terms of the design of our primary processes, our culturally driven behavioural patterns, the competences of our employees and our technical systems? Second, thinking is in terms of partnership with numerous stakeholders, not just business partners but also local and national governments, NGOs and others.

As a final note we shall provide one example of today's business reality with regard to CSR. In the Netherlands there are roughly 470000 companies, of which roughly 500 are multinationals. When one takes a close look at what they are actually doing in the field of CSR, only 50 to 100 are handling CSR in line with the fourth and fifth approaches described above.

Organizing and implementing CSR

Given the various perspectives on CSR it is not surprising that an agreed-upon core definition has yet to be found. Perhaps this is due to the fact that the present debate on CSR was only launched during the last decade. Or perhaps it is due to the fact that it is only now becoming clear what issues are at stake. We suggest a third reason. In our view CSR lacks a theoretical foundation, one that addresses organizational issues in terms of structure, strategy, culture and so on. We therefore dedicate this section to theoretical ideas for exploring CSR as an integrated part of the business strategy.

The aim of CSR is to aid the continuity of the business in terms of results, reputation, network participation and the reduction of risks. This has to be translated into strategies, primary processes, employee behaviour and the development of suitable competences. Until now businesses have primarily drawn on the paradigm developed in the industrial age. The present political, social and organizational situation indicates that a re-examination of this paradigm is necessary.

CSR requires a revaluation and reconfiguration of the relationship between the business and its broader social context. Three fundamental questions need to be addressed:

- What organizational concepts are appropriate for CSR?
- How is the interface between the organization and its context organized?
- What are the fundamental principles and practices used to organize partnerships between business and constituencies of stakeholders?

These questions imply that CSR entails a process of sense making and needs to be better understood before it can contribute to the development of a contemporary theory of the firm in a shifting social context. Addressing these questions will advance our understanding of how to organize CSR in a manner that bridges the gap between emerging practices and current organizational theory.

Theories of the firm in the industrial age placed emphasis on functional design and instrumental practices. In contrast a theoretical approach is needed to investigate the institutionalization of CSR within business as a deliberate construction. In this view three forms of rationality inform choices: functional, substantive and communicative. Functional rationality concerns the differentiation of acts, roles and processes. Substantive rationality refers to the values, norms and identity of the business. Communicative rationality refers to the use of linguistic acts to bring about mutual understanding. This theoretical approach focuses on balancing substantive and functional rationality as guided by acts of communication. It also addresses the core values of the business and the way in which these shape the behaviour of its individual members. These combined theories offer a means of understanding the ways in which businesses and stakeholders interact and make sense of their interactions, with all their complexity and diversity. We therefore introduce a perspective on organizations which view these as a network. This provides a new perspective in order to conduct a more substantive debate on how to institutionalize CSR, to foster its implications for transforming the mental maps that guide organizational decision-making processes and also to elaborate on the underlying change processes that such a perspective entails. Reflecting on these issues and elaborating them in theoretical and practical ways is the task of the chapters to come.

The aim and structure of the book

The current CSR debates need to be deepened in both theoretical and practical terms. The aim of this book is to capture and distil emerging perspectives on CSR and its implementation. This requires consideration of the role and position of organizations and organizational networks in society, their responsibilities, what they should be accountable for, and the way in which they could contribute to the creation of various sorts of capital. In the end this also entails a debate about a paradigm-shift regarding the social and economic tissue of our contemporary society, which does not fall into the scope of this volume. We will describe the changes and consequences of adapting a CSR strategy, both in general terms and in particular business and organizational contexts. It is hoped that this will provide people in the corporate community with building blocks to develop their own implementation strategies. Our principal purpose is to help managers, students, researchers, governments, NGOs and consultants to understand the principles, issues and concepts surrounding CSR and its implementation.

The contributors to this book come from various disciplines and countries around the world, but all are deeply involved with the subject of CSR. As such the book is truly interdisciplinary and truly international.

The book is divided into three parts. Part I considers the evolution of society and business and set the stage for the chapters that follow. Part II focuses on the organization of CSR. It addresses new approaches to stakeholder interaction and the development of competences, networks and standards for CSR. Part III focuses on the actual implementation of CSR. It comprises a mixture of case studies and empirical and applied theoretical research.

Note

1. We have chosen not to use references in this introduction as the ideas expressed and the examples provided are entirely our own. However, we do lean on the work of others. We express our gratitude to Kevin Foley (UTS, Sydney), David Foster (RMIT, Melbourne) and our inspiring colleagues in the Dutch National Research Network on CSR. This network has been made possible by the Ministry of Economic Affairs in the Netherlands.

Part I

CSR in its Context

2
The CSR Landscape: An Overview of Key Theoretical Issues and Concepts

David Birch and Jan Jonker

Introduction

This chapter considers some of the scholarly works and thinkers who have been influential in corporate social responsibility (CSR) debate during the past 50 years or so. It offers an academic narrative of the key social, economic and political concepts and themes from the very diverse and not always coherent discussion on corporate social responsibility. It does not provide a chronological history, but brings together fundamental thoughts in the field of CSR that have considerable resonance for contemporary business practice. Our central proposition is that fundamental change is a prerequisite for the advancement of corporate social responsibility; change that touches at the heart of the established social and economic paradigms.

Capitalism

Thurow wrote nearly 40 years ago that 'Paradoxically, at precisely the time when capitalism finds itself with no social competitors – its former competitors, socialism or communism, having died – it will have to undergo a profound metamorphosis' (Thurow, 1966, p. 326; cf. Harris, 1997). We are hearing increased calls for that metamorphosis now, as more and more people, individuals and groups are calling upon capitalism to be environmentally and socially responsible, to be accountable and transparent, to be inclusive, to be ethical and stable, to be more equitable – to be sustainable. These have been some of the key issues in corporate social responsibility discussions since they began to develop in the 1940s. Thurow recognized that the problems intrinsic to capitalism, such as inequality and instability, had to be faced in order to transform capitalism, as the problems of inequality and instability would continue to 'flow from capitalism's growing dependence upon human capital and man made brain power industries (ibid., p. 325; cf. Zohar, 1997; Hawken *et al.*, 1999). His solution was for capitalism to shift from 'a consumption ideology to a builder's ideology' (ibid., p. 315; see also Halal, 1986). A significant part of building that ideology would be to widen the definition of capitalism from the mere economic to include social and environmental factors in order to bring about what we now call a sustainable society. Put in business terms, it is necessary to move beyond concentration on a single, economic bottom line to encompass multiple bottom lines, including in particular the social and the environmental – what is now often called 'the triple bottom line'.

Elkington (1997) develops the concept of the triple bottom line in terms of economic prosperity, environmental quality and social justice, arguing that the key to establishing the triple bottom line is stakeholder consultation. The reason for doing so is to secure a sustainable future. Sustainable capitalism, to use Elkington's term, therefore requires cultural change in places where influential shareholders are 'so distant, so diversified, and so amorphous that none of them can get any enjoyment out of creating or building. They only see dividends' (Thurow, 1966, p. 315). As a result capitalism 'is going to be asked to do what it does least well – invest in the distant future and make deliberate adjustments in its institutional structure to encourage individuals, firms, and governments to make long term decisions (ibid., p. 309; see also Chomsky, 1999). Investment in the long-term future and in building a sustainable society as part of it – not just a sustainable business in economic terms – has been at the heart of the diverse CSR debates over the last 50 years or so. Hence they have been concerned not only with the survival of capitalism but also with the creation of sustainable capitalism, which is in every business person's interest as well as in every citizen's interest in every society. As Thurow makes clear, 'If capitalism is to work in the long run, it must make investments that are not in any particular individual's immediate self interest but are in the human communities' long run self interest' (ibid., p. 308; see also Piore, 1995). He then asks, 'How can capitalism promote the values that it needs to sustain itself when it denies that it needs to promote any particular set of values at all? Put simply, who represents the interests of the future to the present?' (ibid.; see also Agle and Caldwell, 1999).

Some would still deny a shaping – if not activist – social role for business and the responsibilities that go with it (for example Henderson, 2001; cf. Levitt, 1958; Kennedy, 2000). Business, they would argue, has nothing or very little to do with the social system. However this is not the view of a steadily growing, more highly educated and better globally informed set of people. Unlike the single-issue interest groups of the 1970s, who turned the world's attention to the environment, race, women's issues, disability and sexuality, many of these people are now working in business and not against business. Therefore the lesson for business is that these demands are increasingly coming from within and not from outside, as was the case in the 1970s.

Without actually using the term 'sustainability', one of the key points put forward by Collins and Porras (1994, p. 4) is that a visionary company depends 'on a timeless set of core values and an enduring purpose beyond just making money'. This is an important principle in the corporate social responsibility debate and for companies seeking to make sustainability their 'enduring purpose'. They must 'change in response to a changing world, while simultaneously preserving [their] core values and purpose'. They need 'mechanisms of forward progress, experimentation and entrepreneurship, or continuous self improvement' and should 'create consistent alignment to preserve [their] core values and purpose and stimulate progress'. Above all they require 'resiliency' and an 'ability to bounce back from adversity' (ibid., p. 4; see also Chamberlain, 1972; Cavanagh, 1984; Wood, 1991; Zadek and Tuppen, 2000).

Galbraith argued in 1972 'that there is a deeply embedded view in ... society which maintains that a modern corporation should be free from all interference and is thought to be kept honest by competition, with the market, not the state, as the ultimate regulatory force'. This disguises, he says, the public character of a corporation, and the term 'private enterprise' has led to the view that corporations has 'private affairs that should be protected from public scrutiny'. Instead corporations have 'no natural right to be left alone' (quoted in Steiner and Steiner, 1977, p. 533). This last comment became a central tenet of the corporate social responsibility debate in the 1970s. According to one leading sociologist, 'to think of the business corporation simply as an economic instrument is to fail totally to understand the meaning of the social changes of the last half century' (Bell, quoted in Beesley and Evans, 1978, p. 16). Almost 30 years later many people are saying similar things (see Birch and Glazebrook, 1998; Zadek, 2001b).

Drucker had already said much of this many years earlier. According to him, management has 'become a major leadership group in industrial society and as such have great responsibilities to their own profession, to the enterprise and to the people they manage, and to their economy and society' (Drucker, 1946, p. 247; see also Goyder, 1961; Galbraith, 1968, 1973; Denuyl, 1984). This is now central to the CSR debate (see Zadek *et al.*, 2001; Birch, 2002; WEF, 2002; WBCSD, 2002). Using the term 'industrial citizenship', Drucker argued in 1946 that the major challenge for business was not mechanical or technical but social, because 'the worker has not enough relation to his [*sic*] work to find satisfaction in it. There is no meaning in his work, only a pay cheque. The worker in his work does not obtain the satisfaction of citizenship because he does not have citizenship. For as very old wisdom has it, a man who works only for a living and not for the sake of the work and its meaning, is not and cannot be a citizen' (Drucker, 1946, p. 135; see also Senge, 1994; Casey, 1995; de Geus, 1997; Goyder, 1998). The challenge of course, as it has been for the last 60 years, is to address these concerns in such a way that the underlying economic paradigm actually does shift.

Citizenship

The notion of citizenship is vitally important and has resonances in the various CSR discussions, foregrounding the need to broaden responsibilities to everyone involved in an organization, enabling not only managers and workers but all stakeholders in the organization to obtain the 'satisfaction of citizenship', to use Drucker's phrase, because they enjoy citizenship in the workplace (cf. Moon, 1995; Handy, 1997a, 1997b).

In 1971 at Colombia University a new professorship was endowed in public policy and business responsibility. Brown was the first holder of this chair and a few years later, in his important book *Beyond the Bottom Line* (1979), he brought together (and also critiqued) many of the arguments that had prevailed during the previous two decades, referring crucially to the 'groundswell of change in the societal values that the public holds most important' (Brown, 1979, p. 15; see also Estes, 1966). For the most part this groundswell focused on the environment, but central to Brown's position was the need 'to delineate some of the alterations that may be imposed on the business corporation and its management by the addition, to the traditional single goal of making a profit, of what has come to be called *social responsibility*' (ibid.). Chief among his required changes was a shift 'from an organization conscious of a single purpose (profit) to one conscious of a multiplicity of purposes (economic, social, psychological, educational, environmental, and even political)' (ibid., p. 20; see also Klein, 1977). This is the key both to Brown's understanding of corporate social responsibility – multiple bottom lines – and to the current discussions, although few if any contemporary commentators recognize or refer to Brown's significant contribution. The central issue for Brown was 'not the contest between private enterprise and government for control of the economy, nor the question of the nature and purpose of controls that each might exercise ... but rather the underlying influences at work on society and business' to bring about a modification of the business corporation (ibid.). 'There is urgently needed', he said, 'both a modification of public and government attitudes towards business, and a broadened concept of purpose and social service by business. Both are required to assure that the traditional advantages of the private enterprise corporation will survive' (ibid., pp. 20–1).

While this was written more than two decades ago, few would question its relevance today. His concern was not whether the business corporation had a future but the probable nature of that future, arguing that 'the corporate quest' for 'improved efficiency competitive success, and maximised profits' was no longer sufficient. 'New tasks have been assigned by public pressures, tasks for which executive management in many cases is not prepared' (ibid., p. 5). This observation is as true now as it was then. The challenge, as Brown saw it and as many see it today, was to transform the corporation from being seen and seeing itself 'as a purely profit making organisation ... to a socio-economic institution of society' (ibid., p. 6). That would not be easy as 'The basic legitimacy of the corporation has been and is grounded on stockholder ownership' (ibid., p. 8).

Equality of opportunity was a key social imperative in the 1970s. While it remains very significant, probably the most important (and related) impera-tive now is inclusivity – the right to have your voice heard. The foundations for this were laid in the 1970s, when values inherited from an age of science and reason, such as efficiency and maximum growth, were 'no longer accepted without reservation ... deemed to be too lacking in solicitude for the public welfare, wanting in compassion for the disadvantaged, and lacking in protection for those exposed to exploitation' (ibid., p. 17). The transformation required, therefore, was from an understanding of business that reflected 'the high value society had come to place on rationality, efficiency, competition and growth' (ibid.) to one with a more humanist approach, recognizing the value and worth of human capital (see Zadek *et al.*, 2000).

This was building on a tradition that dated back to the 1950s. The idea of a business with a 'soul' was developed by Kaysen (1957), who wrote of soulful corporations 'discharging social responsibilities' (quoted in Sheikh, 1996, p. 20; see also Bowen, 1953; Tomer, 1999). Even as far back as the 1930s Berle and Means (1933) argued that 'the modern corporation should be transforming itself into a social, rather than an economic institution intent on profit max-imisation alone' (quoted in Sheikh, 1996, p. 20; see also Birch and Glazebrook, 2000). The problem for Brown in the 1970s and for commentators today is that the public perception of business is generally a negative one.

Schwartz and Gibb (1999, p. 12) argue that today many more people consider themselves to be stakeholders in companies and that it is essential for companies to recognize this by 'identifying and acting on opportunities to improve the societies in which they operate' (see also Logan *et al.*, 1997). The public, they argue, is seeking 'a proper balance' (Schwartz and Gibb, 1999, p. 6), and a company's goal has to be 'not the discovery of a model of social responsibility, but development of a process that will create its own living understanding of its place in the wider world' (ibid., p. 82). Corporate responsibility, they suggest, 'should be derived from its stakeholder respon-sibilities' because 'a group whose members trust each other can achieve more economically than a non-trusting group' (ibid., pp. 104, 187). This can cre-ate the corporate dilemma that Brown (1979, p. 143) argued can be found 'in the discomfort of the process of change and the underlying nudging com-pulsions to choose among unfamiliar and often displeasing alternatives'. Recognizing that business is a social invention is key, and 'greater awareness of this fact by business management, by government personnel, and by the public at large would make its passage from a single to a multiple purpose organisation less alarming and painful, and, indeed, more rational' (ibid., p. 144).

Probably one of the most incisive analyses of the business enterprise in the early 1970s was that by Jacoby (1973), who developed a social environment model to explain corporate behaviour as a response to both market and non-market forces that had an influence on costs, revenues and profits (see also Marks and Minow, 1991). Jacoby considered that boards should be made more socially sensitive by including on them 'sophisticated and articulate shareowners' (ibid., p. 226), especially in the case of trust and investment companies and pension funds. This would ensure that 'The total performance of the management will receive a searching audit', thereby alleviating 'the negative perceptions of business as insensitive to social issues' (ibid., p. 267). This could also be achieved, he argued, by employing experts in organizational and public affairs, and setting up 'sensory and feedback social devices linking it with all sectors of society' (ibid.). Communication was essential, with business becoming expert in political as well as social issues. Long before it became common practice he argued that business should establish a social account and be subject to annual social audits.

French *et al.* (1992, p. 50; see also Etzioni, 1988) see corporations as moral agents and business as providing the environment where individuals, themselves as moral agents, 'make choices and take actions'. This business environment, however, is not neutral or disinterested. It conditions many of the choices made there, and as such business has a responsibility 'for the kinds of environments they develop and maintain' (French *et al.*, 1992, p. 51). Moreover, business has to monitor these environments and change them if necessary. Care for the business culture and environment should be a significant tenet of corporate citizenship (see Marsden and Andriof, 1998; Khoury *et al.*, 1999).

The moral zone

French (1984) argued for this position on business as moral agents several years earlier, suggesting that most Western moral philosophers had always positioned individuals, not organizations, at the centre of morality discussions. In this respect it was assumed that, from the moral perspective, 'organisations and collectives do not exist and the notions of corporate and collective responsibility are illusionary' (ibid., p. 8). But for French the key to recognizing the corporation as a moral agent was the concept of 'intentionality' because a corporation's internal decision making was not, as generally thought, the sole responsibility of individuals but was collective in nature (ibid., p. 39). This was contentious of course, especially with respect to corporate governance and liability issues. Yet it did reflect the underlying principle in corporate social responsibility and corporate citizenship discussions that the company was a public and social institution – a coalition of interests – over and above the legal understanding of the company as an individual entity.

According to Galbraith (1971, p. 7), 'To recognise that the great corporation is essentially a public entity, is to accept that its acts have a profoundly public effect.' However, as many participants in corporate social responsibility discussions argued over the years, the traditional model of business as essentially private, despite its public effects, had failed to work because of the often massive differences in power between business and the individual citizen (Medawar, 1978, p. 13). As Beesley and Evans (1978, p. 169) pointed out, 'A continuing problem of the socially responsible company is perceiving, articulating and validating the external goals to which it will respond.'

Carroll, one of the leading authors on the subject in the 1970s and still highly influential today, recognized that management theory needed to take on board some of these difficult issues, particularly as a means of wresting the argument away from the alienating lobbying tactics of single issue interest groups and getting important arguments and issues into boardrooms. In his 1977 work Carroll brought together some of the leading thinkers and writers in the area (Carroll, 1998, 1999).

Davis (1977) – one of the authors in the Carroll collection – argued strongly for recognition that social responsibility arose from social power. That was the first of five propositions. The second was that business 'should operate as a two-way open system with open receipt of inputs from society and open disclosure of its operations to the public'. Third, 'social costs as well as benefits of an activity, product or service should be thoroughly calculated and considered in order to decide whether to proceed with a particular activity or not'. Fourth, the 'social costs of each activity product or service should be priced into it so that the consumer (user) pays for the effects of their consumption on society'. Finally 'beyond social costs business institutions as citizens have responsibilities for social involvement in areas of their competence where major social needs exists' (ibid., p. 57). Davis explained that 'The fifth proposition is based essentially on the reasoning that business is a major social institution so should bear the same kind of citizenship costs for society that an individual citizen bears' (ibid.). This was one of the earliest occasions when the idea of corporate social responsibility was presented as an act of corporate citizenship. Over time all of these propositions have become central to the corporate social responsibility discussions.

In 1972 Dahl argued influentially 'that every large corporation should be thought of as a social enterprise; that is, as an entity whose existence and decisions can be justified insofar as they serve public or social purposes' (Beesley and Evans, 1978, p. 17; see also McDermott, 1991). It was recognized that 'business will benefit from a better society just as any citizen will benefit; therefore business has a responsibility to recognise social problems and actively contribute its talents to help solve them. Such involvement is expected of any citizen, and business should fulfil a citizenship role'. As Polyani had long before made clear, 'the economy requires social institutions which disseminate skills, distribute knowledge and preserve the status of human beings and nature as something other than commodities' (Polyani, 1957, quoted in Glasman, 1996, p. 5). Polyani's position, and one that is increasingly being revisited today, was that the traditional idea of the economy 'as a self-regulating system of exchange grounded in individual choice, governed by prices and constrained by scarcity ... is based on an impoverished conception of the importance of the economy and its institutions in the reproduction of ethics and society' (quoted in ibid., p. 7). Effectively this conception of the economy 'seals off the economy from social institutions and political interference in the name of self-regulation and individual sovereignty while expanding the domain of its analysis to include all elements of culture as conforming with the motivation of rational self-interest' (quoted in ibid., pp. 7–8). Business could not divorce itself from this developing social understanding of economics.

In this regard good corporate social responsibility did not require outside approval, nor was it necessarily a measure of how good or ethical a company was. What was essential was to incorporate social responsibility into all decision making in the company and make it integral to all operations and policies (Beesley and Evans, 1978). This in turn required business to be seen not just as an instrument but also as an organic entity with 'many points of leverage' (ibid., p. 3200; see also Reder, 1995). This led to a both-and, not an either-or situation.

Responsibilities and performance

In the 1980s Anshen argued vigorously that concentrating on corporate social responsibility was too limiting. 'Who', he asked, 'defines the bounds and specific contents of the responsibility of a corporation to deliver benefits to society?' He argued that corporate social performance was a better concept than corporate social responsibility because 'responsibility is outer directed; performance is inner directed. Responsibility is under social control; performance is under management control' (Anshen, 1980, p. 39).

Linowes (1974) argued, as did many around that time (see for example Sethi, 1981) in opposition to traditional business economists, that it was impossible to keep the public and private sectors as separate entities, as corporate actions increasingly affected social conditions. Society, he suggested, was dependent on business, but more importantly business was a dependant of society. The distinction between being dependent and being a dependant is subtle but crucial. Linowes (1974, p. 4) made the point that 'The corporation cannot realistically or rationally divorce itself from society.' 'Socially constructive corporate action', he argued, and reflecting the thoughts of many commentators of the time, 'will in the long run benefit all of society. Irresponsible action – or inaction – will boomerang to harm business as well as the non business sector' (ibid.). This was one of the first times that the term corporate citizenship was used in the literature as a reflection of socially constructive corporate action.

For Miles (1987), corporate social responsibility was an outcome of a corporation's behaviour, and corporate social responsiveness related to the processes that the corporation had developed 'for understanding and responding to development in the corporate social environment' (ibid., p. 74). A few years earlier Engel (1979) had argued that the issue of social responsibility could not 'be debated except against the background of a general political theory'. A classical liberal approach in economics mitigated against good corporate citizenship, while a contemporary managerialist approach recognized the non-economic political and civic duties of business. There seemed to be an element of choice here, but as McIntosh *et al.* (1998) have since made clear, corporate citizenship can no longer be seen as discretionary.

In his seminal 1979 publication, Johnson placed social reporting and disclosure within this larger socioeconomic political context, arguing that corporate social reporting had serious implications for the course of contemporary capitalism. It meant that 'institutional adjustments in the structure and process of the market economy' would have to be made (ibid., p. 2). This raised the spectre, as similar arguments did in the late 1990s, of the growth of socialism, threatening the very foundations of the market economy. Johnson, of course, was not alone in calling for new economic paradigms in the context of corporate social responsibility. Danley (1994) argued very strongly about the failure of the classical liberal and managerialist approaches to understanding corporate social responsibility. He called for a return to Keynesianism and pluralism as they offered 'a dramatically different way of conceptualising the role of government in a free liberal society' (ibid., p. 222). Investment was the key to economic activity, not interest rates, and this required the business world to become much more involved in government, and to move what constituted investment away from the narrow instrumentalist economic definition to a more organic way of thinking about social investment.

Social investment and social reporting required businesses to disclose information on highly organic social goals such as economic justice, stability and freedom (Johnson, 1979) – goals that were not generally associated with the core activities of business. Johnson also stressed that social responsibility required an alternative conception of the business firm: the firm as a shifting coalition of participants in the production process, including executives, employees, dealers, suppliers and stockholders, 'all of whom are held together by the expectation that at least minimum requisites for participation will be obtained out of the fluctuating relationships' (ibid., pp. 9–10).

The problem now, as then, is how to transform business, especially along the lines outlined by Miles (1987), when those responsible for implementing the necessary changes (for the most part line managers) still have to concentrate most of their efforts on meeting exacting economic performance targets each quarter.

Sustainability

The crux of the matter is that if business is to have greater freedom of action to perform economically then this freedom must be used responsibly. In other words there is a moral dimension to corporate social responsibility and performance that involves 'building systems of corporate ethics and values into the enterprise, tackling questions of compliance and governance, meeting the needs of the economically and socially disadvantaged, satisfying responsibilities to the environment' (Cannon, 1994, p. 52; see also Fombrun, 1997; Davis, 2001). As Korten (1995, p. 50) uncompromisingly insists:

> If our concern is for a sustainable human well-being for all people, then we must penetrate the economic myths embedded in our culture by the prophets of illusion, free ourselves of our obsession with growth, and dramatically restructure economic relationships to focus on two priorities: Balance human uses of the environment with the regenerative capacities of the eco system, and allocate available natural capital in ways that ensure that all people have the opportunity to fulfil their physical needs adequately and to pursue their full social, cultural, intellectual and spiritual development.

The argument that business can make a difference to the social fabric is not new. Indeed, it was central to discussions on corporate social responsibility from the 1920s (see Capp, 1950; Bowen, 1953; Heald, 1970; Davies and Frederick, 1984). In the 1970s Hirsch (1976, p. 106) pointed out that society 'is in turmoil because the only legitimacy it has is social justice and the transition to adjust to society is an uncertain road strewn with injustice'. Market capitalism, predicated as it was upon individuals competing, might well raise material productivity, but at what other social costs? (ibid.) More then 30 years later, can it be said that we have tackled that problem?

According to Hirsch, capitalism raised expectations because it could perform so well, but not everyone could be satisfied. He called for a 'managed capitalism' where people would be willing to put social interests 'at a modest sacrifice of their own individualistic interests' (ibid., p. 151), which is still what many in the corporate social responsibility discussions are calling for. The point was that people could not 'act out this preference on their own' (ibid.). What was needed was the formulation of a social ethic. Nowadays that social ethic is emerging out of the successes of the environmental

movement, and even more importantly out of concern that Western capitalism is skewed in favour of the individual and not society as a whole. As
Hirsch argued 'Individual economic freedom still has to be adjusted to the
demands of the majority participation', and 'we may be near the limits of
explicit social organisation possible, without a supporting social morality'
(ibid., pp. 188, 190).

An increasing part of the emerging social ethic is a call for inclusivity.
Hutton (1995, p. 15) pulls no punches about this and states categorically
that 'Altruism and the civilising values of an inclusive society have been
sacrificed on the altar of self interest, of choice, of opting out and of
individualism.' Trust, commitment and cooperation, he suggests, are key
factors in successful businesses creating successful societies, but these are
often missing. He writes of the moral economy, arguing that what is needed
to redress some of the imbalances is 'recognition that firms are formed by
human beings with human as well as contractual claims upon each other
and behind this social world lies the moral domain' (ibid., p. 23). According
to Hutton there is a fundamental amorality in developed societies today and
what is needed is a new citizenship. The need for the latter is reflected in the
writing of Wheeler and Silanpaa (1998, p. 9), who assert that 'the long term
value of a company rests primarily on the knowledge, abilities and commitment of its employees and its relationships with investors, customers and
other stakeholders' (see also *The Copenhagen Charter*, 1999).

To that end Welford (1995, p. 29) argues that we need a new ethics that
'depends on both the values of individuals working within the organisation
and particularly on the culture created by the individual ethics of senior
management and on any codes of conduct which formally exist within the
organisation or standards adopted from external agencies' (see also Graves,
1986). At the heart of this new business ethics is stakeholder accountability
and new democratic forms of organization in the workplace (Welford, 1995).
Adjusting a business strategy to include sustainable development requires a
change in the culture of the organization but it also opens up 'new opportunities to reassess other aspects of business' (ibid., p. 77). The challenge is to
establish a corporate culture that is 'consistent with the concept of sustainable
development' (ibid., p. 114). In Welford's view, business should 'transcend
the limited ideologies and values associated with traditional forms of environmental management' (ibid., p. 198; see also Weiser and Zadek, 2000).

Central to the sustainable corporation is the notion of stewardship, which
is defined by Block (1993, p. 19) as that part of the workplace that has been
most difficult to change in the past, namely 'the distribution of power,
purpose and rewards' (see also Turner and Crawford, 1998). Put simply,
stewardship involves recognition that we 'hold something in trust for
another' (Block, 1993, p. 20). This means presiding over 'the orderly distribution of power' by 'giving people at the bottom and the boundaries of the
organisation choice over how to serve a customer, a citizen, a community'.

'It is the willingness to be accountable for the well being of the larger organisation by operating in service, rather than in control, of those around us. Stated simply, it is accountability without control or compliance' (ibid.).

Hutton (1999, p. 1) continues this theme by arguing that inadequate economic structures 'feed back into our social structures and enfeeble individual wellbeing and social cohesion' (see also Hutton, 2002). We need a more enlightened approach, where 'production and work are key sources of satisfaction and utility', where work 'fosters personal development, deepens skills, humanises and structures lives, above all it makes us cleverer and independent' (Hutton, 1999, p. 10; see also Lane, 1993). 'An interaction between human beings cannot be interpreted in the same way as the supply and demand for dead fish' (Solow, quoted in Hutton, 1999, p. 15). We also have 'to be able to trust the social networks in which we are embedded and unless we can trust them we perform less well. We are not happy simply choosing and maximising our individual preferences which is just as well given that so many of our choices must be mistaken' (ibid., p. 28). We must recapitalize, and as we do so a new language of stakeholding as a political economy will emerge, based on social inclusion, membership, trust, cooperation, long-termism, equality of opportunity, participation, active citizenship, rights and obligations (ibid., p. 80). The core aim should 'be to build a free moral, socially cohesive society based on universal membership, social inclusion and organised around the market economy' (ibid., p. 88).

Postcapitalism

Drucker (1993, p. 68) argues that 'we have moved ... into an employee society where labour is no longer an asset. We equally have moved into a capitalism without capitalists which defies everything still considered self evident truth, if not the laws of nature, by politicians, lawyers, economists, journalists, labour leaders, business leaders, in short, by almost everybody, regardless of political persuasion' (see also Drucker, 1999). The inevitable conclusion is that we are in a process of fundamental change and can no longer seek comfort in the ideologies, terminologies and power distributions of modernism. Drucker, and many others, have been saying for years that 'The economic challenge of the post capitalist society will be the productivity of knowledge work and the knowledge worker' (Drucker, 1993, p. 8). However 'The social challenge of the post capitalist society will however be the dignity of the second class in post capitalist society; the service workers' (ibid.). According to Drucker society, or at least Western developed society, can no longer be considered in unitary terms – it is pluralistic, not only in its make-up but also in its expectations. There is a need to redefine society in terms of social ecologies, where 'every organisation of today has to build into its very structure, the management of change' (ibid., p. 59).

The new challenge of contemporary society is to redefine productivity, because 'the productivity of knowledge workers will in fact require drastic changes in the structure of the organisation of post capitalist society and in the structure of society itself' (ibid., p. 83). These changes lie at the heart of corporate social responsibility discussions. One of the terms that is repeated time and again in this context is partnership. For example 'Partnership with the responsible worker is the only way to improve productivity. Nothing else works at all' (ibid., p. 92). This change in the distribution of power is at the core of effective corporate citizenship. The paradigm shift is from 'a power-based to a responsibility-based organisation' and involves 'a change from asking what we are entitled to, to what are we responsible for?' (ibid., pp. 102, 109; see also Holme and Watts, 2000).

As Tichy *et al.* (1997, pp. 4–6) make clear, 'As we move into the twenty-first century global businesses will find themselves increasingly intertwined with global, political, social and environmental issues that will force them to redefine their role as a potent force for world integration. This force coupled with the pressure being exerted by a burgeoning world population is determining the need for global citizenship.' They argue that there are five cornerstones to corporate global citizenship: 'understanding, values, commitment, actions and cooperation'. Understanding involves human capital, social issues, cultural differences, environmental issues and ecological issues. Values are needed to 'optimise the potential of human capital and to preserve the world's environment'. Commitment involves 'believing in and caring about these values and long term investment'. Actions, if 'institutionalised within the company will reward employees', and cooperation is needed 'with people, with government, with the community' (ibid.; see also Nelson and Zadek, 2000; Waddock and Smith, 2000).

Similarly Handy (1997b, p. 8) recognizes that in a postcapitalist, knowledge-based economy the major asset is people, and 'individuals aren't own-able anymore'. He suggests that we introduce a philosophy of 'selfishness' into the discussions; that is, 'the search for ourselves that paradoxically we often pursue best through our involvement with others' (ibid., p. 9). According to him, 'To be properly selfish is to accept a responsibility for making the most of oneself by ultimately finding a purpose beyond and bigger than oneself' (ibid.). Handy, like many other commentators, recognizes the incompatibility between democracy and capitalism, arguing that we will either have to restrain the free market or limit democracy (ibid., p. 41). As Ulrich and Sarasin (1995, p. 2) remark, 'There is no such thing as "free enterprises" without responsibility and accountability to the community.' It is clear, then, that we will have to abandon our narrow emphasis on economic growth if we are to be sustainable in the future. Handy (1997b, p. 48) suggests that we 'create more activity outside the purely economic sphere where the motivation will be unconnected with efficiency and more to do with intrinsic satisfaction and worth', an argument that is at the core of the corporate social responsibility discussions.

This stands in strong opposition to the very common view 'that life is essentially about economics, that money is the measure of most things and that the market is its sorting mechanism' (ibid., p. 73). However most of us are rejecting this view, and although we may be trapped in the rhetoric of modernist economics 'there is a hunger for something else which might be more enduring and more worthwhile' (ibid.). That hunger has been evident for many years, but as Zadek (2001a, p. 221) says 'corporate citizenship will only be effective if and when it evolves to a point where business becomes active in promoting and institutionalising new global governance frameworks that effectively secure civil market behaviour'. Being hungry for the ideas, as the extensive literature of the last 60 years has demonstrated, does not always mean the effective take-up of related issues into core business. This take-up, then, is the greatest challenge facing business today, and it cannot happen in a serious and sustainable way without a profound change in our thoughts on and processing of the fundamental economics that underlie our understanding and practice of capitalism.

References

Agle, B. R and C. B. Caldwell (1999) 'Understanding Research on Values in Business', *Business & Society*, 38 (3), pp. 326–88.

Anshen, M. (1980) *Corporate Strategies for Social Performance* (New York: Macmillan).

Arthur, D. L. (2001) *The Business Case for Corporate Citizenship* (www.weforum. org/corporatecitizenship).

Beesley, M. and T. Evans (1978) *Corporate Social Responsibility – A Reassessment* (London: Croom Helm).

Bell, D. (1974) *The Coming of Post Industrial Society: A Venture in Social Forecasting* (London: Heineman).

Berle, A. and G. Means (1933) *The Modern Corporation and Private Property* (New York: Harcourt).

Birch, D. (2001) 'Corporate Citizenship. Rethinking Business Beyond Corporate Social Responsibility', in J. Andriof and M. McIntosh (eds), *Perspectives on Corporate Citizenship* (London: Greenleaf), pp. 53–65.

Birch, D. (2002) 'Social, Economic and Environmental Capital: Corporate Citizenship in a New Economy', *Alternative Law Journal*, 27 (1), pp. 3–6.

Birch, D. and M. Glazebrook (1998) 'Rethinking Corporate Responsibility: An Australian Perspective', in D. Hart (ed.), *Visions of Ethical Business* (London: Financial Times Management), pp. 45–48.

Birch, D. and M. Glazebrook (2000) 'Doing Business – Doing Culture: Corporate Citizenship and Community', in S. Rees and S. Wright (eds), *Human Rights and Corporate Responsibility: A Dialogue* (Annandale: Pluto), pp. 41–52.

Block, P. (1993) *Stewardship: Choosing Service Over Self-Interest* (San Francisco, CA: Berrett-Koehler).

Bowen, H. R. (1953) *Social Responsibilities of the Businessman* (New York: Harper).

Brown, C. C. (1979) *Beyond the Bottom Line* (New York: Macmillan).

Cannon, T. (1994) *Corporate Responsibility – a Textbook on Business Ethics, Governance, Environment, Roles and Responsibilities* (London: Pitman).

Cannon, T. (1996) *Welcome to the Revolution: Managing Paradox in the Twenty First Century* (London: Pitman).

Capp, W. K. (1950) *The Social Costs of Private Enterprise* (Cambridge Mass.: Harvard University Press).

Carroll, A. B. (ed.) (1977) *Managing Corporate Social Responsibility* (Boston, Mass.: Little, Brown).

Carroll, A. B. (1998) 'The Four Faces of Corporate Citizenship', *Business and Society Review*, 100 (101), pp. 1–7.

Carroll, A. B. (1999) 'Corporate Social Responsibility: Evolution of a Definitional Construct', *Business & Society*, 38 (3), pp. 268–95.

Casey, C. (1995) *Work, Self and Society, After Industrialisation* (London and New York: Routledge).

Cavanagh, G. F. (1984) *American Business Values in Transition* (Englewood Cliffs, NJ: Prentice-Hall).

Chamberlain, N. W. (1982) *Social Strategy and Corporate Structure* (New York: Macmillan).

Chomsky, N. (1999) *Profit Over People: Neoliberalism and Global Order* (New York: Seven Stories Press).

Collins, J. C. and J. I. Porras (1994) *Built to Last: Successful Habits of Visionary Companies* (New York: Harper).

Dahl, R. A. (1972) 'A Prelude to Corporate Reform', *Business and Society Review*, 1, pp. 17–21.

Danley, J. R. (1994) *The Role of the Modern Corporation in a Free Society* (Notre Dame and London: University of Notre Dame Press).

Davis, K. (1973) 'The Case For and Against Business Assumptions of Social Responsibilities', *Academy of Management Journal*, 16, pp. 312–22.

Davis, K. (1977) 'Five Propositions for Social Responsibility', in A. B. Carroll (ed.), *Managing Corporate Social Responsibility* (Boston, Mass.: Little, Brown), pp. 46–51.

Davis, K. and W. C. Frederick (1984) *Business and Society: Management, Public Policy, Ethics* (New York: McGraw Hill).

Davis, L. A. (2001) 'The Social Responsibility of Corporations', *The Corporate Citizen*, 1 (4), pp. 2–8.

Denuyl, D. J. (1984) *The New Crusaders: The Corporate Social Responsibility Debate* (Bowling Green, Social Philosophy and Policy Center, Bowling Green State University).

Drucker, P. F. (1946) *The Concept of the Corporation* (New York and Toronto: The New American Library).

Drucker, P. F. (1993) *Post Capitalist Society* (New York: Harper).

Drucker, P. F. (1999) *Management Challenges for the 21st Century* (Oxford: Butterworth Heinemann).

Elkington, J. (1997) *Cannibals with Forks: The Triple Bottom Line of Twentieth Century Business* (Oxford: Capstone).

Engel, D. L. (1979) 'An Approach to Corporate Responsibility', *Stanford Law Review*, 32, pp. 1–98.

Estes, R. (1966) *The Tyranny of the Bottom Line: Why Corporations Make Good People Do Bad Things* (San Francisco, CA: Berrett-Koehler).

Etzioni, A. (1988) *The Moral Dimension* (London, Free Press).

Fombrun, C. J. (1997) 'Three Pillars of Corporate Citizenship – Ethics, Social Benefit, Profitability', in N. Tichy, R. Andrew, R. McGill and L. St. Clair (eds), *Corporate Global Citizenship: Doing Business in the Public Eye* (San Francisco, CA: New Lexington Press), pp. 27–61.

French, P. A. (1984) *Collective and Corporate Responsibility* (New York: Columbia University Press).

French, P. A., N. Jeffrey and D. T. Risser, with J. Abbarno (1992) *Corporations in the Moral Community* (Fort Worth, Tex.: Harcourt Brace Jovanovich).

Galbraith, J. K. (1968) *The New Industrial Estate* (London: Penguin).

Galbraith, J. K. (1972) 'The Emerging Public Corporation', *Business and Society Review*, 1, pp. 54–6.

Galbraith, J. K. (1973) 'On the Economic Image of Corporate Enterprise', in R. Nader and M. J. Green (eds), *Corporate Power in America* (New York: Grossman).

Geus, de A. (1997) *The Living Company: Growth, Learning and Longevity in Business* (London: Nicholas Brealey).

Glasman, M. (1996) *Unnecessary Suffering: Managaing Market Utopia* (London: Verso).

Goyder, G. (1961) *The Responsible Company* (Oxford: Blackwell).

Goyder, M. (1998) *Living Tomorrow's Company* (Aldershot: Gower).

Graves, D. (1986) *Corporate Culture – Diagnosis and Change. Auditing and Changing the Culture of Organizations* (London: Frances Pinter).

Halal, W. E. (1986) *The New Capitalism* (New York: John Wiley & Sons).

Handy, C. (1997a) 'The Citizen Corporation', *Harvard Business Review*, 75 (5), pp. 26–7.

Handy, C. (1997b) *The Hungry Spirit: Beyond Capitalism, a Quest for Purpose in the Modern World* (London: Arrow).

Harris, Z. S. (1997) *The Transformation of Capitalist Society* (Lanham: Rowman & Littlefield).

Hawken, P. A. Lovins and H. L. Hunter-Lovins (1999) *Natural Capitalism: Creating the Next Industrial Revolution* (Boston, Mass.: Little, Brown).

Heald, M. (1970) *The Social Responsibilities of Business: Company and Community 1900–1960* (New Brunswick: Transaction).

Henderson, D. (2001) *Misguided Virtue: False Notions of Corporate Social Responsibility* (Wellington: New Zealand Business Roundtable).

Hirsch, F. (1976) *Social Limits to Growth* (Cambridge, Mass.: Harvard University Press).

Holme, R. and P. Watts (2000) *Corporate Social Responsibility: Making Good Business Sense* (www.wbcsd.org).

Hutton, W. (1995) *The State We Are In* (London: Jonathan Cape).

Hutton, W. (1999) *The Stakeholding Society: Writings on Politics and Economics*, edited by D. Goldblatt (Oxford: Polity Press).

Hutton, W. (2002) *The World We're In* (London: Little, Brown).

Jacoby, N. A. (1973) *Corporate Power and Social Responsibility* (New York: Macmillan).

Johnson, H. L. (1979) *Disclosure of Corporate Social Performance – Survey Evaluation and Prospects* (New York and London: Praeger).

Kaysen, C. (1957) 'The Social Significance of the Modern Corporation', *American Economic Review*.

Kennedy, A. (2000) *The End of Shareholder Value* (London: Orion).

Khoury, G., J. Rostami and P. L. Turnbull (1999) *Corporate Social Responsibility: Turning Words into Action* (Conference Board of Canada).

Klein, T. (1977) *Social Costs and Benefits of Business* (Englewood Cliffs, NJ: Prentice-Hall).

Korten, D. C. (1995) *When Corporations Rule the World* (San Francisco, CA: Kumarian Press and Berrett-Koehler).

Korten D. C. (1999) *The Post-Corporate World: Life After Capitalism* (San Francisco, CA: Kumarian Press and Berrett-Koehler).

Lane, R. (1993) *The Market Experience* (Cambridge: Cambridge University Press).

Levitt, T. (1958) 'The Dangers of Social Responisbility', *Harvard Business Review*, Sept.– Oct., pp. 41–85.

Linowes, D. F. (1974) *The Corporate Conscience* (New York: Hawthorn).

Logan, D., D. Roy and L. Regelbrugge (1997) *Global Corporate Citizenship – Rationale and Strategies* (New York: Hitachi Foundation).

Marks, R. and N. Minow (1991) *Power and Accountability* (Glasgow: HarperCollins).

Marsden, C. and J. Andriof (1998) 'Towards an Understanding of Corporate Citizenship and How to Influence it', *Citizenship Studies*, 2 (2), pp. 329–52.

McDermott, J. (1991) *Corporate Society: Class, Property and Contemporary Capitalism* (Boulder, CO: Westview Press).

McIntosh, M., D. Leipziger, K. Jones and G. Coleman (1998) *Corporate Citizenship: Successful Strategies for Responsible Companies* (London: Financial Times and Pitman).

Medawar, C. (1978) *The Social Audit Consumer Handbook: A Guide to the Social Responsibilities of Business to the Consumer* (London: Macmillan).

Miles, R. H. (1987) *Managing the Corporate Social Environment: A Grounded Theory* (Englewood Cliffs, NJ: Prentice-Hall).

Moon, J. (1995) 'The Firm as Citizen? Social Responsibility of Business in Australia', *Australian Journal of Political Science*, 30 (1), pp. 1–17.

Nader, R. and M. J. Green (eds) (1973) *Corporate Power in America* (New York: Grossman).

Nelson, J. and S. Zadek (2000) *Partnership Alchemy: New Society Partnerships in Europe* (Copenhagen: Copenhagen Centre).

Piore, M. J. (1995) *Beyond Individualism* (Cambridge, Mass.: Harvard University Press).

Polyani, K. (1957) *The Great Transformation: The Political and Economic Origins of Our Time* (Boston, Mass.: Beacon Press).

Reder, A. (1995) *Seventy Five Best Business Practices for Socially Responsible Companies* (New York: G. P. Putnam).

Schwartz, P. and B. Gibb (1999) *When Good Companies Do Bad Things – Responsibility and Risk in an Age of Globalisation* (New York: John Wiley & Sons).

Senge, P. M. (1994) *The Fifth Discipline: The Art and Practice of the Learning Organization* (New York and London: Currency Doubleday).

Sethi, S. P. (1981) *Up Against the Corporate Wall – Modern Corporations and Social Issues of the Seventies* (Englewood Cliffs, NJ: Prentice-Hall).

Sheikh, S. (1996) *Corporate Social Responsibilities: Law and Practice* (London: Cavendish).

Solow, R. (1990) *The Labour Market as a Social Institution* (Oxford: Blackwell).

Steiner, G. A. and J. S. Steiner (eds) (1972) *Issues in Business and Society* (New York: Random House).

The Copenhagen Charter. A Management Guide to Stakeholder Reporting (1999) (Copenhagen: Ernst and Young, KPMG, PriceWaterhouseCoopers and the House of Mandag Morgen).

Thurow, L. (1966) *The Future of Capitalism: How Today's Economic Forces Shape Tomorrow's World* (St Leonards, NSW: Allen & Unwin).

Tichy, N. M., R. Andrew, R. McGill and L. St. Clair (eds) (1997) *Corporate Global Citizenship: Doing Business in the Public Eye* (San Francisco, CA: New Lexington Press).

Toffler, A. (1980) *The Third Wave* (New York: Bantam).

Tomer, J. (1999) *The Human Firm: A Socio-Economic Analysis of its Behaviour and Potential in a New Economic Age* (London and New York: Routledge).

Turner, D. and M. Crawford (1998) *Change Power: Capabilities that Drive Corporate Renewal* (Sydney: Woods Lane).

Ulrich, P. and C. Sarasin (eds) (1995) *Facing Public Interest: The Ethical Challenges to Business Policy and Corporate Communications* (Amsterdam: Kluwer).

Waddock, S. and N. Smith (2000) 'Relationships: The Real Challenge of Global Citizenship', *Business and Society Review*, 105 (1), pp. 47–62.

Weiser, J. and S. Zadek (2000) *Conversations with Disbelievers: Persuading Companies to Address Social Challenges* (New York: Ford Foundation).

Welford, R. (1995) *Environmental Strategy and Sustainable Development: The Corporate Challenge for the Twenty-First Century* (London: Routledge).

Wheeler, D. and M. Silanpaa (1998) *The Stakeholder Corporation: A Blueprint for Maximising Stakeholder Value* (London: Pitman).

Wood, D. J. (1991) 'Corporate Social Performance Revisited', *Academy of Management Review*, 16 (4), pp. 691–718.

World Business Council for Sustainable Development (WBCSD) (2002) *The Business Case for Sustainable Development. Making a Difference: Toward Johannesburg 2002* (www.wbcsd.org).

World Economic Forum (WEF) (2002) *Global Corporate Citizenship: The Leadership Challenge for CEOs and Boards* (Geneva: WEF, www.weforum.org).

Zadek, S. (2001a) *The Civil Corporation: The New Economy of Corporate Citizenship* (London: Earthscan in association with the New Economics Foundation).

Zadek, S. (2001b) *Third Generation Corporate Citizenship: Public Policy and Business in Society* (London: Foreign Policy Centre in association with AccountAbility).

Zadek, S., N. Hojensgard and P. Raynard (2000) *The New Economy of Corporate Citizenship* (Copenhagen: Copenhagen Centre).

Zadek, S., N. Hojensgard and P. Raynard (eds) (2001) *Perspectives on the New Economy of Corporate Citizenship* (Copenhagen: Copenhagen Centre).

Zadek, S. and C. Tuppen (2000) *Adding Values: The Economics of Sustainable Business* (London: Corporate Reputation and Social Policy Unit, British Telecommunications).

Zohar, D. (1997) *Rewiring the Corporate Brain* (New York: Berrett-Koehler).

3

Corporate Citizenship, Social Responsibility and Sustainability: Corporate Colonialism for the New Millennium?

Subhabrata Bobby Banerjee

> I see in the near future a crisis approaching that unnerves me and causes me to tremble for the safety of my country ... corporations have been enthroned and an era of corruption in high places will follow, and the money power of the country will endeavour to prolong its reign by working upon the prejudices of the people until all wealth is aggregated in a few hands and the Republic is destroyed. (Abraham Lincoln, 21 November 1864)

Introduction

This chapter describes and critiques emerging discourses of corporate citizenship, social responsibility and sustainability, discusses some of the key assumptions that frame these discourses. It is argued that despite their emancipatory rhetoric the discourses are defined by narrow business interests and serve to curtail the interests of external stakeholders.

The chapter consists of three sections. The first briefly discusses key concepts in corporate citizenship and sustainability, as well as corporate 'triple bottom line' strategies to integrate economic, social and environmental concerns. The fundamental assumptions underlying these concepts are analyzed at the institutional, organizational and managerial levels. The second section provides a critique of stakeholder theory and practice. Understanding and integrating stakeholders' needs are key issues in corporate citizenship and some of the theoretical shortcomings in this area of research will be explored. The final section discusses the implications for critical management studies and suggests directions for future research.

Corporate citizenship and social responsibility: old wine in older bottles?

The vast body of literature on corporate citizenship and social responsibility will not be reviewed here as the other chapters in this book deal with the key concepts in this topic. There is some disagreement about terminology, however: while some writers view corporate citizenship and corporate social responsibility as synonymous (Swanson and Niehoff, 2001; Waddock, 2001), others argue that corporate citizenship focuses on internal organizational values while corporate social responsibility focuses on the externalities associated with corporate behaviour (Birch, 2001; Wood and Logsdon, 2001). Some argue that the roots of the two discourses are also different: corporate citizenship is a more practitioner-based approach whereas the discourse on corporate social responsibility emerged from the academic community (Davenport, 2000).

Regardless of the genesis of corporate citizenship and social responsibility it is should be noted that they are not particularly new ideas, despite what the business press and some parts of the academic literature would have us believe. Corporate citizenship, corporate social responsibility and now sustainability and the 'triple bottom line' address a common theme: the relationship between business and society. Whereas the primary relationship between business and society has and continues to be an economic one, growing public concern about the social and environmental impacts of economic growth and increased legislation in areas of social welfare and environmental protection have led many corporations to assess the social and environmental effects of their business activities. Incidents such as the Bhopal gas leak, the Exxon Valdez oil spill and the issue of Third World sweatshops have periodically focused public and corporate attention on these issues and all transnational corporations today have some form of environmental policy or community relations policy.

The debates on the role and extent of corporate citizenship have arisen because of two distinct assumptions that underly the theory of the firm. The received view of the firm is primarily economic in that it focuses on the efficiencies required to maximize rent-seeking opportunities. The sociological perspective views the firm as a social entity and focuses on issues of legitimacy. The problem with this dichotomy is that legitimacy becomes subordinate to efficiency and the terms of legitimacy are often defined by efficiency criteria. An examination of the literature indicates that the rationale and assumptions behind this discourse are (1) that corporations should think beyond making money and pay attention to social and environmental issues, (2) that corporations should behave in an ethical manner and demonstrate the highest level of integrity and transparency in all their operations, and (3) that corporations should be involved with the community in which they operate in terms of enhancing social welfare and providing community support through philanthropy or other means. These notions of corporate citizenship should be operationalized through engagement and dialogue with stakeholders (another term that seems to be unproblematically and uncritically accepted in the literature) and corporations should always engage with their stakeholders and build relationships with them (Waddock, 2001). The normative core of this discourse is not hard to ascertain: the assumption is that corporations should do all these things because (1) good corporate citizenship is related to good financial performance (despite very weak empirical evidence of this relationship), and (2) if a corporation is a bad citizen then its licence to operate will be revoked by society. Both of these are simplistic assumptions with little theoretical or empirical support. Large transnational corporations that have been responsible for major environmental disasters and detrimental social impacts in the Third World (Union Carbide, Nike, Exxon and Shell, to name but a few), rather than lose their licence to operate have actually become stronger and more powerful, whether through merger, restructuring or relentless public relations campaigns.

There is a remarkable lack of critical examination of these concepts of corporate citizenship in the literature. Works on corporate social responsibility easily identify 'bad' corporate citizens: tobacco companies, weapons manufacturers and environmental polluters. However, the fact that these companies regularly publish corporate citizenship and social performance reports tends to muddy the waters more than a little. For example a recent report released by the vice president for corporate affairs and social responsibility at Phillip Morris states that company's the 'values-based culture' demonstrates 'integrity, honesty, respect and tolerance' while promising 'transparency' and 'stakeholder engagement' (Phillip Morris, 2002). These concepts are echoed by academics. For instance Birch (2001, pp. 59–60) when developing a conceptual framework for corporate citizenship, outlines '12 generic principles of corporate citizenship', including 'making a difference, employee and stakeholder empowerment, transparency, accountability, sharing responsibility, inclusivity, sustainable capitalism, a triple bottom line, long-termism, communication, engagement and dialogue'.

The problem with this conceptual framework, of course, is its operationalization. While stakeholder empowerment is indeed a noble goal, one wonders how this would affect the economic performance of a firm when the stakeholders it is supposed to 'empower' have opposing agendas to industry, as for example in the current conflicts between mining and resource companies and indigenous communities (Banerjee, 2000, 2001a). There is also the question of translating policy into action. Consider the following excerpt from the corporate responsibility annual report of a large transnational corporation:

> The principles that guide our behaviour are based on our vision and values and include the following:
>
> *Respect*: We will work to foster mutual respect with communities and stakeholders who are affected by our operations.

Integrity: We will examine the impacts, positive and negative, of our business on the environment, and on society, and will integrate human, health, social and environmental considerations into our internal management and value system.

Communication: We will strive to foster understanding and support our stakeholders and communities, as well as measure and communicate our performance.

Excellence: We will continue to improve our performance and will encourage our business partners and suppliers to adhere to the same standards.

This corporation – voted by *Fortune Magazine* for six consecutive years as the most 'innovative company in North America' and for three consecutive years as one of the '100 best companies to work for in America', and moreover is on *Fortune Magazine*'s 'All star list of global most admired companies' – is of course none other than Enron (Enron, 2002).

The history of corporate citizenship goes hand in hand with the history of corporate power. For example North American corporations, which were originally conceived in the eighteenth century as entities to serve the public interest, have over the past 200 years systematically diminished the power of the state and federal governments to regulate or govern their activities. There are no legislative requirements for corporations to serve the public interest, thus opening up what Alan Greenspan has called more 'pathways to greed'. Any analysis of corporate citizenship or corporate responsibility must necessarily be seen in the light of corporate abuses of power, and as Mitchell (1989) argues, discourses of corporate citizenship and social responsibility represent a corporate ideology that is intended to legitimize the power of large corporations. These discourses base the business–society relationship on corporate interests, not societal interests (Windsor, 2001). This is quite apparent in the recent discourse on sustainability, which originally promoted sustainable development as an alternate paradigm to the growth model but like the modern Western environmental movement has been hijacked by corporate interests, as we shall see in the next section.

Sustainable development as corporate sustainability

The concept of sustainable development emerged in the 1980s in an attempt to explore the relationship between development and the environment. While there are over 100 current definitions of sustainable development (Holmberg and Sandbrook, 1992), the one most commonly used is that by Brundtland (WCED, 1987). According to the Brundtland Commission, sustainable development is 'a process of change in which the exploitation of resources, direction of investments, orientation of technological development, and institutional change are made consistent with future as well as present needs' (ibid., p. 9). This broad definition is at the root of several controversies and there is considerable disagreement among scholars in different disciplines about how this definition should be operationalized and how sustainability should be measured. The Brundtland definition is really not a definition – it is a slogan and slogans, however pretty, do not make theory. As several authors have pointed out, the Brundtland definition does not elaborate on the notion of human needs and wants (Redclift, 1987; Kirkby *et al.*, 1995) and the concern for future generations is problematic in its operationalization. Given the scenario of limited resources, this assumption becomes a contradiction as most potential consumers (future generations) are unable to access the present market, or as Martinez-Alier (1987, p. 17) elegantly puts it, 'individuals not yet born have ontological difficulties in making their presence felt in today's market for exhaustible resources'.

Apart from attempting to reconcile economic growth with environmental maintenance, Bruntland's sustainable development agenda focuses on social justice and human development within the framework of social equity and the equitable distribution and utilization of resources. Sustainability, as Redclift (1987) points out, means different things to different people. Although theories of sustainability sometimes stress the primacy of social justice, the position is often reversed and 'justice is looked upon as subordinate to sustainability, and since neither sustainability nor social justice has determinate meanings, this opens the way to legitimizing one of them in terms of the other' (Dobson, 1998, p. 242). The terms sustainability and sustainable development are used interchangeably in both academic and popular discourses and the concept is promoted by 'situating it against the background of sustaining a particular set of social relations by way of a particular set of ecological projects' (Harvey, 1996, p. 148). Hence the debate on resource scarcity, biodiversity, population and ecological limits is ultimately a debate on the 'preservation of a particular social order rather than a debate about the preservation of nature per se' (ibid.).

Thus the challenges are to find new technologies and to expand the role of the market in allocating environmental resources in the assumption that putting a price on the natural environment is the only way to protect it, unless degrading it becomes more profitable (Beder, 1994). Rather than reshaping markets and production processes to fit the logic of nature, sustainable development uses the logic of markets and capitalist accumulation to determine the future of nature (Shiva, 1991).

The language of capital is quite apparent in discourses of sustainable development. For instance Pearce *et al.* (1989, p. 124) emphasize 'constancy of natural capital stock' as a necessary condition for sustainability. According to Pearce *et al.*, changes in the stock of natural resources should be 'non-negative' and man-made capital (products and services, as measured by traditional economics and accounting) and should not be created at the expense of natural capital (including both renewable and non-renewable natural resources). Thus growth or wealth must be created without resource depletion. Exactly how this is to be achieved remains a mystery. A majority of the sustainable development literature is of this 'eco-modernist' bent and addresses ways to operationalize the Brundtland concept. Therefore concepts such as 'sustainable cost', 'natural capital' and 'sustainable capital' are developed and touted as evidence of a paradigm shift (Bebbington and Gray, 1993). There is limited awareness of the fact that traditional notions of capital, income and growth continue to inform this 'new' paradigm. The uncritical acceptance of the current system of markets is also problematic: while markets are indeed efficient mechanisms to set prices they are incapable of reflecting true costs, such as the replacement cost of a mature tropical rainforest and the social costs of tobacco and alcohol consumption (Hawken, 1995).

Many large transnational corporations developed environmental and social responsibility policies in response to the broader critique of industrialization that emerged in the 1960s and 1970s. Public perceptions of environmental problems and increased environmental legislation are two key reasons why the environment has become an important issue for corporations, resulting in the need for companies to 'sell environmentalism' in order to be perceived as green (Banerjee, 2001b; Newton and Harte, 1997). Newton and Harte (ibid., p. 91) argue that organizations also paint themselves green to avoid regulatory control: one of the aims of the 'Vision of Sustainable Development' promoted by the Business Council for Sustainable Development is to 'maintain entrepreneurial freedom through voluntary initiatives rather than regulatory coercion'.

Efforts to broaden the scope of greening to include social sustainability are also under way. This 'triple bottom line' approach attempts to assess the social and environmental impacts of business, apart from its economic impact (Elkington, 1999). Elkington describes interactions between the environment, society and the economy as three 'shear zones' that produce a variety of opportunities and challenges for organizations. Many of the advances in cleaner technologies and emission reduction have arisen from the economic–environment shear zone, which is an area that business corporations are most comfortable with since it delivers measurable benefits to them. Outcomes of the social–environment and social–economy shear zones are more ambiguous (for corporations at least), although it is assumed is that organizations need to integrate these as well in order to survive in the long term. Theoretical perspectives of the triple bottom line approach focus on maximizing sustainability opportunities (corporate social responsibility, stakeholder relations and corporate governance) while minimizing sustainability-related risks (corporate risk management, environmental, health and safety audits and reporting). Proponents of the triple bottom line claim that by using these and other parameters it is possible to map the environmental and social domains of sustainability, and ultimately to assess the performance of corporations on a triple bottom line. However, research on the environmental and social dimensions of corporate sustainability is very much in its infancy. Although this approach is proving popular among large transnational corporations the impact on local communities is unclear. The same companies that are being targeted by NGOs and indigenous communities for their detrimental environmental and social impacts are at the forefront of espousing triple bottom line principles, and it remains to be seen whether this approach can deliver real benefits to communities or will become a more sophisticated form of green-washing. There is a real danger that the glossy 'social performance' reports by transnational corporations will deflect attention from the grim realities of their environmental performance.

That corporations play a significant part in sustainability is not in doubt. The question is, are current environmental practices compatible with sustainability? Some researchers caution that the greening of industry should not be confused with sustainable development (Pearce *et al.*, 1989; Westley and Vredenburg, 1996; Schot *et al.*, 1997; Welford, 1997). While there have been significant advances in pollution control and emission reduction, this does not mean that current modes of development are sustainable for the planet as a whole (Hart, 1997). Most companies focus on operational issues when it comes to greening and lack a 'vision of sustainability' (ibid.). In a recent 'Greening of Industry' conference the proposed corporate strategy for sustainable development held no surprises: the focus was on 'scientific innovation, public service and turning the world populations into active consumers of its new products, and expanding global business into the less affluent segments of the world's population' (Rossi *et al.*, 2000, p. 275).

Discourses on sustainable development are becoming increasingly corporatized. For instance in 2000 Dow Jones launched a 'Sustainability Group Index' after a survey of Fortune 500 companies. A sustainable corporation was defined as one 'that aims at increasing long-term shareholder value by integrating economic, environmental and social growth opportunities into its corporate and business strategies' (Dow Jones website). It is interesting to observe how notions of sustainability are constructed, manipulated and represented in both the popular business press and academic literature. As evidence of the deleterious effects of development has mounted the discourse has shifted from sustainable development to the more positive sounding sustainability and then to corporate sustainability. Corporate discourses on sustainability produce an elision that displaces the focus from global planetary sustainability to sustaining the corporation through 'growth opportunities'. What will happen if environmental and social issues do not result in growth opportunities is unclear, the assumption being that global sustainability can be achieved only through market exchanges. Despite framing sustainable development as a 'strategic discontinuity' that will change 'today's fundamental economics', corporate discourses on sustainable development, not surprisingly, promote the 'business-as-usual but greener' line and do not contain any radical change in world-views. As Monsanto's ex-CEO Robert Shapiro has put it, 'Far from being a soft issue grounded in emotion or ethics, sustainable development involves cold, rational business logic' (Magretta, 1997, p. 81). This (post)modern form of corporate social responsibility produces a truth effect that is not unlike Milton Friedman's (1962) concept of corporate social responsibility as involving the maximization of shareholder value, despite the rhetoric of stakeholders and corporate citizenship (Banerjee, 2000, 2001a). The much touted stakeholder approach to corporate citizenship is not without problems and contradictions, as we shall see in the next section.

The complicities of stakeholder theory

A popular framework touted by many management scholars for addressing organization–environment interactions is stakeholder theory. This approach continues to receive a great deal of attention, as evidenced by the publication of dozens of books and more than 100 journal articles (Donaldson and Preston, 1995). While conventional theories of the firm focus on its responsibilities towards its shareholders, the stakeholder perspective takes a broader view and implies that a company should consider the needs of all its stakeholders. Stakeholders are defined as 'any group or individual who can affect or is affected by the organisation's objectives' (Freeman and Reed, 1983, p. 91). This broad view is not without its problems: different stakeholders have differing stakes and balancing the needs of competing stakeholders is not an easy task. Moreover, stakeholder theory is derived from Western notions of (economic) rationality and fails to address the needs of marginalized groups, such as indigenous stakeholders.

A stakeholder perspective is also supposed to be helpful in analyzing and evaluating an organization's 'social performance' in terms of how it manages its relationship with society (Clarkson, 1995). Stakeholder theory is normative with moral overtones. It focuses on what a company should do in order to fulfil its societal responsibilities. It is also instrumental in that it is expected to lead to better organizational performance (a hypothesis that is yet to be tested), and it is descriptive in that it posits a model of the corporation as a 'constellation of cooperative and competitive interests possessing intrinsic value' (Donaldson and Preston, 1995, p. 66).

The normative core of stakeholder theory is said to be a driver of corporate social performance, and once managers accept their obligations to stakeholders and recognize their legitimacy the corporation is well on its way to achieving its moral principles (Clarkson, 1995). This simplistic argument fails to recognize the inability of a framework to represent different realities and the effects of using a single lens to view issues such as legitimacy and responsibility. Proponents of stakeholder theory claim that corporate social performance can be evaluated according to the management of the corporation's relationships with its stakeholders. The fact that social performance has to be 'managed' implies that, as is the case with business ethics, it is deployed as a strategy to benefit the corporation. Who decides what is socially appropriate? Who assesses it? Social appropriateness is often subsumed under notions of progress and development and obscures the fact that somebody is defining appropriateness and somebody else is being appropriated.

The literature on stakeholder theory also distinguishes between a 'social issue' and a 'stakeholder issue'. According to Clarkson (ibid.), a particular society determines what a social issue is and the representative government enacts appropriate legislation to protect social interests. Hence a test of whether an issue is social or not is the presence or absence of legislation. Thus health and safety, equal opportunity and environmental issues are social issues because legislation exists. This is an unsatisfactory argument in that fails to address the fact that segments of society are legislated against. For instance in the case of indigenous communities throughout the world, legislation designed to protect their rights is often a legacy of colonialism, regulated by neocolonial modes of control by neocolonial institutions. If there is no legislation the issue becomes a 'stakeholder issue' that has to be addressed at the corporate level (ibid.).

The argument that business should be socially responsible stems from the notion that 'society grants legitimacy and power to business and in the long run, those who do not use power in a manner which society considers responsible will tend lose it' (Davis, 1973, p. 314). Economic systems, governments and institutions often determine what is legitimate, and this power to determine legitimacy cannot be easily withdrawn. While customers, employees, shareholders and governments may be able to withdraw legitimacy, forcing a corporation either to change its approach or to perish, the power of marginalized communities to do so is severely constrained.

Because the scope and level of application for determining the boundaries of legitimacy are institutional and societal, stakeholder theory urges organizations to be 'publicly responsible for outcomes related to their primary and secondary areas of involvement with society' (Preston and Post, 1975, p. 86; Wood, 1991). This principle of public responsibility is designed to make larger societal concerns more relevant by providing behavioural parameters for organizations. However, social responsibilities should be relevant to the organization's interests (Wood, 1991) and therein lies the problem: these public responsibilities are defined and framed by larger principles of legitimacy, principles that are inimical to certain marginalized stakeholders. Thus the parameters that define a social outcome are determined by a system of rules and exclusions that may not address these concerns. The public–private dichotomy of stakeholder representation does not legitimize stakeholder interests, instead it serves to regulate stakeholder behaviour. Who is seeking stakeholder input, and for what purpose? Public interests are represented by government agencies that seek stakeholder input to obtain information designed to legitimize support for their decisions.

If the institutional and organizational levels of corporate social responsibility are inimical to stakeholder interests, then the principle of managerial discretion (Carroll, 1979) is even more constrained. According to Wood (1991, p. 698), 'managers are moral actors. Within every domain of corporate social responsibility, they are obliged to exercise such discretion as is available to them, toward socially responsible outcomes.' The fallacy of managers being 'moral actors' is revealed by the Foucauldian notion of subjectification, which shows how managers become constituted as subjects who secure their meaning and reality by identifying with a particular sense of their relationship with the firm (Knights, 1992). Individual managers' role in accommodating stakeholder interests is predefined at higher levels, and practices at this level are governed and organized by organizational and institutional discourses.

The search for a legitimate, normative core for stakeholder theory must therefore be conducted with caution, with the understanding that this search, like any other search, is predicated on institutional interests. In an attempt to identify which stakeholders really count, Mitchell *et al.* (1997) have classified stakeholders according to their possession of three attributes: power (the stakeholder's power to influence the company), legitimacy (of the stakeholder's relationship with the company) and urgency (the extent to which the stakeholder's demands require immediate attention). However defining the basis of stakeholder legitimacy is problematic and is typically framed from the perspective of economic rationalism. In the 1960s firms did not view environmental organizations or consumer groups that opposed corporate actions as legitimate stakeholders. As these groups grew in power, corporations were forced to take their claims, into account, to the extent that several movements were co-opted into the economic rationalist framework. The green movement started out as a grass-roots, antibusiness movement; today the environmental agenda is set by corporations, not environmental organizations.

Thus one of the tasks of corporations is to prioritize stakeholders according to an analysis of the corporation–stakeholder relationship. Senior managers of corporations determine the salience of stakeholders, and those which are deemed salient tend to receive management attention. Typically, corporations tend to focus on stakeholders with higher degrees of power, legitimacy and urgency, and the demands of these 'definitive' stakeholders (ibid.) normally receive the attention of top management. Interestingly Mitchell *et al.* (ibid., p. 878) define stakeholders who have urgency and power but lack legitimacy as 'dangerous stakeholders' and condemn their actions as being 'outside the bounds of legitimacy, dangerous both to the stakeholder–manager relationship and to the individuals and entities involved'. They single out 'wildcat strikers' and 'coercive environmentalists' as examples of dangerous stakeholders. They feel duty bound to identify dangerous stakeholders without acknowledging them because they 'abhor their practices'. They argue that by refusing to acknowledge such stakeholders they are 'counteracting terror in all its forms [which] is an effective counteragent in the battle to maintain civility and civilization' (ibid.). While these writers should be applauded for their virtuous stand (the very essence of the white-liberal leftist approach) on violence, it must be remembered that there are very few theoretical frameworks in organization studies to understand the continuing violence that development and management theories impose on indigenous peoples throughout the world. Their argument is both ill-defined and insidious: there is no attempt to analyze the problematic notion of legitimacy (apart from a passing remark that legitimacy is socially constructed) and the power dynamics involved in setting the bounds of legitimacy.

The stakeholder framework developed by Mitchell *et al.* is particularly problematic for marginalized groups trying to negotiate their survival with corporations and governments. Their portrayal of the African National Congress in South Africa as an 'urgent' stakeholder with no 'legitimacy given the ruling South African culture and government' is a case in point (ibid., p. 878). The ANC was made illegitimate by a ruling elite that had the power to make laws governing legitimacy. Mitchell *et al.* claim that the ANC moved from being a demanding stakeholder (possessing urgency but no legitimacy or power) to a dangerous one by using coercive power. They argue that it was only when the ANC relinquished coercive power and became a dependent stakeholder that it achieved success by acquiring the support of more salient stakeholders (such as international investors). Moreover, they state (with very little evidence) that the worldwide disinvestment by stockholders of transnational corporations was a major force in the transformation of South Africa and the legitimization of the ANC. The breathtaking arrogance of this position not only denies years of struggle against colonial domination, but also serves to justify the ruling South African culture and government of the time as legitimate, a flawed and ahistorical argument that displaces attention from the coercive power used by 'legitimate' governments to the coercive power used by the ANC in its resistance (the authors are silent on the former but of course abhor the latter).

If, as Mitchell *et al.* assert, the stakeholder theory of the firm 'holds the key to more effective management and to a more useful, comprehensive theory of the firm in society' (ibid., p. 880), it might be prudent for marginalized stakeholders to change their locks. The stakeholder theory of the firm represents a form of stakeholder colonialism that serves to regulate the behaviour of stakeholders. That the (perceived) integration of stakeholders' needs might be an effective means for a firm to enhance its image is probably true. However, for a critical understanding of stakeholder theory this approach is unsatisfactory. Effective practices of managing stakeholders and research aimed at generating knowledge about stakeholders are less systems of truth than products of power applied by corporations, governments and business schools (Knights, 1992). As Willmott (1995) points out, the establishment of new organizational theories are very much the outcome of the historical development of capitalism and create value only for particular people and institutions. A full picture of the consequences of stakeholder theory and practice requires us to step out of the frame. A more critical examination of stakeholder theory, for instance understanding that stakeholder relations are systematized and controlled by the imperatives of capital accumulation, may produce a very different picture. Notions of power, legitimacy and urgency and the resultant practice of identifying stakeholder salience are contingent on the particularities of nation states, industries, organizations or other institutions (Willmott, 1995), and in the process of stakeholder integration they either negate alternative practices or assimilate them.

A critical perspective on stakeholder theory involves examining how knowledge and theory development in the field constitutes social relations between different stakeholders, and perhaps even sets the ground for a different set of conditions, which in turn needs to be critiqued. It should go beyond structuralist notions of cause and effect. Thus instead of asking the structuralist question – what are the general rules governing stakeholder relations determined in relation to other similar relations? – the question becomes post-structuralist: what gives this particular person the right or power to say this? Why this statement and not some other one? The post-structuralist question is therefore more historical and less universalizing (Muecke, 1992). Popular dimensions of organizations that invoke notions such as diffusion, democracy, market, empowerment, flexibility, trust and collectivity also need to be critically examined and countered by investigating how these corporate objectives, along with the notions of values and ethics, increasingly dominate all other social agendas, giving rise to a new corporate colonialism (Goldsmith, 1997; Grice and Humphries, 1997). Countering positive knowledge is a definite item on the agenda for critical management studies, along with an understanding of 'how management knowledge results from and contributes to a particular disciplinary regime' (Knights, 1992, p. 519). Developing critical ways of thinking about and seeing management theory requires an investigation of forms of domination in locations other than the office or factory; perhaps this could be more effective in initiating revolutionary change (Poster, 1989).

Implications for theory and practice

So what implications does this critique of sustainable development have for the study of corporate citizenship in organizations? It is unlikely that any radical revision of sustainable development will emerge from organizations, given how the discourse is constructed at higher levels of the political economy. For any such rethinking to occur a more critical approach to organization theory is required and new questions need to be raised, not only about the ecological and social sustainability of business corporations but also about the political economy itself. Corporate citizenship practices are informed by the larger debate on sustainable development and therefore radical revisions at this level can only occur if there is a shift in thinking at the macro level. There are three implications for the study of organizations that a critique of sustainable development can provide.

First, we need to broaden our definition of organizations and open up new spaces for critique. An overwhelming proportion of research on management focuses on traditional profit-oriented corporations, and the bulk of research on not-for-profit organizations is framed by similar corporate goals: how can we raise more money for charity, or how can we get more people into our museums or libraries or zoos? There are very few studies in the management literature about the operations of international bodies such as the World Trade Organisation, the United Nations and the World Bank. While these are not corporate organizations in the traditional sense of the term, they are powerful agents in advancing the discourse on sustainability and should come under the purview of organization studies. We must also acknowledge that modern organizations often reflect colonial formations. Employing a postcolonial perspective for the study of organizations might provide new spaces for critique and resistance. Although critical organization theorists portray organizations as structures of domination, legitimacy and 'reflexive social systems' (Leflaive, 1996; Courpasson, 2000), participants in recent debates on modernist and postmodernist forms of organization have been curiously silent on the colonial dimensions that frame organization–environment relationships.

Second, we need to open up new spaces and provide new frameworks for organization–stakeholder dialogues as well as critically examine the dynamics of the relationships between corporations, NGOs, governments, community groups and funding agencies. Contemporary discourses on organizations and their stakeholders are inevitably constrained by 'practical' reasons such as the profit-seeking behaviour of corporations (Treviño and Weaver, 1999). While the vast body of literature on corporate social responsibility, stakeholder integration and business ethics is based on the assumption that business is influenced by societal concerns, the dominance of societal interests in radically reshaping business practices is in some question (Mueller, 1994). The domain of corporate social responsibility cannot be assessed by primarily economic criteria, and neither can an environmental ethic be developed through an 'ethically pragmatic managerial' morality that primarily serves organizational interests (Fineman, 1998; Snell, 2000). While NGOs do serve as important counterpoints, their relationships with corporations and governments are often ambiguous and framed by categories furnished by international institutions such as the UN and the World Bank, categories that are inimical to many groups that are negatively affected by corporations (Spivak, 1999). Increasing the accountability of both corporations and NGOs to local communities and translating 'participation' into more meaningful local contexts without reducing social movements to some other form of domination (the prerogatives of donor agencies, for example) is a challenge for the future (Escobar, 1992; Derman, 1995).

Third, we need to interrogate espoused corporate practices of sustainability. Discourses on corporate greening, whether based on 'deep ecology', 'ecocentric' or 'sustaincentric' management need to be interrogated and their constructs and concepts examined through a critical lens. Despite calls for a 'Fundamental revision of organisation studies concepts and theories' (Shrivastava, 1994, p. 720) there are no suggestions as to how this will occur. It is unclear how alternative conceptualizations of an organization's environment (ibid.) or 'a complete moral transformation within the corporation' (Crane, 2000, p. 673) will naturally lead to social justice or a more equitable distribution of resources. Fundamental changes in organizations cannot occur unless there are corresponding shifts in the larger political economy and fundamental questions are asked about the role of a corporation and its license to operate in society. All the exhortations of green organization theorists do not begin to address the huge impediments involved in restructuring the political economy and abandoning conventional notions of competition and consumption (Newton and Harte, 1997). If organizational analysis involves understanding the way in which organizations are produced in particular societal contexts (Leflaive, 1996) and how 'external constraints of the environment are translated into organisational imperatives' (Knights and Morgan, 1993, p. 212), then a critique of contemporary notions of sustainable development should allow us to examine the emergence of grass-roots organizations involved in resistance movements as to well as to highlight corporate strategies for co-opting and managing the environment. It should also enable us to examine the structures and processes that discursively produce external environmental constraints and how social and cultural relations are changed by organizations. The critique should allow us to broaden the debate to include the political economy and alternative approaches to addressing environmental problems, something that the current environmental management discourse fails to address (Levy, 1997). By placing a critique of capital and capitalisms firmly at the center of the debate rather than the uneasy invisible position it currently occupies in most organizational theories (Pitelis, 1993), it should also allow us to see how nation states, international organizations and transnational corporations support the needs of international capital.

Critical questioning of the sustainability of current economic systems is rarely found in the literature and much of the theorizing on green business is what Newton and Harte (1997) call 'technicist kitsch', laced with liberal doses of evangelical rhetoric. As long as conceptions of sustainable development continue to be driven solely by rationalizations of competitive advantage, no paradigmatic shift in world-views of nature and sustainability can take place. 'Green consumption' will not save the world because rather than attempting to reconstitute politically the mode of modern production to meet ecological constraints, it advocates 'non-political, non-social, non-institutional solutions to environmental problems' (Luke, 1994, p. 158). Corporate 'green marketing' strategies continue to focus on the economic bottom line at the organizational level (Banerjee, 1999) without addressing the macromarketing implications of the relationships between technological, political and economic institutions and their role in environmental decline (Kilbourne *et al.*, 1997). A critical examination of the relationship between the dominant socioeconomic paradigm and the environment will highlight how colonial capitalist development increases social inequalities and, despite its knowledge claims, results in a loss of ecological knowledge. Any attempt to envision alternative ecologies must involve visions of alternative societies and politics as well (Guha, 1989).

The recent North–South conflict over the World Trade Organisation's controversial Trade Related Aspects of Intellectual Property Agreement (TRIPS) is a case in point. The TRIPS agreement legitimizes private property rights through intellectual property over life forms. These rights are for individuals, states and corporations, not for indigenous peoples and local communities. In effect governments are asked to change their national intellectual property rights laws to allow the patenting of micro-organisms, non-biological and micro-biological processes. Two related problems arise from imposing a regime of intellectual property rights on indigenous knowledge. First, traditional knowledge belongs to the indigenous community rather than specific individuals. Second, as indigenous communities all over the world have discovered, national governments are increasingly employing neoliberal agendas (some willingly, a majority through coercion) that have adverse effects on indigenous people's livelihoods by restricting community access to natural resources. Equitable sharing of commercial benefits through mutually beneficial contracts between indigenous groups and transnational corporations is unlikely to occur, given the disparities in resources and capacities to monitor or enforce the terms of any contract.

The TRIPS agreement was developed in large part at the Uruguay Round of GATT by the Intellectual Property Committee (IPC), which consisted of the representatives of many transnational firms, including Bristol Myers, Merck, Monsanto, Du Pont and Pfizer. Monsanto's representative described the TRIPS strategy as follows:

> [We were able to] distil from the laws of the more advanced countries the fundamental principles for protecting all forms of intellectual property … . Besides selling our concept at home, we went to Geneva where we presented our document to the staff of the GATT Secretariat … . What I have described to you is absolutely unprecedented in GATT. Industry identified a major problem for international trade. It crafted a solution, reduced it to a concrete proposal, and sold it to our own and other governments … the

industries and traders of the world have played simultaneously the role of patients, the diagnosticians and the prescribing physicians. (Rifkin, 1999, p. 52)

This is another example of how corporate power is wielded in international trade and why any analysis of corporate citizenship at the level of an individual organization cannot address broader social concerns. The TRIPS agreement sparked in mass protests by indigenous and peasant communities and NGOs in Asia, Africa and South America that continue to this day (Dawkins, 1997). These resistance movements, along with widespread protests by European consumers, have had some effect in slowing the rate at which biotechnology is adopted by transnational corporations. After an aggressive campaign to promote biotechnology in agriculture, several leading transnational corporations have retreated from this arena, or at least temporarily, because of the backlash by European consumers.

The rhetoric of democracy and participation in contemporary discourses on free markets and in international forums on sustainable development also needs to be examined through a critical lens. At the 1992 Rio summit there were open conflicts between corporations, their trade associations, NGOs and indigenous community leaders over environmental regulations. The demands of NGOs were shelved and instead a voluntary code of conduct developed by the Business Council for Sustainable Development (consisting of a number of transnational corporations) was approved in what was supposed to be a democratic process of developing an action plan for sustainable development (Hawken, 1995).

For example an ongoing UN development programme is called 'Global Sustainable Development Facility – 2B2M: 2 Billion to the Market By the Year 2020', a title that embodies what is wrong with current notions of sustainable development in that it reveals the continuities of this alleged discontinuity from prior notions of economic growth and development. The fact that a significant proportion of the programme's team members come from transnational corporations that have imposed environmental and social damage on indigenous and rural populations simply strengthens the notion that international organizations do not and cannot serve community interests. Not one of the several hundreds of UN projects has ever challenged economic globalism or growth-oriented solutions, despite their rhetoric of empowering rural communities. In the current political economy it is simply not possible simultaneously to empower rural communities and transnational corporations and, as we have seen, any compromise tends seriously to disadvantage the former group.

Sustainable development is being managed in the same way as development has been managed: according to ethnocentric, capitalist notions of managerial efficiency that merely reproduce earlier articulations of decentralized capitalism in the guise of sustainable capitalism. The macroeconomic criteria for sustainable development have now become corporatized: development is sustainable only if it is profitable, it is sustainable only if it can be transacted through the market. As Visvanathan (1991) points out, the Brundtland report (WCED, 1987) focuses on uniformity and order, organizing the future into resources, energy, populations, cities and towns, with little place for plurality, difference or multiplicity. There is still a belief that better technology and management and better and more inclusive procedures by international institutions such as the World Bank and the World Trade Organisation can save the planet. As Redclift (2000) points out there is a danger that the current discourses on sustainability, with their focus on what is sustainable and how it is measured, will lose their radical and political edge. Perhaps sustainable development will share the fate of the environmental movement, which is increasingly being depoliticized by environmental policies that translate environmental choices into market preferences.

References

Banerjee, S. B. (1999) 'Corporate environmentalism and the greening of strategic marketing', in M. Charter and M. Polonsky (eds), *Greener Marketing: A Global Perspective to Greening Marketing Practice* (Sheffield: Greenleaf), pp. 16–40.

Banerjee, S. B. (2000) 'Whose land is it anyway? National interest, indigenous stakeholders and colonial discourses: The case of the Jabiluka uranium mine', *Organisation & Environment*, 13(1), pp. 3–38.

Banerjee, S. B. (2001a) 'Corporate citizenship and indigenous stakeholders: Exploring a new dynamic of organizational–stakeholder relationships', *Journal of Corporate Citizenship*, 1, pp. 39–55.

Banerjee, S. B. (2001b) 'Managerial perceptions of corporate environmentalism: interpretations from industry and strategic implications for organisations', *Journal of Management Studies*, 38(4), pp. 489–513.

Bebbington, J. and R. Gray (1993) 'Corporate accountability and the physical environment: social responsibility and accounting beyond profit', *Business Strategy and the Environment*, 2(2), pp. 1–11.

Beder, S. (1994) ' "evoltin" developments: The politics of sustainable development', *Arena Magazine*, June–July, pp. 37–9.

Birch, D. (2001) 'Corporate citizenship: Rethinking business beyond corporate social responsibility', in J. Andriof and M. McIntosh (eds), *Perspectives on Corporate Citizenship* (Sheffield: Greenleaf), pp. 53–65.

Carroll, A. B. (1979) 'A three-dimensional conceptual model of corporate social performance', *Academy of Management Review*, 4, pp. 497–505.

Clarkson, M. B. E. (1995) 'A stakeholder framework for analyzing and evaluating corporate social performance', *Academy of Management Review*, 20(1), pp. 92–117.

Courpasson, D. (2000) 'Managerial strategies of domination. Power in soft bureaucracies', *Organisation Studies*, 21(1), pp. 141–61.

Crane, A. (2000) 'Corporate greening as amoralization', *Organisation Studies*, 21(4), pp. 673–96.

Davenport, K. S. (2000) Corporate citizenship: A stakeholder approach for defining corporate social performance and identifying measures for assessing it', *Business and Society*, 3(2), pp. 210–19.

Davis, K. (1973) 'The case for and against business assumption of social responsibilities', *Academy of Management Journal*, 16, pp. 312–22.

Dawkins, K. (1997) *Gene Wars: The Politics of Biotechnology* (New York: Seven Stories Press).

Derman, B. (1995) 'Environmental NGO's, dispossession, and the state: The ideology and praxis of African nature and development', *Human Ecology*, 23(2), pp. 199–215.

Dobson, A. (1998) *Social Justice and the Environment* (Oxford: Oxford University Press).

Donaldson, T. and L. E. Preston (1995) 'The stakeholder theory of the corporation: concepts, evidence and implications', *Academy of Management Review*, 20(1), pp. 65–91.

Elkington, J. (1999) *Cannibals with Forks: The Triple Bottom Line of 21st Century Business* (Oxford: Capstone).

Enron (2002) *Corporate Responsibility Annual Report* (www.enron.com/corp/pressroom/responsibility/CRANNUAL.pdf).

Escobar, A. (1992) 'Imagining a post-development era: Critical thought, development and social movements', *Social Text*, 31(32), pp. 20–56.

Fineman, S. (1998) 'The natural environment, organisation and ethics', in A. Parker (ed.), *Ethics and Organisations*, pp. 238–252.

Freeman, R. E. and D. E. Reed (1983) 'Stockholders and shareholders: a new perspective on corporate governance', *California Management Review*, 25(3), pp. 93–4.

Friedman, M. (1962) *Capitalism and Freedom* (Chicago, Ill.: University of Chicago Press).

Goldsmith, E. (1997) 'Development as colonialism', *The Ecologist*, 27(2), pp. 60–79.

Grice, S. and M. Humphries (1997) 'Critical management studies in postmodernity: Oxymorons in outer space?', *Journal of Organisation Change Management*, 10(5), pp. 412–25.

Guha, R. (1989) 'Radical American environmentalism and wilderness preservation: A Third World critique', *Environmental Ethics*, 11(1), pp. 71–81.

Hart, S. L. (1997) 'Beyond greening: strategies for a sustainable world', *Harvard Business Review*, Jan./Feb., pp. 6–76.

Harvey, D. (1996) *Justice, Nature and the Geography of Difference* (Oxford: Blackwell).

Hawken, P. (1995) *The Ecology of Commerce: A Declaration of Sustainability* (London: Phoenix).

Holmberg, J. and R. Sandbrook (1992) 'Sustainable development: What is to be done?,' in J. Holmberg (ed.), *Policies for a Small Planet* (London: Earthscan).

Kilbourne, W., P. McDonagh and A. Prothero (1997) 'Sustainable consumption and the quality of life: A macromarketing challenge to the dominant social paradigm', *Journal of Macromarketing*, 14, pp. 23–42.

Kirkby, J., P. O'Keefe and L. Timberlake (1995) *Sustainable Development* (London: Earthscan).

Knights, D. (1992), 'Changing spaces: the disruptive impact of a new epistemological location for the study of management', *Academy of Management Review*, 17(3), pp. 514–36.

Knights, D. and G. Morgan (1993) 'Organisation theory and consumption in a post-modern era', *Organisation Studies*, 14(2), pp. 211–18.

Leflaive, X. (1996) 'Organisations as structures of domination', *Organisation Studies*, 17(1), pp. 23–37.

Levy, D. (1996) 'Environmental management as political sustainability', *Organisation & Environment*, 10(2), pp. 126–47.

Luke, T. W. (1993) 'Green consumerism: Ecology and the ruse of recycling', in J. Bennett, and W. Chaloupka (eds), *In the Nature of Things* (Minneapolis, Min.: University of Minneapolis Press), pp. 154–72.

Magretta, J. (1997) 'Growth through global sustainability; An interview with Monsanto's CEO, Robert B. Shapiro', *Harvard Business Review*, Jan.–Feb., pp. 79–88.

Martinez-Alier, J. (1987) *Ecological Economics: Energy, Environment and Society* (Oxford: Blackwell).

Mitchell, N. J. (1989) *The Generous Corporation: A Political Analysis of Economic Power* (New Haven, CT: Yale University Press).

Mitchell, R., B. Agle, and D. Wood (1997) 'Toward a theory of stakeholder identification and salience: Defining the principle of who and what really counts', *Academy of Management Review*, 22(4), pp. 853–86.

Muecke, S. (1992) *Textual Spaces: Aboriginality and Cultural Studies* (Sydney: University of New South Wales Press).

Mueller, F. (1994) 'Societal effect, organisation effect and globalization', *Organisation Studies*, 15(3), pp. 407–23.

Newton, T. and G. Harte (1997) 'Green business; technicist kitsch?', *Journal of Management Studies*, 34(1), pp. 75–98.

Pearce, D. W., A. Markandya and E. B. Barbier (1989) *Blueprint for a Green Economy* (London: Earthscan).

Phillip Morris (2002) *Listening, Learning and Changing: The Path to Corporate Responsibility at Philip Morris Companies* (www.philipmorris.com/pressroom/executive_speeches/speech_nicoli_fresno.asp).

Pitelis, C. (1993) 'Transnationals, international organisation and deindustrialization', *Organisation Studies*, 14(4), pp. 527–43.

Poster, M. (1989) *Critical Theory and Poststructuralism: In Search of a Context* (Ithaca, NY: Cornell University Press).

Preston, L. E. and J. E. Post (1975) *Private Management and Public Policy: The Principle of Public Responsibility* (Englewood Cliffs, NJ: Prentice-Hall).

Redclift, M. (1987) *Sustainable Development: Exploring the Contradictions* (London: Metheun).

Redclift, M. (2000) 'Post-sustainability', paper presented at the International Sociological Association RC24 Miniconference, Rio de Janeiro, 1–3 August.

Rifkin, J. (1999) *The Biotech Century: How Genetic Commerce will Change the World* (London: Phoenix).

Rossi, M. S., H. S. Brown and L. W. Baas (2000) 'Leaders in sustainable development: How agents of change define the agenda', *Business Strategy and the Environment*, 9, pp. 273–86.

Schot, J., E. Brand and K. Fischer (1997) 'The greening of industry or a sustainable future: Building an international research agenda', *Business Strategy and the Environment*, 6, pp. 153–62.

Shiva, V. (1991) *The Violence of the Green Revolution: Third World Agriculture, Ecology and Politics* (London: Zed Books).

Shrivastava, P. (1994) 'Castrated environment: Greening organisational studies', *Organisation Studies*, 15(5), pp. 705–21.

Snell, R. S. (2000) 'Studying moral ethos using an adapted Kohlbergian model', *Organisation Studies*, 21(1), pp. 267–95.

Spivak, G. C. (1999) *A Critique of Postcolonial Reason: Toward a History of the Vanishing Present* (Cambridge, Mass.: Harvard University Press).

Swanson, D. and B. P. Niehoff (2001) 'Business citizenship outside and inside organisations: An emergent synthesis of corporate responsibility and employee citizenship', in J. Andriof and M. McIntosh (eds), *Perspectives on Corporate Citizenship* (Sheffield: Greenleaf), pp. 104–16.

Treviño, L. K. and G. R. Weaver (1999) 'The stakeholder research tradition: Converging theorists – not convergent theory', *Academy of Management Review*, 24(2), pp. 222–7.

Visvanathan, S. (1991) 'Mrs Brundtland's disenchanted cosmos', *Alternatives*, 16(3), pp. 377–84.

World Commission for Economic Development (WCED) (1987) *Our Common Future* (New York: Oxford University Press).

Waddock, S. (2001) 'Integrity and mindfulness: Foundations of corporate citizenship', in J. Andriof and M. McIntosh (eds), *Perspectives on Corporate Citizenship* (Sheffield: Greenleaf), pp. 26–38.

Welford, R. (1997) *Hijacking Environmentalism: Corporate Responses to Sustainable Development* (London: Earthscan).

Westley, F. and H. Vredenburg (1996) 'Sustainability and the corporation: Criteria for aligning economic practice with environmental protection', *Journal of Management Inquiry*, 5(2), pp. 104–19.

Willmott, H. (1995) 'What has been happening in organisation theory and does it matter?', *Personnel Review*, 24(8), pp. 33–53.

Windsor, D. (2001) 'Corporate citizenship: Evolution and interpretation', in J. Andriof and M. McIntosh (eds), *Perspectives on Corporate Citizenship* (Sheffield: Greenleaf), pp. 39–52.

Wood, D. (1991) 'Corporate social performance revisited', *Academy of Management Review*, 16(4), pp. 691–718.

Wood, D. J. and J. M. Logsdon (2001) 'Theorizing business citizenship', in J. Andriof and M. McIntosh (eds), *Perspectives on Corporate Citizenship* (Sheffield: Greenleaf), pp. 83–103.

4

In Good Company: Reflections on the Changing Nature of the Contemporary Business Enterprise and its Embedded Value Systems

Michiel Schoemaker and Jan Jonker

Introduction

The way in which the business enterprise operates in the global market has become the subject of a lively debate in Western society. Trying to redefine the role of organizations, and particularly the business enterprise, is a crucial element of this debate. The concept generally relates to the need for more responsible behaviour, increased social commitment and greater environmental care – in short, corporate social responsibility (CSR). On the surface the debate is supported by growing awareness of the need to protect the environment, concern about the depletion of natural resources and awareness of social inequality around the world. More fundamentally CSR is about organizations taking greater social responsibility and becoming good corporate citizens. The central notion is that organizations should act beyond their traditional business boundaries, their purpose no longer restricted to generating profit but extended to include a contribution to the cohesion of society and consideration of the social and ecological environment. This challenges the firmly established belief in Anglo-Saxon economies that social issues are secondary to the priority challenges of corporate management.

CSR is a rapidly growing but still rather fuzzy movement. Despite the rich variety of the terms used in the CSR debate and the multitude of items it addresses, its core purpose seems to be to question the role and function of profit-oriented organizations in contemporary society. Different countries focus on different areas (Habisch, 2005), but all are driven by the need to realign the balance between market, state and civil society. The actors and institutions involved are trying to achieve this by engaging in a process of trial and error. A principal reason why the CSR debate is becoming more important is the growing interdependence and increasing interaction between the organization and its social, political, economic and ecological environment. Traditional organizational boundaries have become more or less obsolete or redundant. What was once outside the organization is now inside and vice versa. The organization is being forced to become an open system and operate as part of a flexible network in order to survive in its unpredictable and complex environment. Leaving aside ontological debates on what CSR is or ought to be, there is a number of strong reasons for its present relevance:

- There has been a fundamental institutional shift in the balance of power between the market, government and society. Society is moving from industrial to informational capitalism, and the ability to create an intangible business proposition has become key to business continuity.
- There is a strong ecological purpose. Never before has mankind consumed the world's natural resources at such a rapid pace, and over exploitation and pollution are the most visible consequences of this.
- There are new societal divides, in terms of not only economic access but also of access to technology, information and education. In today's networked world, those who are connected or disconnected constitute the new divides in society.
- Institutional, cultural and societal changes are transforming the society of places into a society based on spaces and structured around items, flows, networks and instant arrangements. It is no wonder that many people are becoming disoriented.
- Geographical and local collectivism is giving way to individualism. The social cohesion and capital necessary to make society work seem to be decreasing at a rapid rate.
- In the past decades there has been a fundamental shift in the general world perspective. Past notions of time and space have become redundant, leading to a confusing global village view of society.
- There has been a decline in the influence of the nation state and other institutional structures. Businesses, NGOs and civil society at large are becoming implicitly responsible for recalibrating the institutions of society.

The order, importance and impact of these developments, how they fit together, how specific configurations reinforce each other and the course these developments will take in the future are not the subject of this chapter, but for our purposes they indicate that doing business in the traditional way is obsolete and new practices are required. The contemporary debate on CSR can be viewed as a sometimes contradictory analysis of symptoms of a society in the midst of a fundamental transition. It implies that organizations are being confronted with developments that have upset the balance of the established market paradigm. Other (and many new) values are at stake, making it necessary to add values that go beyond a one-sided economic perspective.

During the last decade much effort has been expended on developing programmes for and approaches to CSR within and outside organizations. In general these efforts have been piecemeal, aimed mainly at one area (for example the environment, marketing or reporting) and at best leading to superficial local improvements. A survey of the websites of multinational enterprises reveals that to varying degrees they have all adopted the language of CSR and are struggling with the issue of how to combine emergent and often unrelated activities into a coherent strategy (Jonker and van Pijkeren, 2005). We argue that they should now move on from mere awareness of CSR and embed it in the everyday actions of all people in the organization (Jonker, 2003).

Given the nature and complexity of the developments discussed above the direction organizations should take is not entirely clear. In this chapter we suggest that CSR should be viewed as a broad phenomenon that needs to be interpreted and translated on the job by the organizational actors; that is, to find new ways of acting and organizing through trial and error. Embracing CSR requires a different world-view, one that takes into account the fundamental shift in societal balances. The central question we shall explore in this chapter is the changing nature of the contemporary business enterprise and its embedded value system, and the way in which CSR can be turned into a set of organizational values.

In order to gain a clearer understanding of what is happening the following section presents a brief historical background of the development of organizations. It is generally accepted that a modern enterprise operates within a network of societal stakeholders who directly or indirectly influence the operations of the enterprise (Foster and Jonker, 2003). This actor and network approach to organizations leads to the concept that we call the 'community of work', which puts pressure on the organization to reconsider its values. The values and identity of the organization are the subject of the third section. The real challenge of CSR is to reconfigure two fundamentally different internal value systems: the values of the market paradigm and the values of the community of work. As discussed in the fourth section, in order for CSR to progress from talk to walk, it is necessary for an organization to address this, but in most contemporary organizations it has basically begun to happen.

The development of organizations

The roots of today's organization can be traced to the industrial era. The industrial organization was above all a rational–functional entity. In order to engage in mass production, structures and processes were designed and functions created that were based on rational–functional assumptions. As the focus was purely on efficient and effective production, workers' needs and emotions were disregarded. Of course organizations were at the same time communities of workers, but the latter were not regarded individually as important to the smooth operation of the organization, except in terms of their well-being being a necessary condition for optimal performance in the work process. However, since individuals could easily be replaced, their true emotions and needs could be rationalized. Designing and organizing rational and functional work processes was the core issue, the community of workers a separate and disconnected issue.

Since the mid 1980s there has been a fundamental transformation of the way in which organizations function. Today the majority of the work force in developed countries work in service-oriented organizations using information and communication technology (ICT). Computers, e-mails, mobile phones, intranet and internet are firmly embedded in the working environment. The talents of employees and the social capital they bring with them have gained tremendous importance as creating added value is dependent on these factors. As a result the bureaucratic industrial model of organization is becoming redundant. Many authors argue that organizational design in the new information society is based on the network (Hastings, 1993; Nohria and Ghoshal, 1997; Schoemaker, 1998; Brenters, 1999; Castells, 2000a, 2000b), a summary of which is provided in the following subsection. In this chapter we make a distinction between the organization as (1) a way to organize in order to produce products and services and (2) a (social) bond between people in the community of work. The first has tangible properties of design, the second has intangible properties of social capital (Schoemaker and Jonker, 2005).

The rise of the network organization

Providing services has become the driving force of Western economies, and in countries such as Canada, Sweden and the Netherlands roughly 80 per cent of workers are engaged in service provision. Over the past 15 years a new concept has emerged in the service section that can be labelled 'virtual services', the product of which is intangible and requires employees to have the ability to manage other people's needs. Examples of this can be found in banking, insurance, tourism, the media, the entertainment sector and the internet. Thus, countless people now work in organizations where they no longer produce something tangible but provide only intangible services. The nature of work in the service sector tends to be governed by clients' demands and is therefore dynamic in character as expectations and demands constantly change. This is especially true of instant services provided in a virtual environment. It constitutes a striking contrast to labour in industrial organizations where clients are anonymous and hard to envisage. Even traditional production organizations, such as manufacturers of consumer electronics or mobile phones, are concentrating on functions such as R&D, marketing and logistics – all service-related activities – and outsourcing the physical production of goods to low-wage countries around the globe.

The organizational network began to engage in the mid 1980s following technological breakthroughs. With the growing use of PCs, e-mail, mobile phones, and so on the way in which businesses were organized underwent a fundamental change. Since then ICT has enabled the formation of new types of network. For example many consultancy firms, media companies and insurance companies are organizations of professionals using internal and external networks to carry out assignments. Other examples are call centers, which provide a particularly good illustration of standardized mass services via ICT networks. Work for particular clients is not limited to a particular time or place. Thus call centres for European airlines can be found in India and the R&D divisions of multinationals can operate 24 hours a day. The rise of ICT has also resulted more self-regulation in the workplace. Individuals are free to make decisions and to regulate their work processes accordingly, unlike in traditional industrial organizations.

During the last decades of the twentieth century it was often suggested that the traditional hierarchical organization was likely to disappear and be replaced by the network organization, but this is certainly not yet the case. At present the organizational landscape includes organizations in which both functional and network structures are present. These hybrid organizations have built-in structural dilemmas (Schoemaker, 1998), and dealing with the dualities and dilemmas created by the modern organization is one of the new tasks of contemporary management.

Communities of work

An organization can be seen as a set of processes (founded on economic, social and natural capital) in which the competences and skills of employees are put to use to construct a product or deliver a service to customers. The organizational processes are directed in such a way that they create value in the market place. However, organizations are also communities of work. The latter are value-based groups of individuals who collaborate either inside or outside a formal organization. A community of work can but need not be integrated into the organization. This means that those comprising a community of work may work in separate groups in specific organizational processes.

For two reasons communities of work and organizations may not always correspond. First, with the rise of networks and flexible organizations the use of personnel has become more flexible and can be short term. The traditional nine-to-five working day in which functional groups shape the organization and communities of work are integrated into the organization has been partly replaced by fragmented and flexible organizational designs. The latter often correspond more to business, personal or professional networks than to actual organizational processes, and many of these processes no longer foster collectivism in the workplace. Second, individuals often shape their own communities. An organization can therefore consist of many communities, resulting in a fragmented organizational identity. Thus some organizations function as a loosely coupled coalition created for a particular project while others are almost like a sect. Most tend to organize their activities somewhere in the middle of this spectrum and are more like a clan (Schoemaker, 2003a).

The interplay and alignment between organizational processes and communities of work have become important factors in the success of the organization and the motivation of its employees. Organizations as communities of work are to a large extent self-organizing entities held together by a common identity based on shared values. The community of work thus ought to be the fundament used for the information society. 'Ought to be' since management crises are evident in many organizations. What still needs to be established is a design for organizations as communities of work.

Managing contemporary organizations entails paying attention to the nature of the communities of work. In this regard it is assumed that, due to the ongoing development of the information society, the functional concept of an organization does not necessarily correspond to the community of work. People can organize the tasks at hand in the form of a community of work and the organization more or less becomes a facilitative institution. This requires management to pay attention to the membership of communities and to make values and norms explicit in order to create a specific organizational identity. The members need to be organized in a deliberate way through a process of socialization. True membership entails understanding and learning to act according to agreed values and norms. The process of creating membership results in 'intangible' common grounds which create the basis for behaviour with common denominators (Schoemaker and Jonker, 2005). This dedicated management behaviour is essential in order to ground organizational processes on the core competences of the organization. Market-driven performance and added value for customers from the perspective of core competences alone is not sufficient. Value-based management to reinforce the communities of work and the organizational identity is the other side of the coin.

Values and organizational identity

First- and second-order values

People-centred organizing requires a different kind of network. Here a distinction is made between two types of network: networks as an organizational structure to enable the production of goods or services, and social networks between people. The growing attention to social networks is reflected in the ongoing debate on social capital. The concept of social capital places emphasis on the nature and quality of relations between people in the network, between employees and clients, between stakeholders and stockholders, and between what happens internally and externally. As Cohen and Prusak (2001, p. 4) put it, 'Social capital consists of the stock of active connections among people: the trust, mutual understanding, and shared values and behaviour that bind the members of human networks and communities and make cooperative action possible.' Central to the idea of social capital is the existence of a network of relations between (organized) individuals and their social and business environment. These relations are of fundamental importance if the organization is to work, and their durability depends on trust, mutual understanding and shared norms and values. The nature and content of networks are extremely important if all individuals are to carry out their jobs properly and thus benefit the organization as a whole. By investing in networks, social capital is created and maintained.

Networks as structures and social networks operate according to distinctly different sets of values. We call these first- and second-order values. First-order values relate to the business. What makes the business run? What drives our business proposition? How are we being recognized in the market place? First-order values also determine the core competences of the organization, 'the smell of the place' and its success. There are many well-known examples of first-order values; including 'Connecting people' (Nokia), 'We produce anything as long as it sticks' (3M) and 'Sense and simplicity' (Philips). The key factor here is translating first-order values into the core competences required for the business proposition. This means competence development and harnessing appropriate talents in order to maintain the necessary competences and skills for as long as they are needed. First-order values can be considered as core to the market paradigm and as driving the actions of all individuals in the organization. Such values are internalized and govern the behaviour of individual employees *vis-à-vis* customers.

Second-order values support the first-order values. They are not necessarily linked to the business but relate to the desired behaviour of employees towards customers, colleagues and all other internal and external stakeholders. First-order values differ among organizations as they depend on the business proposition, but second-order values are very much the same in all organizations. They apply to human resource management, corporate social responsibility, charity, community involvement and non-mandatory care for the environment, and therefore are separate from the business proposition. Of course there are a few exceptions to the rule, including the emphasis on second-order values at EcoStyle, Kyjugie Jeans and Hagen Dazs, but these companies are niche players and do not operate in the mainstream.

Conflicting values

The paradigm underlying the management of organizational processes (based on core competences and delivering added value and performance for customers) is a market paradigm and is dominant in most organizations. However, the values and norms that hold the community of work together inside and outside the organization do not always correspond to the values and norms that underpin the market paradigm. In many organizations values such as human resource development and CSR are values of the communities of work and are not necessarily useful or applicable to the market. In other words, first-order values (grounded in the market paradigm) can conflict with second-order values (grounded in the values of the community of work). Some organizations use values such as human resource development and CSR as window dressing to show customers and employees that they really care.

But this care is only exhibited if it fits the values that dominate the market paradigm. In such circumstances there is no real link between the first- and second-order values. The question here is whether this kind of behaviour can continue in the long term. We think it cannot as it might lead to undesirable situations, given that recent developments are forcing organizations to change from a purely market value system to a hybrid one, thereby linking first- and second-order values into a system that combines the benefits of the market (doing business) with the social obligations of organizations. An important question in this respect is how can CSR be developed in such a way as to bridge the gap between these values? Exploring this question requires an investigation of organizational identity, which forms the basis of organizational values.

Organizational identity

The behaviour of individuals is anchored in specific values that may also govern the behaviour of a group. Individuals may wish to be a part of a group if their values are the same as those of the members of the group. Membership of the group depends on the congruence of values and norms at the individual and group levels. The stronger this congruence the more likely it is that the group will behave according to a specific set of values (the reinforcement effect). These values also constitute the group's organizational identity. The latter is (1) what the members view as central to the organization, (2) what makes the organization distinct from other organizations, and (3) what is perceived by the members as an enduring feature (Albert and Whetten, 1985). A clear identity gives the group a past, present and future and shapes the boundaries of the group. It also shapes the community of work and the borders of this community with its environment (Schoemaker, 2003b). Communities of work behave as clans, as flexible networks of people for whom organizational identity is the glue. Individuals identify themselves with the communities of work and in the process constantly face a double balancing act: balancing rights and duties (what does the community of work offer me, what does the group ask of me?), and balancing individuality and collectivism (how can I remain a unique individual while being part of the collective community of work?). This balancing act is essential to self-identification and the creation of a community of work with specific values, norms and identity.

We assume that organizational identity, grounded in embedded values, determines everything that happens in a community of work. Therefore management practices in organizations that are value driven, including CSR, must be embedded in the community of work if they are to succeed. Is it possible to develop CSR as an organizational value, thereby linking the community of work to the market-driven organizational processes? Is it possible to bridge the gap between the market paradigm and the organizational identity of the community of work?

Corporate social responsibility as an organizational value

From the perspective of the market paradigm it can be suggested that CSR will only be embedded in organizational processes if it will lead to profit and/or customer satisfaction (apart from compliance, but we shall not consider that issue here). Embedding CSR in organizational processes requires the development of behaviours and collective competences oriented towards CSR while ensuring that these are compatible with the market paradigm. This implies that CSR cannot be regarded as a core competence as such. As with human resource management, environmental care and sustainability, CSR as an organizational value must be linked to business and the market paradigm as well as guiding the behaviour of individuals and therefore communities of work.

This brings us to the issue of bridging the gap between the community of work and the organizational processes. Implementing CSR only in the area of organizational processes may be ineffective or even counterproductive. The key to implementing CSR lies in the community of work, because when its values and norms are developed so too are the values and norms of CSR. From a rational perspective of strategic management CSR can be embedded in organizational processes via a step-by-step implementation programme in which profit, people and the planet are balanced. There is, however, little evidence that this approach has been adopted. Organizations that have implemented CSR have often used a trial and error approach that entails leadership and actions based on specific values and norms (Roome and Jonker, 2005). This indicates that CSR can only be embedded in organizational processes if it is managed as an organizational value. So how can corporate social responsibility be developed as an organizational value, and how can it be linked to the business?

From our point of view three issues are important. First, in the eyes of employees, core competences and organizational identity offer sustainability in the organization. This is because core competences steer the organizational processes and organizational identity provides a foundation for the organization as a community of work. Specific core competences and a specific organizational identity can help to develop CSR as an organizational value.

Second, the growing use of ICT in the workplace offers scope for flexible work and the development of a network organization. Social capital can serve as a binding agent and a driver for the fostering of CSR as a value in this type of organization, and active use of the network between people can promote the developments of the competence needed for CSR.

Finally, fostering a relationship of exchange between the organization and individuals is the key to ensuring commitment, and this relationship must be evaluated on a regular basis. What is put in and taken out – that is, the conditions under which employees work – is as important as the improvement of performance and development of skills. For many employees this will determine whether they feel part of the group and their commitment to it. A relationship of exchange between individuals and the organization can also aid the acquisition of competences for CSR and embed CSR in the organizational processes.

Conclusions

This chapter has emphasized the importance of specific core competences and organizational identity in bridging the gap between first- and second-order values. Whether this gap is bridged also depends on the way in which second-order values are applied and managed in the business. Social capital and a relationship of exchange between individuals and the organization are also important in that they can foster the competences required for CSR.

A significant factor in the development of CSR is the growing interaction between the organization and its social, political and economic environment. The erosion of the traditional boundary between inside and outside means that all the parties involved have to be clear about who is doing what and why things are being done as they are. This requires transparency within the organization and about the way in which the organization conducts its relations with its extended environment. There is a systems side to this transparency – how things are organized in the formal functional system – and a relational side – how people organize their interactions. Relations only exist between people, which implies that transparency is achieved through the actions of people in the course of their relations. A person's actions are always value-based (one cannot act without values). The specificity of CSR thus entails a clear set of values that guide the behaviour of individuals within and across the boundaries of the organization. This behaviour is always expressed in relation to 'the other'. The specificity of CSR is the ability of people to base their behaviour on a defined set of values.

A central value in CSR is responsibility, defined as the ability to behave properly, make the right decisions and take the right actions without having to obtain the permission of others. Responsibility is strongly associated with response and responsiveness. Response is to do with providing an answer and responsiveness is the ability to give that answer. In the CSR debate it is common to distinguish between three types of responsibility: (1) human or social responsibility (inside and outside the organization and involving stakeholders and dialogue with these stakeholders), (2) business responsibility (to run a business according to the market rules of the economic paradigm) and (3) environmental responsibility, particularly in respect of the natural environment. These can be arranged in order of importance but there should be a balance between them, although the nature of this balance and how it can be achieved are unclear. One could argue that a balance can be achieved through the exchange of responsibilities. This implies that a certain weight can be accorded to the various responsibilities, which in turn implies that they can be assessed or measured. It goes without saying that in many situations this will not be the case, and therefore the exchange of responsibilities can lead to internal and external dilemmas.

What we have been discussing here is a fundamentally different perspective on the role of organizations in contemporary society. The rational-strategic, object-oriented management approach needs to be replaced by an approach that is firmly grounded in values. We do not need new values, rather we need to agree on which are most important and to act according to them, both individually and collectively. At the moment organizations that wish to pursue CSR tend to do so within the scope of the market paradigm, and as long as there is no compelling market need to change that paradigm most people in organizations will continue to consider CSR as an add-on feature. This will prevent the development of the communities of work required to make the contemporary network organization operate effectively in its turbulent environment. Among the challenges facing us in the near future is to design hybrid organizations in which first- and second-order value systems are configured in such a way that a balance exists between organizational processes and the communities of work.

References

Albert, S. and D. A. Whetten (1985) 'Organizational identity', in L. L. Cummings and B. M. Staw (eds) *Research in Organizational Behaviour* (Greenwich, CT: JAI), p. 264.

Brenters, M. (1999) *De organisatie als netwerk. Hoe mensen organisaties veranderen en organisaties mensen* (Alphen a/d Rijn: Samson).

Castells, M. (2000a) *The Information Age: Economy, Society and Culture* (Malden: Blackwell).

Castells, M. (2000b) 'Materials for an exploratory theory of the network society', *British Journal of Sociology*, 51 (1), pp. 5–24.

Cohen, D. and L. Prusak (2001) *In Good Company. How Social Capital Makes Organizations Work* (Boston, Mass.: Harvard Business School Press).

Cramer, J., A. van der Heijden and J. Jonker (2004) 'Making Sense of Corporate Social Responsibility', *Journal of Business Ethics*, 55 (2), pp. 215–22.

Davis, I. (2005) 'The biggest contract', *The Economist*, 26 May 2005.

Foster, D. and J. Jonker (2003) 'Third generation Quality Management: The role of stakeholders in integrating business into society', *Managerial Auditing Journal*, 18 (4), pp. 323–8.

Habisch, A., J. Jonker, M. Wegner and R. Schmidpeter (eds) (2004) *CSR Across Europe* (Heidelberg: Springer Verlag).

Handy, C. (1995) 'Trust and the virtual organization', *Harvard Business Review*, 73 (3), pp. 40–50.

Haslam, S. A., T. Postmes and N. Ellemers (2003) 'More than a metaphor: Organizational Identity Makes Organizational Life Possible', *British Journal of Management*, 14, pp. 357–69.

Hastings, C. (1993) *The New Organization* (New York: McGraw Hill).

Hatch, M. and M. Schultz (2004) *Organisational Identity: A Reader* (Oxford: Oxford University Press).

Jonker, J. and D. Foster (2002) 'Stakeholder Excellence?: Framing the Evolution and Complexity of a Stakeholder Perspective of the Firm', *Corporate Social Responsibility and Environmental Management*, 9 (4), pp. 187–95.

Jonker, J. (2003) 'In Search of Society: Redefining Corporate Social Responsibility, Organisational Theory and Business Strategies', *Research in International Business and Finance. SI: Social Responsibility: Corporate Governance Issues*, 17.

Jonker, J. and M. J. van Pijkeren (2005) 'In Search of Business Strategies for CSR: Some reflections on the development of business strategies for corporate social responsibility (CSR) followed by a qualitative analysis of the actual strategies being deployed by the German DAX 30 companies based on publicly available material', unpublished working paper.

Nohria, N. and S. Ghoshal (1997) *The Differentiated Network: Organizing Multinational Corporations for Value Creation* (San Fransisco, CA: Jossey-Bass).

Roome, N. and J. Jonker (2005) *Whistling in the Dark: The Enterprise Strategies of European Leaders in Corporate [Social] Responsibility*, ICCSR Research Paper (Nottingham: International Centre for Corporate Social Responsibility, Nottingham University Business School), pp. 1–39.

Schoemaker, M. (1998) *Organiseren van Werk en Contractrelaties: Tussen Slavernij en Anarchie* (Deventer: Kluwer).

Schoemaker, M. (2003a) 'Identity in flexible organizations; experiences in Dutch organizations', *Creativity and Innovation Management*, 12 (4).

Schoemaker, M. (2003b) *De metamorfose van werkgemeenschappen* (Nijmegen: Katholieke Universiteit Nijmegen).

Schoemaker, M. and J. Jonker (2005) 'Managing Intangible Assets', *Journal of Management Development*, 24 (5–6), pp. 506–18.

Weick, K. E. (1995) *Sense-making in Organizations* (Thousand Oaks, CA: Sage).

Wenger, E. (1998) *Communities of Practice: Learning, Meaning and Identity* (Cambridge: Cambridge University Press).

5
Social Capital and Corporate Social Responsibility

André Habisch and Jeremy Moon

Introduction

This chapter underlines the significance of social capital for business and the contribution that corporate social responsibility (CSR) can make to investment in social capital. We follow Adler and Kwon (2002, p. 17), who state that social capital can be 'understood roughly as the goodwill that is engendered by the fabric of social relations and that can be mobilized to facilitate action'. It generates mutual confidence and stimulates actions that would not otherwise be possible, as noted in Putnam's (1993, p. 167) definition of social capital as a set of 'features of social organization, such as trust, norms and networks that can improve the efficiency of society by facilitating coordinated actions'.

Social capital is thus closely associated with the underpinnings of social relations such as trust and norms, and with their main manifestations: social institutions and networks. The fact that social capital has been deployed in explanations of both broad social problem solving and business success (see below) makes it especially suitable for consideration in the context of CSR. The latter is generally defined as the activities of a business that compensate for its social externalities and other broad social benefits. It is generally regarded as discretionary in that it goes beyond the minimum legal requirements. Traditionally CSR has been regarded as lying outside the organization's main profit-making activity, reflecting its origins in business ethics and business philanthropy. However this dichotomy has been problematized by research that sees CSR either as 'profit-related' (for example Moon and Sochacki, 1996) or as a business strategy (for example McWilliams and Siegel, 2002). These analytical developments have been complemented by the advent of the business case for CSR at the practitioner level. The case for CSR is therefore increasingly predicated upon the assumption that business and societal interests can be consonant.

Social capital and CSR share a number of characteristics. Both concepts are in vogue in the academic and practitioner worlds (Solow, 1995). They are both relatively fuzzy. From the theory of the firm perspective, this reflects their status as intangible assets. From a purely conceptual perspective, it reflects their status as cluster concepts that overlap other equally fuzzy concepts (for example trust and ethics respectively). We have argued elsewhere that CSR is an essentially contested concept (Moon *et al.*, 2004; Habisch, 2004). The task of exploring relations between two fuzzy concepts may therefore seem a vain one from analytical and practitioner perspectives. Our contention is that, like other concepts such as justice and democracy, notwithstanding their fuzziness they are important from the perspective of both individual actors and total systems. Moreover, their importance is not simply in isolation but also in their relationships.

This chapter rests upon the following related propositions:

- In general terms business success is dependent on functioning societies that require mutual confidence (or social capital) among individuals, organizations and institutions.
- Social capital is at risk among and within societies.
- Individual business success is dependent on the confidence (or social capital) of societies and actors therein (particularly the business's stakeholders).
- Social capital between business organizations and other social actors is at risk.
- Large corporations have particular opportunities and incentives to invest in social capital.
- CSR offers means by which businesses can invest in social capital.

There are numerous indicators of a decline in social capital in Western and developing societies and between those societies. While these indicators are complex, society-specific and highly contingent some generalizations are possible. First, in many Western countries people are behaving in a less associative or participatory fashion. This is illustrated by declining political participation, as evidenced by reduced electoral turnout and declining membership of traditional political organizations,[1] and there are growing complaints about certain groups being marginalized from the benefits that democratic citizenship is supposed to offer. Second, and more generally, there is evidence of a decline in wider forms of civic association. This is illustrated by declining membership of a range of associations, from churches to sporting clubs, and is vividly captured by the title of Putnam's (2001) analysis of the decline of sociability in America: *Bowling Alone*. Third, opinion polls indicate a fall in popular confidence in the capacity of political leaders to address basic societal problems. Although these trends do not specifically apply to business, our proposition is that business requires functioning societies for its overall survival and prosperity. This is captured in the maxim 'a healthy high street depends on healthy back streets' (*Economist*, 20 February 1982).

Fourth, and critically from our perspective, the general reduction in trust is illustrated by declining confidence in the probity of business leaders, and in the responsibility of multinational corporations in particular. This is in part a reflection of cyclical bad news about business, ranging from the negative environmental and health impacts of business, such as the *Exxon Valdez* and Bhophal disasters, and corrupt business practices, such as Robert Maxwell's misappropriation of employee pension funds, to more recent accounting frauds such as that by Parmalat. Following the Enron and Worldcom scandals it was reported that whilst Americans retained great faith in each other, their trust in 'CEOs and big business priests' was in decline: 70 per cent distrusted the CEOs of large corporations and 80 per cent believed they would take improper action (*USA Today*, vol. 16, no. 7 2002). More widely, a 15-country study of trust conducted for the World Economic Forum found that whilst 56 per cent of respondents trusted NGO leaders, only 33 per cent trusted the executives of multinationals.

Moreover, there is growing suspicion of the will by national and supranational governments, multinational corporations (MNCs) and international economic institutions (for example the International Monetary Fund and the World Trade Organisation) of the developed world to deal fairly with the developing world. This has been illustrated by the activities of NGOs and the increased reluctance of developing country governments to agree to the developed world's terms of trade. The atmosphere of growing distrust between business and NGOs and between developed and underdeveloped countries is hindering further improvements to global trade and the integration of global markets. Thus the issues dealt with here apply to future economic development on a global scale.

The significance of the fourth and fifth indicators needs no elaboration if it is accepted, as we shall demonstrate below, that trust within and among businesses and between business and society is vital to business success.

The finding that trust in the fabric of modern society is declining corresponds with structural and institutional analyses. In the late nineteenth and the early twentieth century – in some countries more than others – national governments became key players in solving collective problems. Governments provided public goods such as roads and bridges, as well as providing legislation and controlling and punishing law breakers. Citizens contributed by paying their taxes and participating in the public life of democratic society. With globalization and the growing international division of labour, however, the social contract of the industrial society no longer prevails. The experiences of the late twentieth century show that even in developed countries many problems – unemployment, a decline in public education, infrastructure and health care, family dissolution and so on – can no longer be satisfactorily addressed by twentieth century means (see Moon, 2004). This governance deficit is even greater in transitional and developing countries, where a predatory state is often part of the problem rather than its solution. Lack of trust corresponds to a lack of cooperation between different groups in society, between business and society, between the public sector and business, and between the public sector and NGOs. In this perspective even the development problem can be framed in terms of lack of trust within the society of a developing country. Overregulation and the depression of entrepreneurial activities on the one hand and 'hit-and-run' strategies such as tax evasion on the other constitute a behavioural equilibrium of mutual distrust that has to be overcome if development is to be fostered (Habisch, 1998).

We argue that business, and MNCs in particular, should not take a victim's perspective on this state of affairs; rather they are well-equipped to contribute to the renewal of social capital. First, large corporations are not only complexes of contracts but also manifestations of very extended networks of trust. Second, large corporations have numerous resources that are pertinent to investment in social capital: not simply the wealth they can bring to bear in market and non-market activities but also their extended networks with each other and their even wider networks with a whole range of businesses and governmental and social stakeholders. Third, large corporations are increasingly regarded as key players in social governance as governments withdraw from, seek assistance with or simply never had the capacity to meet social expectations of good governance (Moon, 2002; Moon *et al.*, 2004). Fourth, by virtue of their increasingly conspicuous status in new national and global politics, MNCs have most to lose if trust in business in general declines (Habisch, 1999).

It should also be noted that there is a collective action issue here. If, as the secretary general of the OECD recently concluded, '[r]estoring market integrity is essential to winning back public confidence and to helping economies grow' (Johnston, 2003), who is responsible for investing in social capital to that end? Whereas in the twentieth century capitalists were content to rely on governments to meet their collective interest in maintaining social stability, given the current decline in trust in government and the fall in governance capacity, particularly on a global scale, this looks as though it will not be a sufficient solution in the twenty-first century. Thus the imperative for MNCs to address social capital is all the more pressing.

The following sections elaborate on the concept of social capital and relate this to business.

Social capital and business

Social capital is an evolving concept in a number of academic disciplines, particularly sociology, political science and economics. Its significance is usually seen to reside in its capacity to help overcome collective action problems, as recognized by Ostrom and Ahn (2001, p. 8, emphasis added):

> The traditional model of collective action ... assumes atomized individuals seeking short-term selfish goals that lead each individual not to contribute at an overall efficient rate to collective projects. In this view, individuals will not voluntarily tackle a whole host of jointly beneficial projects in both the private and public spheres because they wait for others to take the costly actions needed to benefit them all. Collective action problems have been identified as shirking within private firms, as a lower rate of entrepreneurial activity, as an inability to provide local public goods, and as the likelihood that common-pool resources will be over-harvested or destroyed instead of harvested at an optimal level. Collective action problems are endemic in all societies ... *We see the theory of collective action as a key theory for all of the social sciences and thus view social capital as a crucial factor for all social scientists and policy makers in their effort to understand and promote more effective ways of solving collective action problems in all facets of economic and political life.*

Social capital has been deployed in the analysis of a wide range of issues, including the family, youth behavioural problems, education, public health, community functioning, democracy and governance, and economic development. More narrowly it has also been deployed in the analysis of business organizations, for example, in explanations of career success and executive compensation; job seeking and recruitment; internal resource exchange, product innovation and intellectual capital; the reduction of turnover rates and entrepreneurial success; and strong supplier relations and production networks (see Adler and Kwon, 2002).

Notwithstanding its topicality, the concept of social capital has been criticized because it appears vague and hard to verify empirically. Critics claim that social capital is used to explain too many things at the same time – and in the end nothing at all (for example Solow, 1997). In some respects this reflects the nature of social capital. Like gravity, social capital is invisible. However we can see the effects of both. Gravity enables us to keep our feet on the ground. Social capital enables mutual confidence, which in turn rids us of the transaction costs that would be necessary to alleviate suspicion. Imagine a world in which suspicion replaced mutual confidence: 'If strict controls were imposed on all corporation personnel, then embezzlement, management fraud and other trust violations would be greatly reduced, but very little business would be done' (Cressey, quoted in Shapiro, 1987, p. 650). Or as Arrow (1972, p. 357) puts it: 'Virtually every commercial transaction has within itself an element of trust, certainly any transaction conducted over time. It can plausibly be argued that much of the economic backwardness in the world can be explained by the lack of mutual confidence.'

Similarly, according to Fukuyama (1995) the secret of business growth is the ability to trust employees, managers, shareholders and, wider stakeholders. This informs his analysis of comparative business systems and his conclusion that social and economic systems that do not advance beyond family business cannot produced the large business organizations that are vital to substantial economic growth.

As with any other form of capital, social capital is a resource. More specifically, this resource is the confidence that others have in the subject actor or that the members of a single entity have in each other, be they individuals, groups of people, institutions or organizations.[2] This confidence enables the subject to act without the constraints that suspicion (the antithesis of social capital) might otherwise impose. Coleman (1990, p. 302) equates social capital to other forms of capital because it is 'productive, making possible the achievement of certain ends that would not be attainable in its absence'. Similarly in the political context Putnam (1993) argues that social capital is not only 'nice to have' but is also an asset in terms of economic development, administrative responsiveness and 'making democracy work'.

Adler and Kwon (2002) extend this argument by underlining the extent to which social capital resembles other forms of capital (see also Ostrom and Ahn, 2001). First, like other forms of capital, social capital is 'a long-lived asset into which other resources can be invested, with the expectation of a future (albeit uncertain) flow of benefits' (ibid., p. 19). They note that this asset can be both an 'endowment' of some long-term historical legacy or 'constructible' through deliberate actions. Second, they see social capital as 'appropriable' for other purposes (for example friendship ties can be deployed for information gathering) and 'convertible' in that it can lead to economic advantage. Third, they view social capital as a substitute for or complement to other resources, for example improving economic efficiency by reducing transactional costs. Fourth, social capital resembles physical and human capital but differs from financial capital in that it needs maintenance. However unlike financial and physical capital, social and human capital do not depreciate with use but rather the opposite – the more they are used the stronger they get. Fifth, like environmental capital (for example clean air, safe streets) but unlike many other forms of capital, social capital is a collective good in that it is not owned by those who benefit from it. Moreover, unlike pure public goods, some groups can be excluded from its benefits. Hence Adler and Kwon see social capital as a unique form of capital in that it is located 'among' rather than 'within' the actors and is not amenable to quantification, even though some of its effects can be measured.

Adler and Kwon distinguish social capital from its sources and effects. The substance of social capital is the resource of relations between the actor and other actors, and relations among actors within a collectivity, or networks that are characterized by mutual goodwill and confidence (ibid., p. 19). The sources of social capital are social relations as opposed to market and hierarchical relations, in which favours and gifts are exchanged. The terms of exchange are diffuse and tacit but over time the exchange is symmetrical (ibid.) As noted above this can be in the form of the long-term endowment of propitious social development. However, it can also be something that is consciously constructed given the 'opportunity, motive and ability'. The opportunity resides in different configurations of networks. The motive resides in what Putnam (1993, pp. 182–3) describes as 'generalised generosity': 'Not "I'll do this for you, because you are more powerful than I" nor even "I'll do this for you now if you do that for me now" but "I'll do this for you now, knowing that somewhere down the road you'll do something for me."'

This motive is also captured in Coleman's (1990, p. 307) contrast of Hume's image of farmers not assisting one another 'for want of mutual confidence and security' with a situation in which 'one farmer got his hay baled by another and ... farm tools are extensively borrowed and lent, [and therefore] the social capital allows each farmer to get his work done with less physical capital in the form of tools and equipment'.

These norms and habits and incentives for trust can reside in social institutions and networks, and Adler and Kwon (2002) observe that social capital may not only be a bottom-up process but also that appropriate and responsive leadership can play a part in social capital building.

Adler and Kwon also identify a range of effects of social capital. Benefits include access to information, the improvement of information and the acquisition of new knowledge and skills; capacity (or what they call 'influence, control and power'); and solidarity, particularly in respect of compliance with local rules and norms, reduction of the need for formal controls, speedy dispute resolution and the prevention of long-term griev-ances. In all these cases Adler and Kwon point not only to benefits for the actor but also, through positive externalities, to advantages to the wider social aggregate. They also note the risks of social capital, which tend to be the result of excessive social capital. They warn of redundancy (for example in information stores and network contacts) and overembeddedness (for example in reducing the flow of new ideas and preserving power inequali-ties). They argue out that in social capital there are no invisible-hand mechanisms to deal with these risks.

In sum, the social capital literature argues that social networks of coop-eration and the evolving norms of reciprocity minimize mutual fear of exploitation and help generate public and private goods. The accumulation of these goods instils confidence in further social transactions and even more social capital is accumulated. Cooperation depends on and replenishes social capital. Tables 5.1 summarizes the sources, substance and effects of social capital.

Table 5.1   Social capital: sources, substance and effects

Sources	Substance	Effects
Associative norms, trust, institutions, networks	Mutual confidence among actors, obviation of transactional costs.	Information/knowledge/ innovation, capacity, solidarity (risk of redundancy and overembeddedness)

Source: Adapted from Adler and Kwon (2002).

What can CSR contribute to social capital?

CSR operates between government regulation, social regulation and market incentives. Although it requires more than legal compliance, it assumes that corporations operate within legitimate rules of trade, employment and so on. It also assumes that corporations comply with social values and that these may be passed on to firms through stakeholder relations, and through community relations in particular. Another assumption is that the firm is a functioning and responsive market actor in terms of selling goods and services, providing employment and generating wealth to owners and, through taxation, to the government and society.

There is certainly evidence that CSR has enhanced businesses capacity of for social cooperation, or what Putnam (1993) describes as the 'norm of generalised generosity'. This is most apparent in the case of community involvement, and especially in partnerships with social or community organizations as these provide a tangible framework upon which the fabric of trust can be woven. However, it is also true of other aspects of CSR, such as the responsibility embedded in a company's products, processes and employee relations as this tends to reflect corporate adaptation to social expectations by self-regulation (for example the adoption of codes and principles) or through stakeholder relations with NGOs and employees and their representatives.

However, for these acts to translate into social capital there has to be a positive judgement by society about them. If they are regarded suspiciously or cynically, then trust in the corporation in particular and business in general will hardly be enhanced, and may even be diminished more than if the firm had not embarked on a CSR programme. The question is, how do we know how society regards CSR? Clearly this is not easily generalizable, but research findings from Australia suggest that stakeholders who benefit from community involvement make relatively positive and balanced evaluations.

A survey of Australian school principals was conducted to verify and substantiate an earlier finding that Australian corporations' most prioritized and most frequent focus for non-profit community involvement was education

(Moon and Sochacki, 1996). Not only did 72 per cent of the respondents indicate that they received non-profit support from business, but also 50 per cent claimed to be supported by 10 or more companies and 10 per cent by 50 or more companies (Moon and Sochacki, 1998). In response to a question about the benefits of this support, 92 per cent agreed that this business support benefited students and 42 per cent strongly agreed. This suggests that those responsible for the social purpose, in this case education, did not see the contribution by business as merely tokenistic.

In answer to a question about the motives of business' from supporting their schools the principals offered a relatively nuanced view (the respondents were able to identify more than one motive). Over 50 per cent saw it as motivated by 'community involvement for its own sake'. The respondents also identified forms of social responsiveness, including parental responsiveness (more than 25 per cent) and employee relations (more than 10 per cent). There was some recognition of business-specific motives such as marketing (more than 40 per cent) and recruitment (more than 20 per cent) and of collective business motives, for example vocational education (more than 40 per cent) and education about business (more than 25 per cent).[3]

This nuanced evaluation is reflected in businesses' evaluations of CSR. IBM's 'Reinventing education' and Siemens' *Computer helfen heilen* (Computers help healing) are good examples of how networks of cooperation not only provide positive social benefits but also foster important information. Engineers tend to make product innovations that are smart but do not necessarily reflect the demands of consumers. By working together with schools on organizations for disabled people, R & D departments receive important information on this critical input factor. That is why IBM integrated not trainees but heads of department and chief developers into its 'Reinventing education' programme.

According to Putnam (1993) social capital is signalled not simply by the presence of norms of generalized generosity but also by their having a multiplier effect. There is certainly evidence that CSR initiatives have spread into business coalitions for CSR. These can be local (such as local economic development partnerships), regional (for example group training companies in Australia and the *Initiative für Beschäftigung* in Germany), national (for instance Business in the Community in the UK and D21 in Germany) and international (such as the International Business Leaders Forum and CSR Europe).

The multiplier effect is increased when CSR is extended into wider forms of sociability through employee volunteering. This can bring benefits to the company (in the form of reputational enhancement, new networks and employee loyalty), its employees (in respect of enhanced job satisfaction and a better life – work balance) and the community (in terms of social investment by the company and its employees).

Interestingly the connection between social capital and CSR has been recognized by a major business leader known for his CSR commitment, the

Unilever co-chairman Niall Fitzgerald (2003). He asks, 'How do you ensure a company behaves responsibly and earns and keeps the trust of society?' (ibid., p. 4). His answer is basically that companies are a product of society and are 'part of society, not outside it,' and therefore their fortunes are dependent on society. He goes on to describe CSR as 'not something we "do" to society ... [but as] inherent in everything we do' (ibid., p. 5). He illustrates this in his discussion of creating a more diverse workforce in terms not only of social benefits but also of the business advantages of better understanding consumer needs and enhancing competitive advantage, and of being more adaptive and responsive: 'for us diversity is not only about social responsibility and building trust. It is crucially interconnected with our ability to lead and manage a successful, multinational, multicultural, consumer goods business' (ibid., p. 12). Having described Unilever as a company with a history of social responsibility he observes that 'trust is built by being consistent in how you apply your values' (ibid., p. 5). Unilever's attention to trust is therefore an investment in building social capital from which the company can benefit.

Mutual distrust inhibits cross-sectoral cooperation in many parts of the world. Many business people think that social workers, NGOs and community associations 'just talk' and lack the professionalism of the business world, while many social partners exclude business from their list of potential collaborators because of its profit orientation and perceived lack of ethical orientation. Overcoming those prejudice, would open the door to the enormous advantages of mutual cooperation.

The director of Betapharm, a medium-sized pharmaceutical company in the Bavarian city of Augsburg, started his engagement as one of Germany's leading corporate citizens by building a relationship of trust with the head of a self-help network in the field of home aftercare. In the newly founded BETA Foundation the problem-related knowledge held by the self-help group and the professional know-how of the corporation were merged. Today the Foundation is one of Germany's most important research institutions on after-care and social medicine. One of its major successes has been to bring about a modification of German social law, raising public awareness of the importance of aftercare and including it in the system of public health insurance. However, there have been huge advantages for Betapharm as well. The *BETA-Liste* is a hefty tome containing the addresses of self-help organizations and detailing the legal rights of affected parents. This book, which is produced by the Foundation and circulated by the company's sales representatives, has boosted both the reputation of the company among doctors (as the clients) and the self-esteem of employees. Attractiveness as an employer and motivated sales representatives are crucial factors in Betapharm's highly competitive business. Moreover, as a by-product of its social engagement the company has made considerable savings in its marketing budget whilst preserving its unique reputation among important stakeholders.

It is instructive that in these illustrations of CSR as an investment in social capital upon which business can draw the significance of companies' social contribution lies in its implementation. Companies have recognized that the social impact is best mediated by a socially embedded or networked social medium. We shall now consider some contingencies for CSR implementation as a form of investment in social capital, following Adler and Kwon's (2002) distinction of task symbolic contingencies.

The authors suggest that if the organization's main objective is to develop trust and cooperation then 'embedded ties with repeated exchanges between a small number of the partners are preferred' (ibid., p. 32). This can be contrasted with the objective of building broader awareness, which can be more easily achieved with a larger number of partners and fewer exchanges. Corporations need to be aware of the differences between these approaches to implementing CSR and the different sorts of social capital they can generate. The deployment of employee volunteers to a small number of local community organizations constitutes one extreme of social capital investment. This entails multiple exchanges as numerous employees all have repeated interactions with the community networks. This can be expected to generate social capital in the form of mutual confidence among those immediately affected by the company's operations but it will have little effect on the broader reputation of the company and its products among consumers. Conversely, the implementation of a CSR policy through partnerships with global NGOs can be seen as a social capital investment in key agenda makers and broader stakeholders.

Symbolic contingencies reflect the fact that norms and beliefs are not only sources of social capital but also provide the basis upon which social capital is evaluated (ibid., p. 33). Thus decisions about the implementation of CSR should take account of the values that prevail in the context in question, particularly in respect of the likely evaluation of appropriate behaviour on the part of the business organization. This could also inform the selection of partners according to their legitimacy in the given context. In short a corporation's ability to deploy CSR as a social capital investment will hinge crucially on its understanding of what is socially legitimate in the situation at hand. This is especially the case with global relations as it is very easy to misjudge how social capital will be evaluated in other social settings (see Blowfield, 2004).

Finally, it apposite to apply the managerial implications of social capital in general that Adler and Kwon identify to the more specific task of implementing CSR. First, they point out that social capital investment is not simply a question of establishing more social ties but also of nurturing motivation and providing resources. Nurturing motivation requires a continuous review of the social externalities of the corporation and its evaluation by stakeholders. The allocation of resources requires CSR to be treated not simply as a set of principles but also as a business function whose implementation is consistent with those principles. Second, Adler and Kwon stress that managers should be aware of the different returns from and implications of social capital investment in 'bonding' (internal investment in employee welfare) and 'bridging' (external investments in stakeholder relations). Third, their suggestion that managers map their social capital ties also applies to the implementation of CSR policies. This should include identification of the social networks into which CSR impinges and the location of these in relation to the organization's goals, to the values that characterize their social context and to the social capital resources that are expected to follow.

Conclusion

Social capital is a means of creating incentives for general sociability, thereby avoiding free-rider problems. With regard to CSR, it can be anticipated that – notwithstanding the evidence of multipliers we have presented – some companies will reap the benefits of a generally improved business reputation but not make a contribution themselves while others will contribute disproportionately. This suggests a possible problem for social capital in general terms: can confidence in business be enhanced if CSR is seen to be only selectively invested in by businesses? Moreover, why would any one business make this investment when it knows that others are not doing so? Is the spread of CSR being prevented by the free-rider problem expressed in the 'prisoner's dilemma' of standard game theory?

It can be envisaged that businesses in more competitive markets will be less likely to invest in CSR. This is illustrated by the remarkably Hayekian view held by a representative of an Australian firm engaged in a highly competitive engineering innovation market: 'we have an overwhelming responsibility to the company shareholders to focus our resources towards ensuring the success of our own programs' (Moon, 1995, p. 8). Conversely it might be that some firms will have an individual interest in collective business benefits. Banks, for example, benefit from general economic growth and may have an incentive to support community-based enterprise development initiatives. IT firms already benefit from the acquisition and development of IT skills in the workforce and society at large, and therefore have an incentive to support community-based IT training schemes – the global activities of INTEL are a very good example in this respect. Moreover, some firms have a greater interest in reputational goods than others such as those which are perceived as responsible for or environmental or health risk. Large firms tend to be particularly targeted by NGOs and the media. Furthermore, given that many of their business activities are highly socially networked and dependent they have a particular incentive to convey their trustworthiness to a range of stakeholders in their organization, the community, the government and business.[4] Small- and medium-sized enterprises may wish to build social capital only in their own region or with vital stakeholder groups (Habisch, 2004). All these best practices have enough additional utility to invest in social capital, thus creating positive external effects for other groups and firms. Therefore, we assume that social capital need not be undermined by the differing incentives of corporations to invest in it through CSR.

Another possible threat to social capital is that corporations may proclaim CSR policies but not implement them with any sincerity, coherence or credibility. A cynical investment in social capital would undermine social capital as confidence in it would decline. However, some take that view that the penalties for being found out can act as a disincentive: 'The villains and masqueraders are usually pretty transparent and when consumers discover their insincerity, they clobber them, so from that point of view they can end up in a worse position than if they had not done anything.'[5]

There is a view that 'getting one's homework done' – in the sense of sound internal organization and human resource management – is a prerequisite for eligibility as a CSR partner. A major constraint on masqueraders lies in the fact that companies that engage in CSR activities and invest in social capital will find it problematic to provide an explanation to their partners if they harm the environment, violate human rights or pursue corrupt business practices at home or abroad.

We conclude that CSR can be viewed as an investment in social capital and that there are social, firm-specific and general business advantages to be had from doing so. Acts of social responsibility can contribute to the development of a norm of generosity within networks of civic engagement, and this will be regarded positively by representatives of the social institutions in which the investment is made. Multiplier effects will be evident in an increase in the number of business participants and partnerships with social actors.

When business leaders recognize that their business fortunes are socially contingent and that social capital underpins trust and cooperative relations with society they will also recognize the centrality of CSR to their operations and the importance of living up to their policy claims.

The greatest challenge lies in CSR investment in social capital in societies that are not closely connected to the home society of the corporation and where there are few social institutions and networks in which to invest (Habisch, 1998). The danger here is that if CSR is regarded as tokenistic, no social capital will be yielded. Conversely, if the societal actors perceive CSR as grounded in associative norms and trust, the benefits of social capital in the form of information, knowledge, innovation, capacity and solidarity may be realized for the business as well as its stakeholders. However, this will depend on CSR as an investment in social capital forms a common interpretative device for the investing company as well as the host society.[6] This chapter is an attempt to pave that common conceptual ground in order to strengthen trust in today's globalizing world.

Notes

1. There is increased membership of new social movements but these tend to entail less ongoing engagement than is the case with traditional political parties and pressure groups.
2. Adler and Kwon (2002, p. 19) make a useful distinction between external and internal orientations of social capital.
3. For a more detailed analysis of these findings in the context of social capital see Moon (2001).
4. See McWilliams and Siegel (2002) for an investigation of the business case for CSR.
5. Richard Steckel, quoted in *The Australian*, 23 May 1996.
6. See the results of a large empirical study on German SMEs investing is the Czech Republic in Krizek and Habisch (2005).

References

Adler, P. S. and S. W. Kwon (2002) 'Social Capital: Prospects for a new concept', *Academy of Management Review*, 27, pp. 17–40.

Arrow, K. (1972), 'Gifts and Exchanges', *Philosophy and Public Affairs*, 1, p. 357.

Blowfield, M. (2004) 'Implementation Deficits of Ethical Trade Systems', *Journal of Corporate Social Responsibility*, 13, pp. 77–90.

Coleman, J. (1990) *Foundations of Social Theory* (Cambridge, Mass.: Harvard University Press).

Fitzgerald, N (2003) *CSR: Rebuilding Trust in Business* (London: Unilever and London Business School).

Fukuyama, F. (1995) *Trust: The Social Virtues and the Creation of Prosperity* (London: Hamish Hamilton).

Habisch, A. (1998) 'Social Capital Investment, Property Rights and the Ethics of Win-Win. Why Multinational Enterprise Management should Engage in Institution Building of their Host Countries', in H. Steinmann and B. Kumar (eds), *Ethics in International Management* (Berlin and New York: De Gruyter), pp. 109–27.

Habisch, A. (2002) *Corporate Citizenship: Gesellschaftliches Engagement von Unternehmen in Deutschland* (Heidelberg and Berlin: Springer Verlag).

Habisch, A. (2004) 'Social Capital, Corporate Citizenship and SMEs', in L. Spence, A. Habisch and R. Schmidpeter (eds), *Corporate Citizenship in Small and Medium Companies* (London: Palgrave).

Hardin, R. (1991) '*Trusting persons, trusting institutions*', in R. Zeckhauser (ed.), *Strategy and Choice* (Cambridge, Mass.: MIT Press), pp. 185–209.

Johnston, D. J. (2003) 'Building Trust', *OECD Observer*, 9. December 2003.

Krizek, P. and A. Habisch (2005) *Gesellschaftliches Engagement Deutscher Untemehmen in der Tschechischer Republik*, Vorstellung and Ergebnisse einer Studie (Prague: Publisher).

McWilliams, A. and D. Siegel (2002). 'Corporate Social Responsibility: A Theory of the Firm Perspective', *Academy of Management Review*, 26(1), pp. 117–27.

Moon, J. (1995) 'The Firm as Citizen?', *Australian Journal of Political Science*, 30(1), pp. 1–17.

Moon, J. (2001) 'Business Social Responsibility as a Source of Social Capital', *Reason and Practice: the journal of philosophy and management*, 1(3), pp. 35–45.

Moon, J. (2002) 'Business Social Responsibility and New Governance', *Government and Opposition*, 37 (3), pp. 305–408.

Moon, J. (2004) 'Government as a Driver of Corporate Social Responsibility: The UK in Comparative Perspective', *International Centre for Corporate Social Responsibility*, 20.

Moon, J., A. Crane and D. Matten (2004) 'Can Corporations be Citizens?: Corporate citizenship as a metaphor for business participation in society', *Business Ethics Quarterly*, 15(3), pp. 429–53.

Moon, J. and R. Sochacki (1996) 'The Social Responsibility of Business in Job and Enterprise Creation: Motives, Means and Implications', *Australian Quarterly*, 68(1), pp. 11–30.

Moon, J. and R. Sochacki (1998) 'New Governance in Australian Schools: A place for business social responsibility?', *Australian Journal of Public Administration*, 55(1), pp. 55–67.

Ostrom, E. and T. K. Ahn (2001) '*A Social Science Perspective on Social Capital: Social Capital and Collective Action. Gutachten für die Enquete-Kommission 'Zukunft des Bürgerschaftlichen Engagements'*, Bloomington, Indiana University.

Putnam, R. D. (2001) '*Bowling Alone: The Collapse and Revival of American Community'* (London: Simon & Schuster).

Putnam, R. D., R. Leonardi and R. Nanetti (1993) *Making Democracy Work: Civic Traditions in Modern Italy* (Princeton, NJ: Princeton University Press).

Shapiro, S. (1987) 'The Social Control of Trust', *American Journal of Sociology*, 93 (3), pp. 623–58.

Solow, R. M. (1995) 'But verify! Book review on F. Fukuyama, Trust', *The New Republic*.

6

An Anatomy of Corporate Social Responsibility: Causal Factors in CSR as a Social Movement and Business Practice

Nigel Roome, Robert-Paul Doove and Marcel Postema

Introduction

An increasing number of businesses are applying the concept of corporate social responsibility (CSR) to the organization of their activities. While the idea that companies should have an explicitly stated approach to CSR is relatively new in continental Europe, examples of responsible business practice can be traced back nearly two centuries in many European countries. These earlier examples often focused on the provision of good working and/or living conditions for employees or, as in the case of the cooperative movement, sought to ensure that consumers' demand for products of reliable quality was met. In contrast the practices that contribute to contemporary CSR are found in a wider constituency of companies and CSR has gathered support in the form of policy commitments by national governments and the European Commission.

Thus CSR is no longer the realm of isolated companies but has become part of a broader social and business movement that includes companies, policy makers, advocates, knowledge institutes (universities and consulting companies), business associations and sections of the investment community. In the eyes of many managers the rationale for CSR is complex, the phenomenon is multifaceted and the managerial and organizational responses seem to run counter to traditional business logic. In fact the modern CSR movement, with its many actors, interests, statements and guidelines, while fostering a climate that supports CSR is also contributing to its growing complexity.

This chapter examines the factors, or drivers, that have given rise to the movement that supports this new style of CSR in Europe and shape the processes of learning and change that constitute the practice of CSR in contemporary business. The perspective we adopt focuses on the interaction between business and society. We take the view that CSR is emerging simultaneously as a social and a business phenomenon. It is emerging as an aspect of business practice and in the fabric of ideas and experience of the society in which businesses are embedded. This open-complex systems perspective is made more complicated by the fact that CSR does not deal simply with business and its interface with the economic system or the political economy. The interface for CSR is between business and many other actors in society who represent an array of economic, social and environmental concerns. Indeed, we contend that the present attention to CSR is symbolic of a broader critique of the role and responsibilities of business in modern society. While business will remain true to its core purpose of generating value for shareholders, that purpose is increasingly conditioned by the need to take account of social and environmental as well as economic concerns and responsibilities. This constitutes a move towards a 'reformed capitalist model' that is more in concert with the demands of the present and the challenges of the future than the models of business that have dominated during past century.

Some commentators might suggest that CSR is a management fad or a question of image management. However, we argue that the emergence of CSR is part of a broader process of reform taking place in the light of changes in the nature of business and the way in which business interacts with its many contexts. Against this background the key purpose of this chapter is to analyze the trends and events that have contributed to the emergence of CSR in its present form. These are examined in two stages. In the next section we take a macro view of the CSR movement in Europe and portray its wider adoption as the outcome of numerous causal factors. The analytic framework used to discuss the phenomena that contribute to globalization is provided by the notion of meta-problems. An introduction of this concept is followed by a discussion of the phenomena that are contributing to globalization. The section closes with a discussion of the instabilities in the global business system that we contend provide the basis for the modern CSR movement.

The subsequent section provides a meso-level analysis by considering the factors that combine with one another to foster CSR policies and practices in specific business organizations. These factors derive from the core issues of globalization, which open up and reveal gaps in corporate governance that require a response through CSR. The first set of factors relates to the processes of innovation that contribute to CSR. The second concerns the changing ideas and practices in business organizations that foster the move towards CSR. The third involves the emergence of institutions that shape the context in which businesses increasingly operate with CSR in mind. The final set includes the stimuli that provoke institutional attention or the allocation of time and resources to CSR. These individual and structural, formal and informal elements of institutions and organizations are informed by, and in turn inform, the trends that make up the broader global context. The last section discusses the main implications of our analysis of the routes and pathways for CSR.

The causal factors of CSR: a macro view

CSR arises at the interface between business and society. The agenda of CSR and the response by companies to that agenda is shaped at this interface. It seems that the CSR movement has emerged out of a growing realization that the world in which business operates increasingly presents an array of demands and pressures that are not signalled through markets or the traditional political processes up on which companies have relied for so long (Roome, 2004). In this regard the CSR movement is symbolic of the emerging role and responsibilities of business in a changing society. CSR thinking therefore involves reframing the position of business in society, while CSR practice is concerned with the way in which companies manage their present and future relationships with actors within and outside the company. Fundamentally, then, we view CSR in terms of the ties or relationships between business and other actors in society, as seen from a business perspective. Companies that are involved in formulating and implementing CSR policies are engaged in processes to learn about these relationships and in change that reshapes them.

The implication of this is that a variety of factors (trends, countertrends and events) have influenced the emergence of the CSR movement by affecting the position of business in society, the most profound of which is globalization as this affects European companies as well as those in the rest of the world. A framework for our discussion is provided by the notion of meta-problems.

Chevalier and Cartwright (1966) first discussed meta-problems in the context of public policy issues. Conceptually meta-problems are examples of open complex systems. In their view meta-problems are interconnected problem sets in which attempts to resolve or change one part of the set affects the other issues in the set. Moreover, they argue that organizational interests are frequently tied to different elements of the problem set. The interconnection of issues, coupled with the multiplicity of interests, means that changes in any part of the set will positively or adversely affect different organizations and their interests. The complexity of the problem sets implies that the pursuit by one organization of its interests is frequently a matter for dispute and contest with other organizations. This contest is not trivial and it is not simple to resolve. Contest does not arise just because interests contradict, rather it often arises because there is little if any agreement between organizations on the relationship between the issues that make up the set, and they do not necessarily agree on the courses of action open to them or the outcomes of those actions, whether intended or unintended. Meta-problems are therefore characterized by ambiguity, uncertainty and contest between organizations and interests.

Moreover, when organizations pursue their individual interests in complex systems without reference to the interests of others there is a tendency to create turbulence or instability in the system. A tyranny of small decisions can arise, in which choice is informed by too narrow a view of outcomes and consequences. Suggested responses to turbulence include the establishment of common rules for organizations operating in the system. More specifically there is a need for new governance procedures that improve communication between organizations, give greater attention to the legitimate interests and concerns in the set and the knowledge and perspectives held by actors. Initiatives such as the Global Compact, the forum provided by Corporate Social Responsibility Europe and the Global Reporting Initiative are examples of attempts to establish common rules for organizations, especially business, and there are many other forums and initiatives that seek to foster change and new codes and guidelines for business.

The concept of globalization

Chevalier and Cartwright (1966) identified pollution, poverty and ill-health as typical examples of meta-problems. The importance of this characterization is that it highlights that what were seen 40 years ago as distinct meta-problems have now merged into larger, more complex problem sets. What has caused this increasing complexity? To pursue this issue we shall analyze the claim that the globalization of economic and financial systems is a more recent example of a meta-problem. Here the interdependence and interconnection of global financial and economic markets – facilitated by linked digital technologies and improved global communications and transport – together with more open markets means that what happens in one region of the world has potential repercussions for economic and financial interests and organizations in other parts of the world. More critically, instability in one region can destabilize the overall (more) global system.

This is consistent with Castells' (1996) argument that a technological revolution has brought us into the networked information age, which combined with the progressive liberalization of the world market has fuelled the process of (economic and financial) globalization. From an environmental perspective it has led other authors to suggest that economic and financial globalization has resulted in a world-wide increase in wealth, but also in a world characterized by interdependency and vulnerability, in which a local problem today can turn into a global (environmental) crisis tomorrow (Elkington, 1998).

However, Roome (2000) suggests that economic and financial globalization is a rather narrow conceptualization of globalization. He advances the view that globalization describes a class of complex phenomena where by interdependence and interconnectivity between locations around the world arise from human agency. The causes of globalization are the actions and choices that create these ties and interdependence. The primary drivers of globalization fall into three categories: technological, such as the internet and rapid, cheap transport; organizational and institutional, such as the span of multinational companies and of trade and supply-chains, and the practices of international organizations such as the WTO; and concepts or idiolect, such as a universal model of progress and development, or words that we use to describe the economic system, such as open, global markets for products and services. These categories may overlap, for example when companies expand their business globally on the basis of their technologies, using the argument of free trade and drawing on the support of global institutions such as the WTO.

These primary drivers are themselves composed of smaller technological, organizational or institutional innovations. For example advances in digital technology have enabled the interconnection of computers and communication media, while silicon technology and miniaturization have led to rapid increases in the power and diffusion of telecommunications and computing. Moreover advances in aeroplane engines, lightweight metals, composite materials and radar technology, together with the organizational ability to move vast numbers of passengers through airports and on to planes, have facilitated the mass movement of travellers by air.

However, economic and financial globalization, as experienced in the late 1980s and beyond, is only one part of what we call 'broad definition' globalization. This also includes changes in environmental systems arising from the demands of developed economies and the model(s) and experiences of development in developing countries during the 1950s and 1960s, as well as the increasing pace of social and cultural globalization, as evidenced by global migration and the emergence of multicultural, multiethnic communities around the world.

In conceptual terms globalization, as interdependence and connectivity arising from human agency, has outcomes that are often manifested as events, trends, or patterns. These take a number of forms. First, events in one part of the world affect other parts of the world. For example in environmental terms the demand for hardwood has led to deforestation; in economic terms defaults on loans can lead to a broad collapse of financial markets. This can occur rapidly or may unravel over an extended period of time. Second, spatially diverse events or changes around the world form patterns because they share common causal factors, such as migration from environmentally impoverished and politically disputed territories. Third, some changes are so ubiquitous that they affect many global locations, such as the spread of persistently toxic chemicals. The interconnections between human and natural systems mean that there are often second-, third- and higher-order effects to take into account.

The perception that some of the outcomes of globalization are undesirable has prompted demands for new forms of governance. The environmental consequences of development were addressed at the Stockholm Environment Conference in 1972, the Earth Summit in Rio de Janeiro in 1992 and the Johannesburg Summit in 2002. These events led to a raft of new approaches to global and local governance: the Montreal Protocol on ozone-depleting substances, Agenda 21, the Kyoto Protocol and so on. Financial and economic instability due to globalization has given rise to the WTO and the Basel Accord, led by the International Bank for Settlements. Cultural and social globalization has caused national governments to impose controls on the flow of migrants and refugees.

Roome (2000) suggests that we are now experiencing a collision between and a combining of these waves of globalization. The implication is that the forms of governance that have emerged in response to each successive wave of globalization are no longer adequate as new forms of globalization have added to the complexity and interdependence of issues. In terms of our earlier analysis we have entered a period in which previous meta-problems are combining to form a more complex and turbulent meta-problem.

We can list some examples of this complexity and turbulence. The disparity in economic opportunity between rich and poor countries is giving rise to a number of issues. Countries with low labour costs are attracting inward investment from companies based in developed countries, with a consequent loss of jobs in the developed world. This raises a number of CSR concerns in respect of labour and environmental standards in developing countries, the loss of jobs and closure of plants in developed economies, and the overall environmental burden of material flows around the world. The demand for food, timber and materials and the need for export-driven growth in developing countries are stimulating overfishing, deforestation and resource extraction. Poor people in developing countries and countries in conflict are migrating to the richer countries of North America and Europe, with the consequent problem of cultural adaptation. The growing wealth in developing economies is supporting the spread of cars and other energy-consuming devices, thereby increasing the demand for fossil fuels and metals and provoking global climate change.

The broad recognition among politicians, business leaders, consumers, citizens and non-governmental organizations of the environmental stresses and social and cultural tensions that are accompanying global production and consumption is putting pressure on business to consider new forms of responsibility, either reactions to existing events or actions taken in anticipation of perceived risks.

Instabilities in the system and CSR

If 'broad definition' globalization is the canvas upon which modern CSR is being painted, and if CSR is a governance response by business to the knots and tears in the relationships between business and the societal actors that make up this canvas, then it is possible to identify where in the weft and warp of this canvas that better governance is required. The weft of the canvas is composed of the demands that actors place on relationships. The threads here are simple. A growing number of informed and sceptical citizens are seeking to defend their concerns but at the same time are experiencing disempowerment as their jobs, health and safe and secure environments are being affected by the decisions of those who seem more and more remote. This is leading to a wider perception in society of the potential risks associated with some technologies and some aspects of modern lifestyles, as well as a lack of trust in relationships with [remote] others.

The threads that make up the warp of the canvas are technological, organizational and conceptual in nature. We have become dependent on complex technologies to meet our daily needs, and the technologies that underpin globalization (transportation, communication and computing) are bringing images of and information about distant places and issues closer to our lives. They provide both information and disinformation and offer a means to mobilize and organize interest movements. At the same time the organizational span of businesses and the length of global supply chains are distancing corporate decision makers from the complex issues that prevail in locations of production or consumption around the world. This is a source of concern for decision makers, who need much more detailed information about an increasing number of local settings. It is creating new axes of governance, from global to multilocal. At the same time individuals are able to access powerful, but often simple images of issues that cause concern among citizens, interest groups, consumers and producers. There is an asymmetry between the informational aspects of protest and the informational demands of good governance. Similarly globalization is distancing consumers and others from what is involved in the production, manufacture and supply of the products they use, wear and eat. While some wish to know more about the provenance of these goods and services, this is being rendered more difficult by the ever lengthening supply chains. In terms of concepts or ideas, recognition of the value of company logos and brands, made possible by global markets and communication, exposes these assets to vulnerability.

Added to this are highly publicized events such as the industrial accident in Bhopal, the oil spill from the *Exxon Valdez* and the nuclear accidents at Three Mile Island and Chernobyl, as well as trends such as global climate change, fears about genetic manipulation and food safety, concern about child labour and poor working conditions at Nike's suppliers in the Far East, scandals over the fiduciary responsibilities of senior executives and the dubious practices of some leading corporations.

There is a growing recognition among policy makers, business leaders and others of the fault lines arising from our economic system and economic activity. These fault lines have gradually developed over time and so far few see them as a consequence of the system that is being created. Nevertheless there is a growing call for better governance in general, and for better governance in business in particular. In our view, while the market economy has the value of rapidly informing producers about consumers' wants and it promotes efficiency in the allocation of resources between competing economic interests, it is not good at revealing the environmental, social, cultural and economic instabilities created by the system as a whole, as these mostly lay outside the market. These require different capacities in governance.

For the cynical, CSR is an attempt to conceal the knots and tears in modern business practice, while for advocates of CSR it is a means of repairing these flaws so that the economic system can continue to provide the many benefits we have secured. In that sense CSR, in common with all human activities, has the capacity to be both a mask and part of the search for a more authentic form of capitalism that will fit the demands of the modern world.

A model of CSR in business

Against the above backdrop of globalization and the CSR movement, we shall now explore how CSR is formulated and implemented as a business practice (European Commission, 2002). Four sets of factors serve as drivers and facilitators of CSR in companies (Figure 6.1). The first set consists of

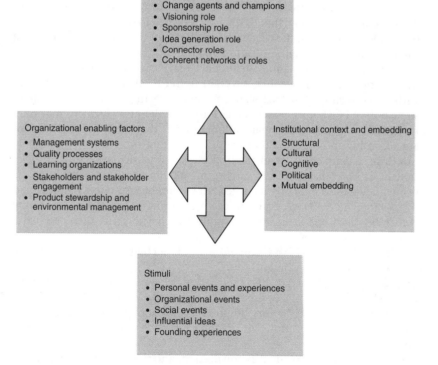

Figure 6.1 Causal factors in CSR as a business practice

individual actors in business organizations as agents of change and innovation, as successful CSR is essentially an innovation process. Set two relates to changing ideas and practices in business organizations that facilitate or enable CSR to take root. The third set involves the emergence of institutions that provide the context within which business is embedded. The final set consists of stimuli that prompt organizations to pay attention to CSR. We use these to identify the different ways in which CSR practice is formulated and implemented in business organizations.

Individual actors: change and innovation

In organizations committed to CSR the roles played by individual actors are similar to the roles identified in learning and change or innovation processes by authors such as Tushman and Nadler (1996) and Roome (2001). This similarity is not surprising given that in most companies CSR involves innovation in the relationships between the firm and others in its social and environmental context. These roles include visioning, sponsorship, idea generation and connecting, and in combination they provide the basis for 'change agents' in organizations (Roome and Bergin, 2000). Rarely is one individual responsible for all roles. Rather they are normally performed by different actors working in concert. In large organizations the roles tend to be performed recursively; that is, they are repeated in different business units or at different levels in the organization (ibid.). In this situation connecting roles are essential to communication and the ultimate coherence of CSR.

Visioning is the means to construct an image of a future desired state. In the case of CSR this image includes changes in the relationships the firm has with other organizational actors or the environment. A CSR vision includes some notion of what a new set of relationships might involve. This may originate from recognition by organizational leaders that there is a need to operate according to principles that are different from those in conventionally run firms, a conviction about the importance of particular qualities in relationships, or realization that environmental processes and resources are being undervalued or poorly managed. The source of this concern may be personal experience, the necessity of responding to crises or events or turning constraints into opportunities, or simply a conviction that there are better ways of doing business.

When individuals with a vision of the need for changed relationships have formal authority in the organization, such as a CEO, some of the other roles are less important. When there is a separation between visionary managers and those who provide capital or the organizational 'space' to develop these ideas, then sponsorship roles become important. Sponsors provide organizational space and resources for those with vision so that the vision can be developed and implemented.

Visionary leaders may identify the need for and the direction of change, or determine the principles required to govern the process of change, but they are rarely equipped with all the necessary ideas and/or competences to translate the vision into practice. Ideas to support or fill out visions can be drawn from many sources: technological, organizational and cultural. These can be used alone or in combination. Ideas can be generated internally or through the injection of new resources into the company, for example by hiring new staff, engaging consultants or conferring with NGOs. Ideas are necessary in the formulation and implementation of an original vision or to overcome obstacles to the attainment of the vision. Over time a combination of ideas can be transformed into a single concept, providing a basis for strategy and organizational development, and serving as a strong symbol for communication.

Whether the CSR approach and its content are directed from the top, supported by ideas from outside or facilitated and coached inside the organization, it is necessary to communicate the content and instill an understanding of the approach throughout the organization. The larger the organization, the more likely it is that the development and diffusion of the content of the CSR innovation will have to be communicated through networks or via recursive processes that affect all departments and functions, formal structures and systems. Irrespective of whether these networks are informal or institutionalized, as in the case of formal knowledge management systems, they require managers with network skills or the ability to design information and communications systems to link others.

The visioning, idea generation and connecting roles are part of the process of formulating and implementing a CSR approach. Clearly, if the vision and ideas that provide the content of the CSR vision are facilitated or coached within the organization, then this process, if handled well, will support the development of commitment and shared understanding and begin to develop a network of CSR champions within the organization. Participation is also a source of ideas and a basis for employees to begin collectively to test the meaning of the concept and practice of CSR so that it becomes a theory in practice. A participative approach of this kind is also consistent with the view that CSR is founded on and leads to strong ties of engagement and trust within an organization and with other organizations in its business context.

Organizational enabling factors

A number of contemporary ideas and practices in business enable innovation and change in general, and through that facilitate the move towards CSR in particular. These include management systems that emphasize missions, goals, targets, resource allocations, performance measurement and reviews. They also include quality management tools, techniques and processes, learning organization practices based on visioning, creative tension and the identification of key points of leverage, cross-functional teams, flat and open organizational structures, knowledge management systems and an organizational culture based on explicit principles or values.

Prior experience of these concepts and systems fosters the formulation and implementation of CSR. It provides the ducts across organizations along which information and ideas flow, it guides individual and organizational knowledge and choice and offers accumulated experience upon which to draw. These ideas and practices, with their emphasis on learning and change, can be seen as building blocks for processes that support the formulation and implementation of CSR policy and practice.

Other ideas or concepts that have gained currency in management are supporting the move towards CSR. There is a tendency how to speak of stakeholders rather than shareholders (Freeman, 1984), including the identification and determination of stakeholder salience (Mitchell *et al.*, 1997), stakeholder mapping (Wartick and Wood, 1998) and processes of stakeholder engagement (Sharma and Vredenburg, 1998). Similarly, the wide spread of the notion of 'product stewardship' has shifted the focus of companies away from strictly limited responsibility for the functionality of products to joint responsibility with others in the supply and value chain, including consumers. This has in turn led to the development and use of a raft of techniques that capture the environmental profile of products and services throughout their life cycle (Roome, 1999). These ideas have all contributed to a management language and approach that has improved understanding of the relationships between firms and others in society and equipped managers with the concepts and tools required to deal with those relationships.

The capacity to identify CSR as an opportunity and to build on this to shape a new context for the organization and its CSR practices is also important. By so doing the organization's CSR approach is recognized and can flourish; attracting customers, suppliers and employees is important in building success and aligning relationships between the business, its context, supply-chains and markets (for capital, customers and labour). Indeed it is consistent with CSR as a vision-led activity and this vision can be as powerful in shaping the external context as it is in shaping the internal context and processes.

Institutional contexts and embedding

Institutions are defined here as (1) sets of organizational actors and (2) the rules and belief systems that guide the behaviour of organizations and individuals. Institutions provide the context in which individual organizations are embedded (Granovetter, 1985). That embedding can have a number of dimensions (Zukin and DiMaggio, 1991); structural, for example when economic exchange is contextualized in patterns of interpersonal relationships; cultural, when shared collective understandings develop to shape economic strategies and roles (Spender, 1989; Phillips, 1994); cognitive, when structured regularities of mental processes limit the exercise of economic reasoning; and political, where economic institutions and decisions are shaped by a struggle for power that involves economic actors and non-market institutions.

Our earlier observation that the rise of CSR is a governance response to the fault lines of globalization, and particularly the role and position of business in contemporary society, suggests that CSR has the character of a social movement. In this regard it has influenced thinking and practice in business. In other words CSR has structural, cultural, cognitive and political significance as a social movement. The structural and cultural aspects find expression in, for example, business leaders' and managers' forums when greater attention is given to the notion of CSR (Holliday *et al.*, 2002). Cognitive processes are shaped by the claims and arguments of CSR advocates and the tools, techniques and rationality they propound. These include the claim that CSR contributes to or at least does not detract from performance in terms of profitability and shareholder returns (Burke and Logsdon, 1996; Epstein and Roy, 2001; SustainAbility/ENEP, 2001; Johnson, 2003). Politically there is growing support for CSR as a way to curb the perceived excesses of corporate behaviour and as part of a wider movement to reorder the joint governance of social, economic and environmental systems based on voluntarism by business (Holliday *et al.*, 2002). In continental Europe this social movement only began to take shape in late 1990s, whereas it emerged in the UK in the early 1980s. The movement lends support to companies and managers that are pioneering new approaches to CSR, success is recognized and rewarded by awards and publicity, and new participants in CSR are brought onto the bandwagon.

After an initial period of experimentation the tendency of all social movements is to move towards standardized practice and the professionalization of management by developing codes and guidelines. The development of CSR as a social movement is no different, although it involves a complex development of institutions and individual organizations. In this sense organizations are embedded in these institutions and the institutions are composed and derivative of the CSR practices and commitments of individual organizations. It is this synergistic embedding that qualifies CSR as a social movement that is shaping or attempting to shape mainstream business institutions and is in turn being shaped by them. An example of this the responsible investment community, which began as a fringe activity but has become institutionalized and incorporated into mainstream investment funds and banks. It has the power to influence the mainstream but is also influenced by it.

Stimuli for CSR

The final elements in our discussion of the drivers of CSR are the ideas, events and experiences that draw the attention of change agents to CSR and stimulate the development of new visions based on CSR ideas. There are many sources of stimuli, including a daughter who asked her father what his company was doing to protect the environment, a textile company that faced increasingly stringent environment controls, a CEO who chose to see this as an opportunity to reconfigure his business on environmental principles,

CEOs who respond to ideas from their employees and then oversee the emergence of a new vision for the company, and a managing director with many years of experience in pharmaceuticals with a new vision of a way of doing business that valued employees as people rather than numbers.

The development of CSR as a social movement means that ideas, codes, books and consultants are increasingly available to inject ideas to be taken forward by business leaders. Important, too, have been the repercussions of catastrophic accidents such as Bhopal and *Exxon Valdez*, and the revelation of child labour and poor working conditions in Far Eastern factories, which not only propelled individual companies to consider their own CSR position but also contributed to the growth of CSR as a social movement.

Pioneers emerge in response to different combinations of events, ideas and experiences. Follower companies are then attracted to CSR because it has become fashionable or they wish to be seen as leaders in their industry. Yet even in follower companies there are passionate advocates of CSR, just as there are in pioneering companies.

Motives for adopting CSR

We consider that all companies are reactive rather than proactive in terms of the formulation and implementation of CSR in response to the emerging fault lines in the globalizing economy and society. All companies react, through their managers, to events or ideas they witness or experiences they have. Since the beginning of capitalism there have been companies that have sought to find more responsible ways of operating, and more recently this has been extended to the use of environmental resources and the relationship companies have with natural systems. There have never been more dimensions to corporate responsibility and it is now emerging as a strategic concern. Our analysis suggests that the development of CSR as a social movement and a corporate practice is part of a complex restructuring of the role and position of business in society.

A range of reasons for adopting CSR can be identified. These are pioneering companies that are driven by the desire of senior managers or owners to do something different. There are synergistic companies for which CSR is in accord with a longstanding commitment to values, or principles such as quality or leadership, where the systems and ideas they utilize are conducive to CSR. There are reactor companies whose practices have been questioned and whose reputations have suffered as a consequence. There are companies that merely follow the trend. And there are uninterested companies that have yet to be persuaded of need to adopt CSR.

We maintain that there is no superior way to formulate and implement CSR, which is a continuously unfolding canvas and has so many dimensions that no one company can be master of them all or attend to all the issues that provoke attention to CSR. It has been suggested that the agenda for CSR is shaped by national and local concerns and circumstances, which means that what is viewed as responsible is socially constructed (Roome, 2004).

Whatever drives CSR in an organization and whatever route it takes, the key factor is the success with which CSR is formulated, implemented and embedded in the organization's practices. CSR is a strategic and operational concern that requires attention across the organization, is a motor for innovation and a force for change (CSR Europe, 2002). It is a concept and practice that draws together the owners of capital, senior managers and all other employees in a quest for quality relationships with others in the economic, social and environmental systems of which they are part. The ultimate challenge for CSR is to foster such relationships while ensuring profitability.

We have suggested that there are many motives for adopting CSR. In its most extreme form CSR is emerging in response to the need to reposition the role of business in society. The paradox of this repositioning is that managers and others are often searching for a business case to justify the development of a CSR approach. This business case is rooted in the logic of traditions capitalism, but we maintain that CSR should be founded on the logic of 'reform capitalism'. We also maintain that in the case of CSR, for those who understand no explanation is necessary, and for those who do not understand no explanation will suffice.

References

Burke, L. and Logsdon, J. M. (1996) 'How corporate social responsibility pays off', *Long Range Planning*, 29, pp. 495–502.

Castells, M. (1996) *The Rise of the Network Society* (Oxford: Blackwell).

Chevalier, M. and T. Cartwright (1966) 'Towards an action framework for the control of pollution', paper presented at the National Conference on Pollution and our Environment, Canadian Council of Resource Ministers, Ottawa.

CSR Europe (2002) *Exploring Business Dynamics: Mainstreaming Corporate Social Responsibility in a Company's Strategy, Management, and Systems* (Brussels: CSR Europe).

Elkington, J. (1998) *Cannibals with Forks: The Triple Bottom Line of 21st Century Business* (Gabriola Island: New Society Publishers).

Epstein, M. J. and M. J. Roy (2001) 'Sustainability in action: Identifying and measuring the key performance drivers', *Long Range Planning*, 34, pp. 585–604.

European Commission (2002) *Corporate Social Responsibility: A Business Contribution to Sustainable Development* (Brussels: European Commission).

Freeman, R. E. (1984) *Strategic Management: A Stakeholder Approach* (London: Pitman).

Granovetter, M. (1985) 'Economic action and social structure: The problem of embeddedness', *American Journal of Sociology*, 91, pp. 481–510.

Holliday, C. O., S. Schmidheiny and P. Watts (2002) *Walking the Talk: The Business Case for Sustainable Development* (Sheffield: Greenleaf).

Johnson, H. H. (2003) 'Does it pay to be good? Social responsibility and financial performance', *Business Horizons*, Nov./Dec., pp. 34–40.

Mitchell, R., B. Agle and D. Wood (1997) 'Toward a theory of stakeholder identification and salience: Defining the principle of who and what really counts', *Academy of Management Review*, 22 (4), pp. 853–86.

Phillips, M. (1994) 'Industry mindsets: Exploring the cultures of two macro-organisational settings', in J. Meindl, C. Stubbart and J. Porac (eds), *Cognition Within and Between Organizations* (London: Sage), pp. 475–507.

Roome, N. (1999) 'Integrating environmental concerns into corporate decisions', in K. Sexton, A. Marcus, K. Easter and T. Burkhart (eds), *Better Environmental Decisions: Strategies for Governments, Businesses and Communities* (Washington, DC: Island Press), pp. 267–88.

Roome, N. (2000) 'Globalization and sustainable development: Toward a transatlantic agenda', in C. Bonser (ed.), *Security, Trade, and Environmental Policy: A US/European Union Transatlantic Agenda* (Dordrecht: Kluwer), pp. 161–86.

Roome, N. (2001) 'Meta-textual Organizations: Innovation and adaptation for global change', professorial inaugural address, Erasmus University, Rotterdam (available from Erasmus Centre for Sustainable Development and Management, Erasmus University, Rotterdam).

Roome, N. (2004) 'A pan-European approach to CSR: Some implications of national agendas for corporate social responsibility', paper presented at the CSR Discovery Colloquium, Wildbad Kreuth, Bavaria, January, pp. 29–31.

Roome, N. and R. Bergin (2000) 'The challenges of sustainable development: Lessons from Ontario Hydro', *Corporate Environmental Strategy*, 7 (1), pp. 8–19.

Sharma, S. and H. Vredenburg (1998) 'Pro-active corporate environmental management strategy and the development of competitively valuable organizational capabilities', *Strategic Management Journal*, 19 (8), pp. 729–53.

Spender, J. (1989) *Industry Recipes* (Cambridge: Basil Blackwell).

SustainAbility/UNEP (2001) *Buried Treasure: Uncovering the Business Case for Corporate Sustainability* (London: SustainAbility).

Tushman, M. and D. Nadler (1996) 'Organizing for innovation', in K. Starkey (ed.), *How Organizations Learn* (London: Thomson).

Wartick, S. L. and D. J. Wood (1998) *International Business and Society* (Malden: Blackwell).

Zukin, S. and P. DiMaggio (eds) (1991) *Structures of Capital: The Social Organization of the Economy* (Cambridge: Cambridge University Press).

Part II
Organizing CSR

7
Reinventing Social Dialogue

Robert Beckett and Jan Jonker

Introduction

The theory of social dialogue and practice of public engagement are founded on democratic ideals of participation that remain elusive, despite a connection with established principles of Western democracy, a century of social science enquiry and more recently the growing practice of corporate stakeholder consultation. In theory and practice, dialogues are difficult to characterize and actual evidence for their effectiveness is difficult to separate from interrelated drivers of change. As the explicit communication technique behind many newly minted statements of corporate social responsibility, the latest practice of social dialogue appears too weak to maintain the questioning attitude that dialogue implies. This chapter draws on Jürgen Habermas's (1968, 1984, 1987) discourse ethics and some original research techniques to assess the controversial issues behind corporate dialogue practice. We conclude that new forms of public consultation offer some promise of change by employing democratic communication processes implied in dialogue and through this a promise to further restore fundamental human rights, or at least the values that lead and protect them. To restore freedoms and define new rights through dialogue is a practice to be welcomed, even while practitioners are challenged to prove the ability of dialogue to deliver such promise. Still, where claims for dialogue are insufficiently evidenced, or imbalanced by inappropriate power relations, public consultation may be considered not as a liberating, democratic communication technique but merely an extension of the power, privilege and control that mark many forms of Western political and economic activity and their miscommunication. This chapter offers a unique approach to identifying key concepts in dialogue practice, through graphic modelling, enabling corporate and community managers to identify and examine their own critical thinking, thereby to support the stakeholder consultation processes that they may undertake.

Dialogue for corporations

For corporations entering into dialogue with stakeholders implies not only listening and responding, but also making a moral commitment to address the human rights of those citizens whose lives they affect by their actions or inactions (Rawls, 1972; Habermas, 1984; Benhabib, 1992). Dialogue offers hope in the same way that the principle of justice offers hope, in terms not only of participants being heard (as with the less onerous activity of consultation) but also of changes actually being made. In the twentieth century, large corporations became powerful actors in a new global society, taking or being granted substantial resources, rights and powers (Korten, 1995). For many world citizens, fairness and equality of outcome were diminished while privilege was accorded certain groups (shareholders, employees) supported by the ideologies and technologies of capital, particularly over the less explicit moral codes of human community (Habermas, 1968; Suzuki and Dressel 1999). The question that stands before all corporations is whether their actions further reduce the ideals of community held in human rights and social morality, or whether they support the opportunity for people to live and work in just and sustainable world communities.

The corporate social responsibility (CSR) movement, driven largely by corporations themselves, can be judged by its responsiveness to specific arguments made by world citizens to further the aims of social justice, information transparency and organizational accountability. Our research suggests that less than 5 per cent of corporations publish the transcripts of their dialogues, clearly reducing the possibilities of dialogue in establishing differences between community and corporation that may be understood and challenged. The second critical question is, do corporate and stakeholder dialogues comply with a more rigorous definition of dialogue – what we call just and fair communication defined as protecting and extending the human right to self-determination, or are corporate dialogues merely organization self-publicity, aimed at improving corporate reputation through sophisticated perception management? The social accounting project which links dialogue with the measurement of corporate performance can be judged similarly. Is citizen-stakeholder self-determination enhanced by corporate dialogue measured by social accounts (despite the potential of dialogue to aid rights resistance), and do dialogues support a counter culture that may actually limit corporate objectives or even profits? The future cry for all citizens must be self-determination and corporations that practise CSR should be judged by how they help to build the capacity for self-governance by citizens through all levels of society. The public interest decided by civil servants equates to no interest at all, nor should the sustainability of communities be left to decisions by private corporations. In practice, as in democratic theory, the public interest may only be decided by citizens who support both government and market with legitimacy, taxes and profit.

A clear danger with corporate dialogues is the closing off of the questioning attitude, the *docta ignorantia* of Socrates, where according to Gadamer (2003, p. 361) 'Openness to the other ... involves recognizing that I myself must accept some things that are against me, eventhough no one else forces me to do so'. In reality, just and fair dialogue implies a situation that most organizations might find difficult to cope with, as proposals for change, or questioning from the bottom up, go against all notions of management expertise, control and efficiency (Argyris, 1990). Western business and administrative management still appears to be mired in the nineteenth-century certainty of expertise and control, as held in the heads and hands of privileged elites, an antiquated model that in the global network society no longer appears sustainable. Information communication technology (ICT) has established a revolutionary new 'information space' founded outside the traditional institutions of civil society and where individual citizens constitute network nodes of a vast web of social relations. While this transformation substantially increases the capacity of individual actors for self-determination, it equally threatens the traditional structures and ruling assumptions of powerful organizations by undermining the need for them and the dependence of citizens on narrow channels of highly prized and controlled information sources. Businesses, in particular, have enjoyed vast gains in efficiency and performance from ICT, gains that have often been achieved at the expense of democratic principles, for instance in the ruthless marketing of economic consumption at the expense of sustainable alternatives (Monbiot, 2000). Because it enhances all other technologies, ICT is almost certainly the greatest technology the world has ever known, despite its relatively recent appearance (McLuhan, 1964). Ideally, the next phase in the information revolution would see the benefits of technology reassigned to the citizen stakeholder – those whose right to justice, well-being, care and self-determination has, in previous generations, regularly been suspended in the name of progress, special dispensation and elite control. In the age of sustainability the arguments for privilege are redundant as they dangerously limit the vast changes necessary to ensure an equitable and sustainable future for all. Dialogue is one of the few constitutionally valid procedures for making democratic decisions. This implies the reconstitution of existing modes of governance, more effectively combining multiple self-governing communities joined together through dialogue and electronic communication and complying with transparent principles of justice. Neither governments nor corporations can make all the changes required to sustain human life on earth. Only individual citizens empowered to create just communities are able to achieve this end. In doing so, the role of corporations and institutions is likely to be transformed in ways that may be anathema to powerful organizations founded in and operating with assumptions that may no longer remain viable.

Dialogue defined

Rehg has described dialogue in terms of ethical discourse and 'as a vehicle for systematic reflection on the problems attaining consensus in pluralistic societies'. (Rehg, 1994, p. 2). In probably its most sustained examination Habermas (1990, p. 79) describes a moral essence for dialogue: 'I call communicative those interactions in which the interlocutors agree to coordinate in good faith their plans of action.'

Habermas offers those who engage in public consultation a theory for assessing the value of corporate dialogues. According to him dialogue is not something that can be achieved by writ or decree, requiring 'freedom from influence or autonomy in will formation' (ibid., p. 71) founded on the universal principle that any dialogue should consider if 'all affected can accept the consequences and side effects its general observance can be anticipated to have for the satisfaction of everyone's interests' (ibid., p. 65). The purpose of practical discourse is described in the principle of discourse ethics: 'Only those norms may claim to be valid that could meet with the consent of all affected in their role as participants in a practical discourse' (ibid., p. 66). In the case of corporate dialogues it is worth remembering the Habermasian rules summarized by Alexy and quoted by Habermas himself:

> 1. every subject with the competence to speak and act is allowed to take part in a discourse
>
> 2a. everyone is allowed to question any assertion whatsoever
> 2b. everyone is allowed to introduce any assertion whatever into the discourse
> 2c. everyone is allowed to express their attitudes, desires and needs
>
> 3. no speaker may be prevented, by internal or external coercion, from exercising their rights as laid down in 1 or 2 (ibid., p. 89).

In Benhabib's theory of enlarged thought, taking responsibility for self action identifies the moral position of participants in dialogue and the opportunity within institutions to generate moral outcomes:

> There is thus a fundamental link between a civic culture of public partic-ipation and the moral quality of enlarged thought. Enlarged thought, which morally obligates us to think from the standpoint of everyone else, politically requires the creation of institutions and practices whereby the voice and the perspective of others, often unknown to us, can become expressed in their own right (Benhabib 1992, p. 140).

Benhabib criticizes earlier Habermasian claims to create universal standards and procedures for dialogue as too ambitious. Nonetheless, the value of

Habermasian ideas lies not in their idealism but in their pragmatic grounding in universal human values or norms (truth, well-being, trust, goodwill and so on) and a universally shared rationality. These universal pragmatic values, enhanced and protected by communication, are being held in suspension by laws, regulations and management systems, and are often distorted, limiting the historic move 'from legislative to interactive rationalism' (ibid., p. 2).

In his theory of the public sphere, Habermas (1984, 1987) identifies distortions built into the systematic resources of politics, government and business, while linking the notion of a public sphere to the privileged status of dialogue. He sets out the ground for a 'moral discourse' in a 'lifeworld' that is free from politicization and economic forces of control. These are summarized as a discussion of technical interests and the effects of a 'system world' in which bureaucratic and other special interests rationalize culture and human interaction in an attempt to control them. Over time the 'mediatization of the lifeworld *turns into its colonisation*' (Habermas 1987, p. 318, emphasis in the original) as rational technical interests diminish the ability of citizens to effectively represent themselves through public discourse. For any theory of social dialogue this analysis has a profound implication. Interhuman communication is the underpinning technique or 'praxis' for social dialogue and the *de jure* (principle of justice) means by which all social democratic processes are built. Without legally protected and viable social dialogue, democracy may simply not exist. Hence, none of us may actually live in a true democracy where citizens rights are held above elite control over any debate. Paradoxically, without the right to equitable dialogue linked to forms of citizen power that control political outcomes, most Western political processes, by their own terms, would be too restricted to be viewed as either democratic or offering a complete picture of justice.

Dialogue as a complex communication process is also hinted at in the concept of 'argumentation' put forward in Habermas's (1984) theory of communicative action. Habermas describes different styles of discourse:

- theoretical
- practical
- aesthetic
- therapeutic
- explicative

These can be read as dialogue types, indicating different principles, structures and motivations for dialogue. Corporate dialogues may more or less conform to the notion of practical discourse, but without a relationship with other discourses, practical discourse can become removed from the morality embodied in linked debates, for instance those on ethics or sustainability. There is still much research to be undertaken in the field of dialogue typology and classification, though this is beyond the scope of this chapter. For corporations, the essential point is that dialogue may not be controlled by anyone, that dialogue is a measure of human moral emancipation and must not be interrupted or reduced in the name of convenience by 'systemworld' initiatives that still motivate political and economic action in most Western countries.

Dialogue democracy

One branch of theory identifies dialogue as a language concept situated in people's capacity and right to communicate. For Apel ([1973] 1980 p. 425) communication is the foundational relationship people have with each other, the 'unlimited communicative community of all rational beings (alle denkenden Wesen)', thereby to govern their own lives and respond to the impact others have on them. Such a right to tell and be heard (inform and communicate) is not straightforward, particularly when working assumptions and dialogue conditions are very different, as between individuals and corporations. At the very least, corporations are likely to privilege their own viability and methodologies above those of individuals, groups or even communities; certainly until the evidence to the contrary is so overwhelming that change is impossible to deny and government allies to refute. For social justice campaigners, stark lessons have been learnt about how organizations (public and private) respond to community demands through dialogue, suggesting that dialogue is often employed as a valve to release social tension while the organization works against the direct interests of communities, or more particularly in its own self-interest (Korten, 1995). If dialogue is to be effective, particularly when linked to principles of self-determination by citizens and community self-governance, it has to be grounded in political and legal structures that are able to protect both the process and the outcomes of dialogue. Self-certification by large organizations hardly fits this model, and in fact can be viewed as a form of crude publicity to ensure that action is not taken and the full implications of dialogue are actually avoided.

According to the philosopher John Rawls (1972) distributive justice is the human right above all others and lies at the heart of democracy. In reality, justice is the main principle behind communication, in its deeper sense 'the privileging of the other' (Buber, 1947; Levinas, 1996; Christians and Traber, 1997). Benhabib (1992, p. 100) draws together dialogue and the communication of justice as an underpinning concept: 'rather public dialogue means challenging and redefining the collective good, and one's sense of justice as a result of the public foray'. Benhabib considers the link between justice and dialogue founded on the liberal value of neutrality as insufficient to protect the true value and role of dialogue:

> The liberal principle of dialogic neutrality, while it expresses one of the main principles of the modern legal system, is too restrictive and frozen in application to the dynamics of power struggles in actual political processes. A public life, conducted according to [this] principle ... would restrict the scope of the public conversation in a way which would be inimical to the interest of oppressed groups (ibid.).

Communication between citizens and corporations without coercion or manipulation is a fitting goal for CSR, ensuring justice in democratic societies by protecting free communication among citizens who are equal before the law, if not preferentially before the moral order. A crucial question is whether in its many guises corporate dialogue can be fitted into a framework of extended or extendable human rights in order to protect the principles of dialogue from legally constituted misappropriation? Rawls (1993, p. 8) defines the principle of 'free public reason' to enable the evaluation of justice in a public forum: 'The maxim that justice must not only be done, but be seen to be done, holds good not only in law, but in free public reason.' In these circumstances, the citizen may ask of a corporation whether its claims to be socially responsible conforms to its actions, and whether these can be judged against an ideal model that rebalances the market power and legal rights of the collective enterprise, with the often suspended rights and lack of power generally displayed by dispersed human communities. Crucially, dialogue (and dialogic tools such as the internet) are a potential means to achieve this rebalance, although dialogue must be supported by conditions and rights that protect the participants. Rawls is credited with refining the social contract theory of society that began with the Greek sophists and was taken up by Thomas Hobbes (1651), John Locke (1693) and Jean Jacques Rousseau (1764), arguing that human rights enabled by an explicit and dynamic social contract appear to offer the firmest foundation for the construction of a shared moral order. While this accords with the oft-stated purpose of social dialogue, to support human rights, it is self-evident that the moral order underlying all human community has largely been replaced by laws that disembody moral territory and reduce the capacity of communities to protect themselves from manipulation by corporations (Habermas, 1968; Foucault, 1972; Bourdieu, 1992). By employing broad and enforceable notions of human rights to support the moral order rather than appealing to legal ends, there is a faint hope that social justice can be served. Even so, human rights should be recognized as a 'soft' means of directing social outcomes, while legislative frameworks, often used to protect the rights of power and wealth, are recognized as harder and more enforceable. According to Rawls (1972) human rights must conform to five necessary conditions:

- generality
- universality
- publicity
- rightness
- finality

Still, the problem with rights-based argumentation is that in so many areas human rights lie suspended, or are subsumed in legal, regulatory and corporate powers. Participants in dialogues are in theory protected by rights laid down in the UN Charter of Human Rights in 1948. Despite the clear right to free expression, recognition before the law, self-determination and freedom, there is still deep injustice in the treatment of citizens and systematic reduction of human rights by governments and corporations alike (Monbiot, 2000). In theory, at least, participation in social dialogue is an essential means of affecting change, with rights and responsibilities being held equally by the community of citizen actors, while institutions and corporations remain under democratic control. However, the right to engage in dialogue is a weak form of democratic participation unless those taking part recognize its binding nature as part of a commitment to universal human justice. The problem with this moral argument and the practice of corporate dialogue itself, is that those with legally constituted corporate or institutional power are able to counter arguments, negate human rights and avoid moral norms to suit their own purpose. In this case the only alternative to self-justifying, legally protected institutional power is morally constituted citizen power. Although hardly prioritized except as an ideal of constitutional democracy, it is citizen power that is the ultimate seat of authority in every state. Despite such a clear commitment democracy remains dull. Aristotle, in *The Constitution of Athens*, makes the point that democracy was even then a battleground between have and have-nots, the powerful and the powerless. In two and a half thousand years little appears to have changed (Barnes, 1984).

Corporate dialogue managers should take this analysis into consideration. For instance, social accounting, with its claim to objectivity and neutrality (Gray *et al.*, 1996), cannot protect dialogue from interference and manipulation, as no such theoretical or practical position can be maintained, at least according to post-structuralist critique and Habermasian public sphere injunctions (Foucault, 1972; Lyotard, 1979; Habermas, 1990; Bourdieu, 1992). For social accountants and auditors, whose competence to support or protect dialogue must surely be questioned in respect of both self-interest and constitutional legitimacy, this should be troubling. The claim of social accounting to offer objective (measured) knowledge to all parties in the evaluation of corporate social performance can be questioned as scientific dogma, promoted by commercial interests as a 'communication token', offering corporations control over a measurement process that finds what it seeks and to dialogue participants a quasi-technical response to their demands that is overwhelmingly imbalanced. A number of questions are worth asking a socially responsible corporation: Do you publish the transcripts of your dialogue? On what terms do you employ independent facilitators of dialogue? How does your social report address the contested questions that are part of your wider operating remit? Does your social report contain a commitment to individual participants in dialogue? The chances are that when using social accounts the powerful and wealthy remain in control of both the agenda and the resources. Public debate is not enough. Procedures of engagement must be equitable and just and corporations must defer to the legitimate right of citizens to self-determination. This may require corporations to reduce their commercial interest in any community that expresses dissatisfaction with corporate involvement, or to act in other ways that secure the public interest. Such actions are difficult to determine inside the corporations itself.

Dialogue and communication ethics

Communication ethics is a theoretical and practical discipline reformulated from a number of traditions from the European social sciences. Defined as 'an ethics of communication and communication of ethics' (ICE, 2001) it privileges theories of human communication, language, well-being and moral reasoning (Christians and Traber, 1997). The position of the communication theorist is startlingly informative, according to Thomas McCarthy (1996, p. 282): 'Since speech is the distinctive and pervasive medium of life at the human level, the theory of communication is the foundational study for human sciences: it discloses the universal infrastructure of socio-cultural life.' Likewise ethics is seen as foundational human response to being together, *feminist* ethics particularly privileging the self-other relationship (Greer, 1970; Gilligan, 1982), and by the European tradition of ethics (Buber, 1947; Levinas, 1996; Bauman, 1993) which takes into consideration the need for self-identity and self-expression while balancing construction and maintenance of cultural and community relations. Since Socrates, the self and community dialectic has been the most important of ethical concerns and it is apparent that the intervention of powerful organizations can distort this relationship, reducing community life while capturing individuals as economic units to be exploited for economic gain. In communication ethics, dialogue is understood both as a technical form of group communication (debate is another) and as a necessary agent for intersubjective human agreement. The intercultural and multimoral dimensions of human communication are, according to Christians and Traber (1997), the basis of a universally shared conception of socially constructed and linguistically mediated reality, where 'communication is not the transference of knowledge but a dialogic encounter of subjects creating it together' (ibid., p. 9). Such a moral insight challenges the very basis of an economic system designed to reduce all effective social conduct to discrete, accountable units that can be rationalized, manipulated and owned.

Examining the role of social dialogue, an understanding of language is clearly essential. For Habermas (1984, p. 275) language agreement precedes dialogue by virtue of its being the foundation for dialogue where '... it can be shown that the use of language with an orientation to reaching understanding is the original mode of language use, upon which indirect understanding, giving something to understand or letting something be understood, and the instrumental use of language in general are parasitic'. This implies a crucial role for linguistic analysis in assessing and identifying the terms upon which dialogue is founded. For instance language complexity may reveal disagreement in several fundamental dimensions of language use:

- semantics
- linguistics
- semiotics
- decisionistics
- psychodynamics

Added to language complexity are cultural factors and the different traditions and values held by gender, ethnic and economic groups (Makau and Arnett, 1997). Contingency and diversity are dominant and apparent across human action and require consideration as the background for all dialogue, as do sub-languages (politics) and technical language sets (professions):

- language
- culture
- relations
- media
- systems

For those entering dialogue the implications are that complexity in human culture and social organization, information and communication are often displaced via processes of ideological reduction in order to achieve practical ends. In the information age this is no longer necessary, or appropriate, as the technological capacity to produce, evaluate and disseminate information ensures that resources are available to enable thorough and appropriate investigation into the implications of undistorted dialogue.

Professional dialogue

A particularly important factor in assessing social dialogue is recognition for the part played by professionals and technocrats, who through their involvement in dialogue potentially gain special privilege for those they represent (and incidentally themselves) at the price of the democracy they carefully uphold as their source of power and wealth. According to Larson (1977) the 'professional project' should be considered in terms of power and the enclosure of rights, a point made by Max Weber some time earlier and quoted by Larson. Professional '... purpose is always the closure of social and economic opportunities to outsiders' (ibid., p. 342). In a study of the medical professions, Friedson (1970, pp. 159–60) describes the 'organized autonomy' of professionals and their role in creating 'barriers to communication and co-operation within a functional division of labour, structures of evasion and the reduction of the client to an object. This imperialistic ideology hardens when an occupation develops the autonomy of a profession and a place of dominance in a division of labour'. Decades of academic enquiry into the professions have revealed a set of practices that professional groups use to establish their own agenda over others:

- social stratification
- structured inequality
- ideology
- rule formation

When considering professional involvement in dialogue it should be borne in mind that there are class and special interests which professional bodies have historically enjoyed to gain privilege and power over citizens. The clustered problems of professional dependency are commented on by Thomas McCarthy (1996, pp. 9–10) who describes the transfer of power from politician to professional:

> The dependence of the professional on the politician appears to have reversed itself. The latter becomes a mere agent of a scientific intelligentsia which, in concrete circumstances, elaborates the objective implication and requirements of available techniques and resources as well as of optimal strategies and rules of control. The politician would then be at best, something like a stop-gap in a still imperfect rationalization of power, in which the initiative has in any case passed to scientific analysis and technical planning.

In the case of dialogue, there are several issues to consider. How do the professionals install themselves in the process of dialogue, for instance as facilitators? Why should special privilege be accorded any professional group to influence the central communication procedure at the heart of democratic life? In whose name do these professions work? And how do they ensure their concordance with legitimate claims made by citizens in dialogue? These professionals include civil servants, accountants, auditors, public relations personnel and managers.

According to Habermas, (facilitation of) social dialogue requires absolute independence. It is, however, unlikely that any professionals, employed by institutions or corporations, could ever have such independence. The main form of weak authority a professional group might claim is derived from the notion of public interest, one of the key dimensions of professionalism cited by many professional groups and potentially compromised as a result. Should we conclude that lawyers, accountants or (even less likely) public relations professionals can be trusted to protect fundamental human rights without inserting their own private interests or those of their clients? The only solution is for the citizen through the state to protect all forms of dialogue against intervention by professional interests. This accords with the broadest purpose of dialogue to allow citizens to manage their own lives through acts of self-governance and to define their own rights and responsibilities from a position of equality, unmediated by institutional and professional authority. Thus, dialogue can be defined as dialogue in which citizen's control their own issues and debates free from professional interference. Anything less should be viewed with deep scepticism, particularly when professional groups seek to bolster their own power and authority over the process of democratic debate. This point is made clear by McCarthy (1997, p. 15):

> the enlightenment of political will can become effective only within the communication of citizens. For the articulation of needs in accordance with technical knowledge can be ratified exclusively in the consciousness of the political actors themselves. Experts cannot delegate to themselves this act of confirmation from those who have to account with their life histories for the new interpretation of social needs and for accepted means of mastering problematic situations.

Tools for dialogue

The graphical modelling that is part of this analysis is a means of transparent communication, allowing key concepts to be opened to common dispute or agreement. The aim is that a graphic language be understood by general and specialist users as part of a process of opening up underlying communication concepts to democratic debate by participating in the design and development of the thinking itself (for a fuller presentation of the graphic language visit www.5systems.net).

For instance, language use appears to be directed by a dialectical logic that shapes much of Western thought. Issues of dimorphism (duality) have been noted since the time of Heraclites, Plato and Aristotle. More recently in the field of semiotics, de Saussure (1919), Eco (1974) and many linguists and communication scholars have used various forms of dialectical reason to identify key tensions in information-communication and language-meaning. Levi Strauss (1958) called this phenomenon 'binary opposition' and Barthes

(1967) has described the 'duplex structure' that lies at the root of language and thinking. The following are examples of binary opposition in language:

langue	parole
sign	signified
diachronic	synchronic
text	intertextual
discourse	recit

A critical role for social dialogue is to outline the public space to evaluate and balance concepts the exhibit duality, concepts that may reflect worldly conception, but which may still be disputed and contested. Tensions are created in distinctions, a fact recognized by Aristotle whose syllogistic logic is one of the earliest attempts to give substance to dialectical reason and remains one of the most profound class of rules to distinguish know from unknown. In the twentieth century, Bertrand Russell's logical atomism offered a renewed effort to ground dialectical reason with formal laws.

In moral dialectics, how are right and wrong decided from numerous cultural and moral oppositions? Or when does the class bad turn to the class good? These questions point to a critical issue in any discussion of dialogue that structural misunderstanding implicit in our languages may deny agreement through dialogue or any other means. Perhaps it is time to reassess the values imposed by binary logic? One of these is the primacy that logic has over ethics. The language of science (underpinned by mathematics) and the language of values in human relationships and ethics might usefully be rebalanced to emphasize human wellbeing over economic efficiency and social rights promoted over other forms of instrumental self-interest. The primary forms of human rationality are:

logic	ethics
conclusive control over facts (minima)	non-conclusive values in relationships (maxima)

Dialogue can be viewed as a process that encourages a deeper examination of shared, although not necessarily agreed, meanings. For dialogue participants, bringing together twin binary structures initiates a simple heuristic model, the QUAD, thereby generating a deeper evaluation of dialogue content (Figure 7.1).

Even shared concepts, words and beliefs can be open to dispute. For instance, 'polysemy' describes the situation in which different words mean

Dialogue forms using CE dialectics	values	rights
Medium	dialogue-lite	just dialogue
Message	Corporate dialogue	Community dialogue

Figure 7.1   Example of a QUAD
Source: ICE (2004).

different things at different times to different people' (Bruhn-Jensen, 1995). Which values are fundamentally in opposition? Which are aligned, which are redundant and which are flawed? Social dialogue, if it is to be successful as a process to achieve the social good, must be founded on a methodological evaluation grounded in communication ethics that are freely available to everyone (not held by authorities), a practical ethics of communication that can be used to examine multiple realities, traditions and cultural values by all those concerned. Descriptive dialectical reason achieves this through openness to being examined and by encouraging examination of underlying concepts and definitions.

Communicative relations

The model of communicative relations (PMOGI) is a tool designed by the Institute of Communication Ethics (ICE, 2001) to assess the integrity and operational values that exist in acts of communication such as dialogue. It is a standpoint model that situates human relationships as both interdependent and morally founded, with 'viewpoint emerging from standpoint'. In the PMOGI

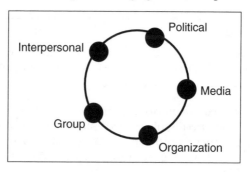

Figure 7.2   PMOGI heuristic
Source: ICE (2001). The 5circle is a trademark of Communication Ethics Limited.

model, dialogue participants use five relational groups to contrast and examine various dimensions of communication and their respective ethics (Figure 7.2).

- Political (P): the political dimension of dialogue relates to human rights, statutory instruments and regulations devised to protect individuals against coercion and manipulation by corporations or indeed government institutions.
- Media (M): dialogue is traditionally associated with face-to-face communication but far more information is now disseminated through mediated systems, which has both positive and negative implications for consultations practice. For example using the internet to report public consultations may actually reduce dialogue by setting technological limits, or it may improve it by bringing new constituencies into it.
- Organization (O): dialogue between organization and others is clearly fraught with competing paradigms, for example personal versus corporate interest and community rights versus commercial imperatives.
- Group (G): dialogue can be viewed as a convenient term to describe group communication that promotes justice, although the question remains whether dialogue is possible outside face-to-face contact in groups, and even in these encounters can dialogue be limited by expedience? When is it a dialogue and not a debate or a consultation?
- Interpersonal (I): individual relationships lie at the centre of dialogue but corporate dialogue reports rarely if ever reveal individual circumstances, dynamics or opposition.

The PMOGI model identifies how different interests, language and powers affect the way in which people communicate. Even when group dialogue exists it can be seriously distorted if political, media, organization or personal interests interfere with the dialogue in process. One particular factor rarely mentioned in reports of public consultation is the group-interpersonal relationship. This relates to the opportunity for coercion of the individual by the group, or coercion of the group by an individual, for example by the facilitator.

The binary relational tensions in the PMOGI model presented in Figure 7.3 indicate a degree of communicative complexity that is rarely acknowledged in communications at any level of society. For instance an organization–organization discourse has a completely different complexion to that of an organization–individual communication. The variety of communicative relations and assumptions that exist increase the complexity of corporate dialogue and make communication a far more powerful and meaningful task than is usually identified by solely pragmatic interests.

In communication ethics, dialogue conflicts are often regarded as language conflicts, revealing logical assumptions with a positivist agenda. For example feminine ideals are often subjugated to masculine ones (Alia, 2004). The following analysis of dialogue is by no means comprehensive and is intended only to show that the 'dialogue on dialogue' is in the early stages

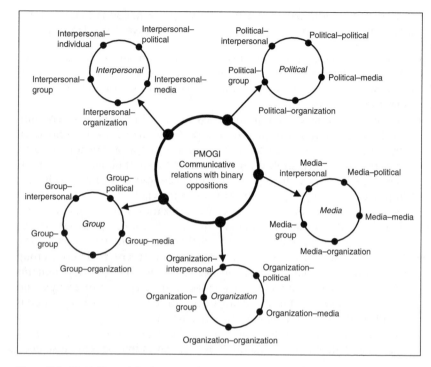

Figure 7.3   PMOGI model of communicative relations
Source: ICE (2001).

of its critical development and lacks key conceptual tools. The neglect of communication-based linguistic analysis tends to reduce communication while potentially exercising control by simplification or reducing complexity through expedience. The media dimension of the PMOGI model exemplifies this simplification. For instance, when addressing ethical issues the media are often guilty of reducing complex reality to black and white 'conditions of certainty' (Alia, 2004) in order to create a 'lite-communication' able to be effectively transmitted through multiple media channels.

Figure 7.4 displays some of the dilemmas in social dialogue. These can be read (graphed) alongside Figure 7.3 to produce a picture of the complexity that is inherent in all dialogue. For instance knowledge of interpersonal issues involving gender, language, personal control, wellbeing and ability are essential to understand how individuals perceive and react in a group dialogue. Each of the PMOGI relational groups has its own dilemmas that are part of a matrix of tensions that lie behind dialogue and may reduce its effectiveness, particularly if not opened to examination by the participants.

Each assessment made of formal dialogues should account for a deeper level of complexity founded in communication theory and a practice of moral engagement. Participants should be fully enabled to appreciate the

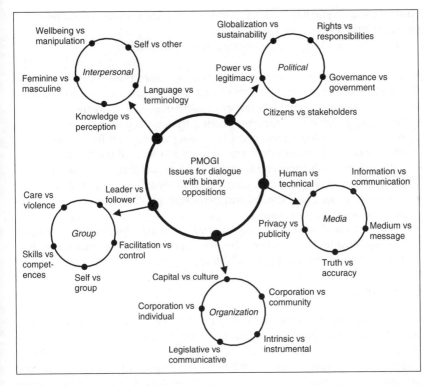

Figure 7.4 Binary paradox in social dialogue
Source: ICE (2004).

deeper issues concerned. For organizations that initiate dialogues this implies a substantial responsibility to educate the citizens whose lives they touch (and sometimes dominate) and to enable maximum responsiveness from participants in order to safeguard the implied ethic of dialogue. Despite being the reverse of how most systematic dialogues are presently conducted, we argue that the real purpose of dialogue must be to help citizens to make decisions that are fundamentally ethical rather than merely procedural, and that in addition, protect them from the overwhelming power of enormous public institutions and massive multinational corporations.

Applications

A comparison of these dialogue models with the everyday management of corporate responsibility programmes reveals that current dialogue practices are largely removed from citizens. Without programmes to teach communities to hold and maintain their own dialogues it is difficult to see how they can engage in dialogues with corporations. Armed with appropriate tools for dialogue preparation, participants should increasingly be able to deal with complex issues. Further research is being conducted on the effectiveness of the particular tools presented in this paper.

Meanwhile we offer the following hints for managers:

- Dialogue is a social process of questioning assumptions and promoting social justice that corporations should actively encourage and resource, thus making them enablers rather than managers of dialogue.
- Dialogue groups should themselves select leaders from their communities to manage their dialogues and provide training and support for ongoing community communication that is open to all members of the community.
- Participants in dialogues can be supported by providing them with as much information as possible, including expert analyses where appropriate.
- Dialogues should be recorded and transcripts published to ensure fairness in presentation of the results.
- Corporations should encourage participation by representative samples of communities, even where the potential for dialogue outcomes goes against the interests of the corporation.

Conclusions

Communication and dialogue are quite different concepts. Dialogue is a special class of communication that uses questioning and dialectical reasoning to protect 'otherness' and ensure justice, principles that are not always central to corporate interests, where more expedient values often take precedence (for example efficiency, cost, resources). While communication techniques such as social reports, public relations events and so on, may benefit from the use of the term dialogue, the citizens involved should be made aware of the limitations imposed by corporate expedience on all communication. A preference for the term consultation should be required where expedience is determined by the corporation.

Corporate dialogues can be assessed on the basis of whether they answer the following questions:

- Does dialogue by corporate mandate promote human rights and effect change that is responsive to the needs of all affected citizens for self-determination?
- Is the language used in the CSR movement ethical, does it fulfil the task of communicating the real objects and interests of powers that may or may not be present?

Social dialogue is a practice that, like communication itself, is fundamental to the functioning of a healthy democracy. Communication is at the centre of human life and is a necessary condition for examining the workings of democratic states. Ethical communications exemplify what Benhabib (1992, p. 70) has described as 'a paradigm shift in critical theory from the critique of instrumental reason to the critique of communicative rationality'.

This is where corporate stakeholder consultation may fall below standards of democratic participation, or even notion of ethical communication. In the current model of public consultation, dialogues appear methodologically flawed because they privilege instrumental rationality and systemic initiatives over the deeper principle of human self-determination.

The last word is given to Benhabib (1992, pp. 101–2) who is deeply critical of notions of political ideology free from public scrutiny and where:

> The idea that the justice of institutions be 'in the public's eye,' so to speak, for the public to scrutinize, to examine and reflect upon is fundamental. That it recognises the legitimation of power or the examination of the justice of institutions to be a public process. Open to all citizens to partake in is one of the central tenets of liberalism and one which has its roots in the political primacy of consent in social contract theories. From the standpoint of the discourse model of legitimacy as well this is crucial.

References

Alia, V. (2004) *Media Ethics and Social Change* (Edinburgh: Edinburgh University Press).

Apel, K. O. (1980) *The A Priori of the Communication Community and the Foundation of Ethics: The Problem of a Rational Foundation of Ethics in the Scientific age. In towards a Transformation of Philosophy* (London: Routledge & Kegan Paul).

Argyris, C. (1990) *Overcoming Organizational Defences* (Englewood Cliffs, NJ: Prentice-Hall).

Barber, B. (1988) *The Conquest of Politics: Liberal Philosophy in Democratic Times* (Princeton, NJ: Princeton University Press).

Bames, J. (ed.) (1984) *The Complete Works of Aristotle* (Oxford: Oxford University Press).

Barthes, R. (1967) *Elements of Sociology* (New York: Hill & Wang).

Baudrillard, J. (1972) *For a Critique of the Political Economy of the Sign* (St Louis, Mo.: Telo Press).

Baudrillard, J. (1973) *The Mirror of Production* (St Louis, Mo.: Telo Press).

Bauman, Z. (1993) *Postmodern Ethics* (Oxford: Blackwell).

Beckett, R. and J. Jonker (forthcoming) 'How Social Reporting omits key data Ethical Space', *Journal of Communication Ethics*.

Benhabib, S. (1992) *Situating the Self: Gender, Community and Postmodernism in Contemporary Ethics* (Princeton, NJ: Prince University Press).

Benhabib, S. (1996) 'Toward a deliberative model of democratic legitimacy', in S. Benhabib (ed.), *Polity Democracy and Difference: Contesting the Boundaries of the Political* (Princeton: Princeton University Press) pp. 67–94.

Bourdieu, P. (1992) *Language and Symbolic Power* (Cambridge: Polity Press).

Bruhn-Jensen, K. (1995) *The Social Semiotics of Mass Communication* (London: Sage).

Buber, M. (1947) *Between Man and Man* (London: Kegan Paul).

Buber, M. (2004) *I and Thou* (London: Continuum).

Carey (1992) *Communication as Culture: Essays on Media and Society* (New York: Routledge).

Christians, C. and M. Traber (eds) (1997) *Communication Ethics and Universal Values* (London: Sage).

Derrida, (1973) *Speech and Phenomena of Grammatology and Writing and Difference* (Evanston, Ill.: Northwestern University Press).

Dostal, R. (ed.) (2002) *The Cambridge Companion to Gadamer* (Cambridge: Cambridge University Press).

Eco, U. (1976) *A Theory of Semiotics* (Bloomington: Indiana University Press).

Foucault, M. (1969) *The Archaeology of Knowledge* (New York: Pantheon).

Friedson, E. (1970) *Profession of Medicine* (New York: Dodd, Mead).

Gadamer, H. G. (2003) *Truth and Method* (New York: Continuum).

Gilligan, C. (1982) *In a Different Voice* (Cambridge, Mass.: Harvard University Press).

Gray, R., D. Owen and C. Adams (1996) *Accounting and Accountability* (Hemel Hempstead: Prentice-Hall).

Greer, G. (1970) *The Female Eunuch* (London: Paludin).

Habermas, J. (1984) *The Theory of Communicative Action: Reason and Rationalization in Society* (Oxford: Polity Press).

Habermas, J. (1987) *The Theory of Communicative Action: The Critique Functionalist Reason* (Oxford: Polity Press).

Habermas, J. (1989) *The Structural Transformation of the Public Sphere* (Cambridge: Polity).

Habermas, J. (1990) *Moral Consciousness and Communicative Action* (Cambridge: Polity Press).

Hobbes, T. (1968) *Leviathan* (London:Penguin).

Institute of Communication Ethics (2001) Lewes: Conference proceedings.

Kennedy, H. (2004) *Just Law: The Changing Face of Justice and Why it Matters to Us All* (London: Chatto & Windus).

Korten, D. (1995) *When Corporations Rule the World* (CT: Kumarian Press).

Larson, M. S. (1977) *The Rise of Professionalism* (Berkeley, CA: University of California Press).

Levinas, E. (1996) *Levinas: Basic Philosophical Writings*, ed. by A. Peperzak, R. Bernasconi and S. Critchley (Bloomington: Indiana University Press).

Levi Strauss, C. (1963) *Structural Anthropology* (New York: Anchor).

Locke, J. (1990) *Essay Concerning Human Understanding* (London: Penguin Books).

Lyotard, J. F. (1979) *The Postmodern Condition: A Report on Knowledge* (Minneapolis, Minn.: University of Minnesota Press).

Makau, J. M. and R. C. Arnett (1997) *Communication Ethics in an Age of Diversity* (Ill.: University of Illinois Press).

McCarthy, T. (1996) *The Critical Theory of Jurgen Habermas* (Cambridge, Mass.: MIT Press).

McLuhan, M. (1964) *Understanding Media: The Extensions of Man* (London: Routledge & Kegan Paul).

Monbiot, G. (2000) *Captive State: The Corporate Takeover of Britain* (London: Macmillan).

Pasquali, A. (1997) 'The Moral Dimension of Communicating', in C. Christians and M. Traber (eds), *Universal Values and Communication Ethics* (London: Sage), p. 32.

Rawls, J. (1972) *A Theory of Justice* (Oxford: Oxford University Press).

Rawls, J. (1993) *Political Liberalism* (New York: Columbia University Press).

Rehg, W. (1994) *Jurgen Habermas Between Facts and Norms: Contributions to a Discourse Theory of Law* (Cambridge, Mass.: MIT Press).

Rousseau, J.-J. (1764) *The Social Contract* (New York: Knopf).

Sanders, K. (2004) *Media Ethics* (London: Sage).

Saussure, F. de [1916] (1974) *Course in General Linguistics,* trans. by W. Baskin (London: Fontana/Collins).

Suzuki, D. and H. Dressel (1999) *Naked Ape to Superspecies* (Sydney: Allen & Unwin).

Weber, M. (1958) *The Protestant Ethic and the Spirit of Capitalism* (New York: Charles Scribner's Sons).

Wood, L. and R. Kroger (2000) *Doing Discourse Analysis* (London: Sage).

Yanklelovitch, D. (1999) *The Magic of Dialogue* (New York: Simon & Schuster).

8
Stakeholder Engagement in and Beyond the Organization

David Foster and Jan Jonker

Introduction

The involvement of stakeholders in organizations has been the subject of considerable research and debate since Freeman wrote his seminal work in 1984. Building on the work of contingency theorists, engagement with stakeholders has come to be seen as a mechanism by which the organization can learn to adapt to what is happening in the world around it. This adaptation is often viewed in an adversarial way as the organization tries to steer its way towards its own ends. In this regard stakeholders have generally been perceived as a negative force that can disrupt the operations and goals of the organization. This perspective reflects a particular organismic view of an organization as an isolated, self-contained entity that interacts with its (hostile) environment through the auspice of various (organismic) stakeholder groups in order to achieve its legitimate goals.

There is growing evidence to support the notion that an enterprise does operate within a societal network of stakeholders that have the power to influence directly or indirectly its success. Operating in such a societal context requires a fundamental reconsideration of the nature of the business enterprise and the way it engages with its wider societal context. Even though society's provision to business of a 'licence to operate' may continue to be based on profit, businesses are now part of the complex web of social relations and must deal with the multiplicity of issues and concerns expressed by stakeholders with varied backgrounds and interests. Increasingly, they cannot remain aloof from these issues while achieving their organizational goals.

This chapter acknowledges the changed nature of this engagement process and suggests that it can be best understood through a reconceptualization of the organization, leading to a clarification of its *raison d'être*. It is suggested that the reactive and a sometimes manipulative relationship that often characterizes organization–stakeholder interactions arises because stakeholders are viewed as external to the organization and as an obstacle to, rather than a facilitator of, the achievement of organizational goals. This is in turn based upon a particular view of the nature of power, authority and political activity, which appears to result from a functional view of organizations where the boundary of what is and is not within the organization is very clear and organizational goals are viewed individualistically.

The chapter does not present the idea of a fundamental change in relationships with society as a simple ideal that should be adhered to. Instead it argues that organizations already pay attention to the needs and expectations of all stakeholders in order to ensure their long-term sustainability. It is the nature of the interaction that has started to differ greatly. It also suggests that what has been missing is a solid theoretical basis upon which this changing need to interact can be understood. To develop such a basis requires an analysis of the assumptions and world-view upon which such a theory can be built.

Stakeholders

There is a considerable research and anecdotal evidence that some organizations recognize the role of stakeholders and take them into account when strategic directions in organizations are being established (Zadek, 2001). This is particularly the case with not-for-profit, charitable or public organizations (Vinten, 2000). In the corporate sector acceptance is still patchy but it is certainly recognized by some (Scholes and Clutterbuck, 1998; Vinten, 2000). More importantly, the management literature has accepted that stakeholders play an important role in the overall performance of organizations.

As noted above, the contemporary stakeholder literature can be traced back to the seminal work of Freeman (1984), who articulated a stakeholder model to replace the managerial model of the firm. The latter, which had served managers well for many years, focused on the role of employees, suppliers, shareholders and customers. He defined external stakeholders as 'any group who can affect, or is affected by, the accomplishment of organisational purpose' (ibid., p. 25). He proposed a new conceptual model of the firm that had up to then incorporated only a limited number of groups or interests. But this conceptual proposition was more than the establishment of a simple model incorporating some new groups. It was rather a call for real understanding of the needs and expectations of all stakeholders, taking into account their increasingly diverse and sophisticated ways of influencing the firm's behaviour and effectiveness.

Freeman laid the foundation for reconceptualizing the nature of the firm to encourage and legitimize new forms of managerial action in the changed circumstances of contemporary society. In the older managerial view of the firm the external environment was conceptualized as anything that did not include the corporation itself, the owners, the suppliers and the customers – an environment that could be managed and controlled across the boundaries of the organization. The proposed stakeholder view of the firm expanded the conceptual organizational boundaries – made them less rigid – to incorporate other external parties.[1] Instead of regarding them as external to the firm, Freeman suggested that they should be integrated into the firm in some way. While managers had developed ways of understanding and addressing the dynamics of the traditional stakeholders, he suggested that managers needed to develop this same understanding of those stakeholders that were previously perceived to be external to the firm. This suggestion was more than a boundary-definition problem. Rather it concerned the way in which the whole organization functioned and achieved its objectives, given the embeddedness of a wider societal context.

The stakeholder theory that has developed since then can be viewed as a logical extension of contingency theory, which has its roots in Lawrence and Lorsch's (1967) open systems approach. In their view an important function of the organization was to adapt to what was happening in the world around it. They saw the organization as an internally differentiated system that needed to achieve sufficient integration to adapt to the situation in its external world. Their suggestion that different organizational principles should be applied in different environmental circumstances challenged the basic canons of both classical (scientific) management and human relations theories. Building on those ideas, scholars such as Osborn (1974) argued that the organization and its environment operated in a state of mutual influence and interdependence. Moreover, the relationship between the organization and its environment could be seen in terms of the organization's need to survive.

Stakeholder theory emphasizes one aspect of the external environment: the conceptualization of external interests into groupings under the common title 'stakeholders'. Organizations can engage with much of this external environment by means of dialogue with stakeholders. A dialogue is viewed as the ultimate instrument by which needs and expectations can be communicated in a fair and reliable way. In this view it is assumed that continuity depends on the firm's relationships with those stakeholders, and in particular its ability to satisfy their needs and expectations. It is the mutual satisfaction of various and sometimes paradoxical needs and expectations that in the end creates profit.

Towards a stakeholder theory of the firm

The role of stakeholders has been the subject of an impressive amount of research since Freeman (1984) published his work. While he only sought to develop a general approach to strategic decision making, it has subsequently become the basis of a new theory of the firm (Donaldson and Preston, 1995). This stakeholder theory of the firm was originally proposed by Brenner and Cochran (1991) and was subsequently developed by Brenner (1993), Donaldson and Preston (1995) and Jones (1995). It has provided a framework for research in the business and society field (Carroll, 1989) and taken on the status of a 'master theory in its own right' (Rowley, 1997, p. 889) by describing how organizations operate under certain conditions. It is presented by many as an alternative theory of the firm, one that should replace the traditional Friedmanite economic theory of the firm (Andriof and Waddock, 2002). However, Key (1999) has suggested that although recognition of identifiable actors in the external environment is a valuable strategic tool, it does not warrant the status of a theory, especially not one that seeks to be regarded as a new theory of the firm. In particular, it does not provide an adequate theoretical basis for explaining a firm's behaviour or the behaviour of individual internal or external actors. Key suggests that also missing is a methodology to explain the dynamics that link the firm to identified stakeholders. While the motivations of profit and efficiency may be what Freeman and subsequent scholars had in mind, these are not made explicit and could easily be replaced by alternatives such as Davis's 'iron law of responsibility' (Davis, 1973) or some normatively based social responsibility (Wood, 1991).

These legitimate theoretical and methodological issues appear to have stalled the development of a more solid stakeholder theory of the firm. However, rather than continuing to focus on a methodology to link the firm and its stakeholders through dialogue it may be more productive to investigate the way in which the firm is conceptualized through the notion of stakeholders. The rationale for doing this can be better understood when the nature of theory is explored.

Key (1999, p. 317) defines theory as 'a systematic attempt to understand what is observable in the world. It creates order and logic from observable facts that appear tumultuous and disconnected'. Good theory would 'identify relevant variables and the connections between them in a way that testable hypotheses can be generated and empirically established' (ibid.). The essence of a theory is the demonstration of associations between variables within a conceptual framework. In a similar vein Bacharach (1989, p. 496) defines theory as 'a statement of relations among concepts within a set of boundary assumptions and constraints'. He suggests that a 'good' theory in the social sciences should meet the following criteria: it must be falsifiable, logically coherent, operationalizable, useful and possess sufficient explanatory power in terms of scope and comprehensiveness. Ideally it should have both explanatory value and predictive value. It should also include the underlying logic and values that explain the observable phenomenon, and be supported by a plausible or logical explanation of how it happens (Labovitz and Hagedorn, 1971). These are particularly rigorous requirements that are either not met or ignored by many scholars working in the social sciences. Indeed Sayer (2000, p. 147) suggests that theories are 'few in number, monolithic and distinct'. Yet reference to almost any scholarly journal would provide evidence of a multitude of theories that do not meet these criteria but are still accepted by refereeing committees and devoured by readers.

Llewelyn (2003) has provided a particularly interesting answer to this conundrum that is relevant to the issue being addressed here. She proposes a broader understanding of the term theory and introduces the criterion of utility rather than truth in assessing their value in the social sciences. Given the concept-dependence of the social world, she argues that what she calls 'grand theory' is affected by the basic conceptual framing that supports it. Drawing on the work of Sayer (2000), she argues that 'there is no perception without conceptual schemes within which to locate perceptions' (Llewelyn, 2003, p. 666). Given this link between what is often regarded as the only form of theory (grand theory) and the conceptualizations and perceptions of social phenomena involved in that theory, Llewelyn suggests that five levels of theory can be identified (Table 8.1). She argues that all five levels are significant and that each can be seen as a necessary stage in the ascent to grand theory (level five). This ensures that any grand theory that does ensue is not disconnected from empirical reality.

These ideas are particularly relevant to the development of a stakeholder theory of the firm. Most of the work on this issue has focused on the higher levels of theory without clearly addressing more fundamental issues that would ground that theory on empirical reality. For example, Brenner's (1993, p. 206) investigation of what constitutes a theory of the firm suggests that a theory should 'posit either a single decision principle or set of principles which explain a significant aspect of the organisation's behaviours'. He proposes that a theory of the firm should have three components: (1) a world-view, (2) basic propositions and (3) choice process(es) (Brenner and Cochran, 1991). If there is no analysis of more fundamental questions about how a firm is conceptualized in the first place and what metaphors this conceptualization is based on, it is rather difficult to take any theoretical endeavour a step further.

Table 8.1 Five levels of theorization

Level	Theory	Focus
One	Metaphor theorizes	By image-ing and grounding experience
Two	Differentiation theorizes	By 'cutting the pie' of experience
Three	Concepts theorize	By linking agency and structure through practice
Four	Theorizing settings	Explaining how contexts for practices are organized
Five	Theorizing structures	Explaining impersonal, large-scale and enduring aspects of social life

Source: Llewelyn (2003), p. 667.

In order to move our understanding forward it is worthwhile revisiting the more fundamental question of how we conceptualize and differentiate the complex social phenomenon that we call a 'firm' from its social surroundings. This will shed light on how and why relationships exist and what makes these relationships different enough to require a conceptualization of the firm as a distinct form of social collective. Most scholars embrace the Friedmanite view of the firm as a set of assets owned by shareholders, with managers acting as agents to maximize the returns on those assets. The supporting metaphor is that of an organism with individualistic needs and goals and a clear boundary between it and the outside world. This is a classical liberal economic view of organizations, a view that is now recognized as being only one of many. This view is based on a structuralist sociological theory in which the nature or structure of the organization determines the behaviour of those within it (Jones, 1987). The management of stakeholders is, like any other activity in the organization, determined by the need constantly to maximize the returns to shareholders. Depending on one's perspective, this can be the result of learned behaviour and socialization within the firm (supported by structural consensus theory) or the result of inequality of power and privilege between the shareholders and other stakeholders (supported by structural conflict theory).

It is possible, however, to adopt a totally different perspective based on interpretive sociological theory. Adapting this to the context of organizations, firms or corporations are the end result of social interactions that lead to a dynamic nexus of contracts; they are not the cause of such interactions. By looking at the way in which individuals and groups interact inside the organization and across its boundaries we are able to understand how a firm is created and functions. Adopting this perspective suggests that a firm or business enterprise can be seen as a social collective in which various interests come together to achieve mutually acceptable goals. As a social collective rather than an organism, the goals are those created *for* the collective not *of* the collective.[2] While the goals of shareholders may include profit, this should be seen in relation to the goals of others involved in the achievement of those profits. If those others were not required for goal achievement then the collective would not exist. The owners of capital would operate through the marketplace. Likewise the goals of individuals involved in the collective (even individuals regarded as belonging to the same stakeholder group) are neither all the same nor permanent or unchanging. Where such a collective (that is, a corporation) does exist the focus is on the way in which the collective, with its complex goals and interests, acts to achieve this array of goals.

Human action, in the context of a firm or any other social collective and resulting from a conscious intention to act, is based on a thought process and is aimed at some goal or objective (perceived in various ways by various people). Human action in this context is purposive, meaningful and aimed at achieving certain chosen goals. These goals are derived from individuals' interpretation of the world in which they exist. This includes an interpretation of the actions of others both within and outside the formal boundaries of the firm, an interpretation that is based on the formal and informal communication that takes place between those involved in the situation. The social order that is created is the result of this interaction, 'carried on by interpreting meaning-attributing actors who can make sense of the social settings in which they find themselves and who choose courses of action accordingly' (Jones, 1987, p. 18). The structure does not determine the social order that ensues in the way that structuralists would suggest. Formal or legal requirements may constrain the actions of those in the social collective called a firm, but they do not determine the human action that ensues in any particular situation. Using stakeholder terminology, this means that a corporation or business enterprise is composed of a nucleus of stakeholders with diverse and sometimes conflicting interests who come together to achieve goals that would not be possible individually (Jonker and Foster, 2002). Management is the group within this collective that has the role of steering it towards those goals. The way in which management engages or interacts with the stakeholders is therefore crucial in determining whether the goals are achieved. The goals can be of various types (economic, social, deontological and so on) and their alignment is not always assured. Achieving them is part of a transactive process (see below).

Based on this conceptualization, it is argued here that an organization necessarily operates through interactions among participants, resulting in a stream of benefits generated by their collective action. These interactions can range in type from the very informal to the contractual. If the result of cooperation is not mutually beneficial the participants can withdraw their support and involvement. Likewise, the collective action is focused on a particular purpose at a particular point in time. The purpose can change over time as the influence of different stakeholders varies and/or other stakeholders join or leave the temporarily coalition. This view is consistent with other stakeholder conceptualizations of the firm based on a 'nexus of contracts' (Key, 1999). However, it more thoroughly explains why these contracts exist without relying on the deontological explanation of formal reciprocal rights and duties. They exist because without them goal attainment would not be possible. Moreover, while the relationships are influenced by identifiable economic incentives, possible explanations of behaviour extend beyond these to the social, emotional, sociopsychological and political. This approach appears to fit more closely with the reality of organizational life.

Unlike the contingency theorists, who are concerned to demonstrate that the external world provides a context within which management decisions should be made, Freeman's stakeholder theory focuses on a fundamental engagement with that context. It is one thing to point out that a firm exists within a broader social context that needs to be considered. It is quite a different thing to draw attention to the need for active engagement with entities that exist in that context. It is with regard to why such engagement occurs that a theoretical foundation is missing.

Categorizing organizations on the basis of their approach to stakeholder engagement

If the firm is theorized as a social collective in which the achievement of goals is dependent on the interaction of those involved, it is obvious that the nature and depth of that interaction will vary. It is, therefore, appropriate to categorize organizations in terms of the way in which – conceptually at least – they interact with their stakeholders. This is in line with Llewelyn's (2003) second level of theory. If it is done well it could become the basis of empirical research to identify whether there is a relationship between the approach adopted and the success of the organization. This would move the research agenda beyond the issue of whether corporations engage with stakeholders to the impact that the way they interact has on their long-term survival. What are the possible boundaries and limitations of this interaction? How is this interaction organized inside the firm or across its boundaries? It may be that successful firms are those that manage this interaction in a particular way.

The literature includes various 'ladders of participation' designed to demonstrate that participation in decision making can be at various levels (Arnstein, 1969). Most begin with what could be described as 'tokenism' and then move on to actual involvement in decision making (often described as 'codecision making'). These ladders generally look at the situation from the perspective of the stakeholder rather than the organization. Moreover, most of them are one-dimensional, as though there were a simple linear relationship between the type of involvement, the nature of the issue at hand and the impact on decisions (Coenen *et al.*, 1998). Cowie and O'Toole (1998) argue that the extent of participation also needs to be considered. That is, one situation may have a real impact on a wide array of relatively unimportant decisions while another may have real impact on a few important decisions. Others suggest that the level of the decision is another important dimension to consider. That is, participation may be more influential if it affects strategic decisions as opposed to decisions at the operational level (Flynn, 1998). The extent of participation can therefore be seen as multifaceted.

The following is an attempt to create a similar ladder, but this time from the perspective of management (Table 8.2). Rather than viewing this ladder as a series of stages where the ultimate goal is to identify those that achieve the highest level, it should be regarded as the basis for categorizing different organizational types. In other words, while there are numerous ways in which organizations can be categorized, this diagram is very useful when such categorization is based on stakeholder involvement in decision making. Implicit in the categorization is the understanding that the role of management within the organization is to establish and achieve certain collective

Table 8.2 Ladder of stakeholder involvement

Group	Management activity	Characteristics of the process	Level of decision	Extent of decision making	Type of organization	Stakeholder communication	Stakeholder engagement
1	Management *of* stakeholders	Manipulation, non-participation	Operational focus	Covers many unimportant areas	Traditional, reactive	None	None
2	Management *for* stakeholders	Information, consultation, placation	Operational and instrumental	Fewer areas of focus	Proactive	Strategic	Calculated
3	Management *with* stakeholders	Partnership, participation	Instrumental and strategic	Limited focus but significant issues involved	Learning, quality	Dialogic	Transactive

goals. The difference is the way they go about doing this, given the earlier elaborated perspective of the firm as a social collective.

Group 1 organizations

Organizations in group 1 tend to be run by management as an isolated group that seeks to operate with minimal interaction with the stakeholders, and when an interaction does take place it is generally on terms dictated by management. Organizational goals are achieved through management decisions in isolation. Any attempt to engage stakeholders usually involves low-level operational decisions that have very little impact on the organization's long-term survival. At this level actions are aimed at ensuring that management perspectives dominate. Management operates in an environment that has to be confronted and manipulation is part of the armoury. The measure of success is whether the wishes of the managers are achieved. The development of agency theory can be seen as a response to this approach as in many situations manipulation and control extends to all stakeholders, including shareholders.

Group 2 organizations

Organizations in group 2 recognize that stakeholders do have a role to play in organizational decision making, but this role is neither active nor direct. It involves recognition that stakeholders may have needs and expectations that could be affected by the achievement of organizational purpose. However, management seeks to interpret those needs and expectations. Parasuraman *et al.*'s (1985) gap model is a good example of this. Customers' needs and expectations are researched and interpreted by management as part of the process of establishing appropriate service standards. The emphasis is on management's interpretation of those needs in an asymmetric communication exercise that could not be described as open dialogue (Grunig and Grunig, 1992). Moreover, the decisions in which stakeholders are involved tend to be merely instrumental. That is, they are about the implementation of a strategy and its direction rather than the establishment of the strategy itself. This group includes organizations that have adopted many of the principles and techniques promoted by the quality movement, as exemplified by total quality management (TQM). A characteristic of this approach to management is its emphasis on the importance of unity and the creation of an appropriate corporate (organizational) culture. Much of the literature on the subject promotes the idea of developing a culture in which everyone agrees to the direction and purpose of the organization and all pull together through a shared vision and mission. Great effort is expended to achieve this, and even the use of coercion and direction. Lack of unity is regarded as an organizational weakness. Engagement with the external world is within the context of this unitary culture.

According to Cope and Kalantzis (1997) this represses essential differences and ignores the complexity and diversity that characterizes the real world of the organization and the wider society. The metaphor that guides this organizational perspective is that of life in a village where homogeneity is the primary characteristic and village life is held together by shared values, interests and experiences.

> Every member buys into the values of the community, shares the way of life of the community, and joins in the tasks of the community. There might be the odd squabble, but if the community is to hold together, most of what happens has to be based on shared meanings and cooperative activities. (Ibid., p. 15)

While this may have many benefits, differences may appear disturbing and thus frightening. When a culture is strong and uniform, then anything that is different or any person or entity that sees the world differently is wrong, holds inappropriate views, is not worth listening to or is possibly even subversive.

In this situation, an organization's stakeholder relationships are recognized as important but they are still often hands-off and driven by the organization. Stakeholder engagement is focused on finding out as much as possible about the needs and expectations of the 'other'. While the metaphor 'know thy enemy' may be too strong, stakeholder engagement is certainly about gaining an understanding of where the 'other' stands so that the organization can accommodate its views, but only in the light of its own goals and perspectives. An analogy with recent US foreign policy may be appropriate in this regard. The Bush administration is so sure of the value and superiority of the American culture that its engagement with other nations (especially those with a different culture) is aimed at understanding them so that they can be brought into line with its view of what is right and appropriate. There is no attempt to change the nature of its own culture in this process, rather the objective is to determine how the 'other' can be brought into this dominating and encompassing world-view. Organizations are not nation states, but the approach of some of them to controversial issues is along the same lines.

Group 3 organizations

The organizations in group 3 are similar to what Andriof and Waddock (2002) describe as a 'network organization', which is defined as an open system that seeks greater interdependence with its environment to ensure survival and goal achievement. This increased interdependence can be described as the stakeholder transactivity process. 'Increased interdependency makes it necessary to focus on a firm's strategic relations to a set of actors – stakeholders – in the task environment and to increase awareness of relevant contextual aspects behind the market scene' (ibid., p. 39). The authors argue that stakeholder engagement recognizes the benefits of strategic networks that arise 'from cumulative processes including both increased dependency through exchange and the development of social capital (ibid.). Mutual trust is developed through the 'incorporation of deeper personal commitment among participants' (ibid.). Interpersonal affiliation and respect are extremely important. While the general thrust of this description is true for this group, it differs in a very significant way from what Andriof and Waddock and many others have proposed. It is based not on the development of shared values or norms, but on recognition of the diversity and complexity that exists in contemporary society. Instead of investing energy in developing a common denominator under the heading of a unifying culture, the basic premise is that the network operates on the basis of recognized differences.

A crucial notion in this conceptualization is transaction, the nature of which determines the continuity of the organization. Management is responsible for coordinating this collective action by negotiating transactions with and between participants. This engagement becomes part of the goal achievement activities of management and is not a negative reaction to an external threat. It recognizes that human action is affected by individuals' interpretation of the social world in which they operate. Influencing this subjective interpretation is part of transactivity.

The organizations in this group are managed in a manner that takes into account the needs and expectations of stakeholders from the perspective of the stakeholders themselves and with respect to their fundamental differences. These organizations recognize that the existence of a diversity of views and perspectives creates strengths and leads to better outcomes and decisions. They do not thrive on the creation of uniformity and sameness. Diversity and difference are seen as normal and part of the reality of society within the organization and beyond. They do not accept that diversity and difference necessarily produce fragmentation but view them sources of productivity and energy. Difference is not feared, rather it is regarded as part of the reality of a modern society and the organizations operating in it.

Transactivity is fundamentally based on willingness to understand. The focus of understanding is developing 'meaning-in-action' aimed at pulling differences together in such a way to enable collaborative action. Part of this involves identifying and achieving goals for the organization based on the different interests, aspirations and experiences of those involved. This is a collective responsibility in the sense that their achievement affects all concerned. It builds on recognized interdependency, which accepts the value of difference and is quite different from dependency (Harrison and St. John, 1996). The focus of this understanding extends to the strategic level, where values and other broad mega issues and directions are considered. The focus also moves from consideration of the organization in isolation to the broader issues of value diversity and the complexity of societal change. This does not mean that management simply abdicates its decision-making role. Rather its role changes to one of communicative action, where success is measured by the ability to create unity out of diversity in order to define and achieve goals. Instead of management being held to account by one stake-holder (the shareholder), as in the case of agency theory, management must ensure that all stakeholders are considered, even though the principal objective is to generate profit for shareholders. This is very similar to what Freeman and Phillips (2002) describe as the principle of 'stakeholder cooperation', according to which there is no need for all parties to adopt a common view about everything.

Interestingly, this terminology reflects the difference being suggested here. No longer is engagement about consultation, with its connotations of gathering information. Rather it becomes a collaboration in which the parties interact in a mutually respectful manner and the process involves sharing differences and generating new knowledge. The process assumes not only that the differences will never be resolved, but also that their resolution would not be in the interests of either party. Maintaining differences may also be of value to society as a whole. Of course underpinning this is the necessity to achieve organizational goals. This is not simply a debating club where debate alone is the goal.

Conclusion

This chapter has offered a theoretical basis for understanding the true nature of stakeholder engagement in a firm and the latter's multifaceted relationships with its social environment. To this end, it has built on insights developed by the corporate social responsibility movement. The key message is that taking a stakeholder perspective on the corporation does not exclude the achievement of increased shareholder value or profit. Consideration of the needs and expectations of stakeholders is simply a means to achieve those goals in a manner that is more sustainable in the longer term.

At the root of this argument is the fact that a corporation is a social collective that exists within a broader societal framework that is highly diverse, rapidly changing and extremely complex. Those who have adopted a more organismic view of the corporation would also argue that it exists within a societal framework, but viewing it as a social collective explicitly acknowledges and focuses on these links. If the corporation is viewed as a distinct form of social collective then the role and diverse interests of its members (stakeholders), together with their links with other aspects of society, become crucial. No corporation can be immune from this societal framework in the longer term and its very survival is dependent on the way in which it engages with that framework. However, there are many organizations where such engagement does not exist (group 1 organizations), or where the engagement is of the type described as characteristic of group 2 organizations. Old habits die very slowly. Nonetheless, the continued existence of these groups does not run counter to the basic stakeholder theory of the firm. Rather it describes the different ways in which some go about managing relationships.

Our typology of organizations addresses a criticism that is often levelled at conceptual developments of the type outlined here: that arguments of this type are essentially normative – an attempt to tell others what should happen rather than an empirical analysis of what does happen. Given the undeniable fact that corporations exist within a societal framework that provides them with a licence to operate in that framework, the typology demonstrates how some corporations engage with the framework while still achieving the fundamental goal of profit for shareholders. The mechanism by which they do this can be described as 'transactivity' with stakeholders who represent the face of the societal framework.

This opens up an opportunity for empirical research aimed at investigating the relative success (measured in terms of long-term survival) of corporations that fit into the three categories. Do corporations that adopt the transactive approach that is characteristic of group 3 organizations have greater long-term success than others? Is the transactive approach adopted the principal factor in their success, or are other factors compounding the situation? What variations are there amongst the corporations that belong to this group? What are the implications for structuring and managing these organizations? And what kinds of management and leadership are required to manage them? These important questions can be addressed as we move closer to an understanding of the modern corporation, which is acknowledged as one of the most significant social phenomena of our times.

Notes

1. Freeman wrote about expanding the boundaries of the firm in figurative terms. He explained how the external environment could be 'assimilated into the relatively more comfortable relationship with suppliers, owners, customers and employees'. Neither suppliers nor customers were internal to the firm in the true sense of the word. However, they are internal in the sense that they had been incorporated into a 'framework for managing the firm'. Looking at it in a different way, stakeholder relationships became crises 'because we have not incorporated the idea of their existence into our day-to-day routine' (Freeman, 1984, p. 13).
2. Keeley (1980) has argued convincingly that while organizations may have many properties, welfare-entailing properties (defined as goals, needs, interests, etc.) are not among them. He argues that the 'purpose as well as the binding element of social organisation is the satisfaction of diverse individual interests; and collective welfare, to the extent that the term is meaningful at all, is a direct function of individual welfares' (ibid., p. 343). Organizations do have goals; but these are goals *for* the organization not *of* the organization.

References

Andriof, J. and S. Waddock (2002) 'Unfolding Stakeholder Engagement', in J. Andriof, S. Waddock, B. Husted and S. S. Rahman (eds), *Unfolding Stakeholder Thinking*, vol. 1 (Sheffield: Greenleaf).

Arnstein, S. B. (1969) 'A Ladder of Citizen Participation', *Journal of the American Institute of Planners*, 35, pp. 216–24.

Bacharach, S. (1989) 'Organizational Theories: some criteria for evaluation', *Academy of Management Review*, 14, pp. 496–515.

Banerjee, S. B. (2000) 'Whose Land is it Anyway? National Interest, Indigenous Stakeholders, and Colonial Discourses', *Organisation and Environment*, 13 (1), pp. 3–38.

Brenner, S. N. (1993) 'The Stakeholder Theory of the Firm and Organisational Decision-Making: Some Propositions and a Model', *Proceedings of Fourth Annual Meeting of the International Association for Business and Society* (San Diego, CA: IABS).

Brenner, S. N. and P. L. Cochran (1991) 'The Stakeholder Theory of the Firm: implications for business and society theory and research', *Proceedings of Second Annual Meeting of the International Association for Business and Society* (Utah: Sundance).

Carroll, A. B. (1989) *Business and Society: Ethics and Stakeholder Management* (Cincinnati, OH: South-Western Publishing).

Claycomb, C. and C. Martin (2002) 'Building Customer Relationships: an inventory of service providers' objectives and practices', *Journal of Services Marketing* 16 (7), pp. 615–35.

Coenen, F. H. J. M., D. Huitema and L. J. O'Toole (1998) *Participation and the Quality of Environmental Decision Making* (Dordrecht: Kluwer Academic).

Cope, B. and M. Kalantzis (1997) *Productive Diversity: A New Australian Model for Work and Management* (Sydney: Pluto).

Cowie, G. M. and L. J. O'Toole (1998) 'Linking Stakeholder Participation and Environmental Decision-Making: Assessing Decision Quality for Interstate River Basin Management', in F. H. J. M. Coenen, D. Huitema and L. J. O'Toole (eds), *Participation and the Quality of Environmental Decision Making* (Dordrecht: Kluwer Academic).

Davis, K. (1973) 'The Case for and against Business Assumptions of Social Responsibilities', *Academy of Management Journal*, 16, pp. 312–22.

Donaldson, T. and L. E. Preston (1995) 'The Stakeholder Theory of the Corporation: Concepts, Evidence and Implications', *Academy of Management Review*, 20 (1), pp. 65–91.

Flynn, B. (1998) 'Is Supranational participation possible? The European Union's attempt to enhance participation in Dublin's Transport Initiative', in F. H. J. M. Coenen, D. Huitema and L. J. O'Toole (eds), *Participation and the Quality of Environmental Decision Making* (Dordrecht: Kluwer Academic).

Foster, D. J. and J. Jonker (2002) 'Quality Management Beyond the Enterprise: Moving towards the societal embeddedness of the firm' Proceedings of the 7th World Congress on Total Quality Management, (Verona: University of Verona).

Freeman, R. E. (1984) *Strategic Management: A Stakeholder Approach* (Boston, Mass.: Pitman).

Freeman R. E. and R. A. Phillips (2002) 'Stakeholder Theory: a libertarian defense', *Business Ethics Quarterly*, 12 (3), pp. 331–49.

Fukuyama, F. (1995) *Trust, Social Virtues and the Creation of Prosperity* (London: Hamish-Hamilton).

Gronroos, C. (1994) 'From Scientific Management to Services Management', *International Journal for Service Industry Management*, 5 (1), pp. 5–21.

Gronroos, C. (2000) 'Relationship Marketing: The Nordic School Perspective, in J. N. Sheth and A. Parvatiyar (eds), *Handbook of Relationship Marketing* (London: Sage), pp. 95–118.

Grunig, J. E. and L. A. Grunig (1992) 'Models of Public Relations and Communication', in J. E. Grunig, D. M. Dozier and W. P. Ehling (eds), *Excellence in*

Communication and Communication Management (Hillsdale, NY: Lawrence Erlbaum), pp. 285–325.

Harnesk, R. (2002) 'Partnership with Internal Customers: A way to achieve increased commitment', *Proceedings of the 7th World Congress on Total Quality Management* (Verona: University of Verona).

Harrison, J. S. and C. H. St. John (1996) 'Managing and Partnering with External Stakeholders', *Academy of Management Executive*, 10 (2), pp. 46–60.

Jones, P. (1987) *Theory and Method in Sociology* (London: Unwin).

Jones, T. M. (1995) 'Instrumental Stakeholder Theory: A synthesis of ethics and economics', *Academy of Management Review*, 20, pp. 404–37.

Jonker, J. and D. J. Foster (2002) 'Stakeholder Excellence? Framing the evolution and complexity of a stakeholder perspective on the firm', *Change Management: Proceedings of the 7th International Conference on ISO 9000 and TQM* (Melbourne: RMIT University).

Keeley, M. (1980) 'Organizational Analogy: A Comparison of Organismic and Social Contract Models', *Administrative Science Quarterly*, 25 (June), pp. 337–62.

Key, S. (1999) 'Toward a new theory of the firm: a critique of "stakeholder" theory', *Management Decision*, 37 (4), pp. 317–28.

Labovitz, S. and R. Hagedorn (1971) *Introduction to Social Research* (New York: McGraw-Hill).

Lawrence, P. R. and J. W. Lorsch (1967) *Organization and Environment* (Cambridge, Mass.: Harvard University Press).

Llewelyn, S. (2003) 'What counts as "theory" in qualitative management and accounting research? Introducing five levels of theorizing', *Accounting, Auditing and Accountability Journal*, 16 (4), pp. 662–708.

Liljander, V. and I. Roos (2002) 'Customer-Relationship Levels – from spurious to true relationships', *Journal of Services Marketing*, 16 (7), pp. 593–614.

Osborn, R. N. (1974) 'Environment and Organizational Effectiveness', *Administrative Science Quarterly*, 19, pp. 231–46.

Parasuraman, A., V. A. Zeithaml and L. L. Berry (1985) 'A Conceptual Model of Service Quality and Its Implications for Future Research', *Journal of Marketing*, 49 (Fall), pp. 41–50.

Park Dahlgaard, S. M. (2002) 'A Critical Rethinking on Motivation', *Proceedings of the 7th World Congress on Total Quality Management* (Verona: University of Verona).

Patching, A. and D. Waitley (1996) *The Futureproof Corporation* (Singapore: Butterworth-Heinemann Asia).

Rowley, T. J. (1997) 'Moving Beyond Dydactic Ties: A Network Theory of Stakeholder Influences', *Academy of Management Review*, 22 (4), pp. 887–910.

Sayer, A. (2000) *Realism and Social Science* (London: Sage).

Scholes, E. and D. Clutterbuck (1998) 'Planning Stakeholder Communication', *Long Range Planning*, 31 (2).

Vinten, G. (2000) 'The Stakeholder Manager', *Management Decision*, 38 (6), pp. 377–83.

Webster, F. E. (1992) 'The changing role of marketing in the corporation', *Journal of Marketing*, 56 (4), pp. 1–17.

Wood, D. J. (1991) 'Corporate Social Performance Revisited', *Academy of Management Review*, 16 (4), pp. 691–718.

Zadek, S. (2001) *The Civil Corporation: The New Economy of Corporate Citizenship* (London: Earthscan).

9

A New Direction for CSR: Engaging Networks for Whole System Change

Ann Svendsen and Myriam Laberge

Introduction

In recent years a number of multinational companies, including Ikea, Home Depot and Nike, have become agents of social change by convening or joining networks of stakeholders to address complex socioeconomic and environmental issues. In attempting to deal with sustainability and corporate responsibility they have gradually shifted their change efforts from their own operations (that is, improving eco-efficiency) to upstream and downstream stakeholders (that is, supply-chain compliance with environmental and social policies) and, finally, to working with networks of governments, civic societies and businesses to change entire economic or social systems.

Nike's vice president of corporate responsibility, Hannah Jones, recently wrote:

> In the early 1990's we had a 'go it alone' attitude ... When we came under scrutiny for the labor practices in our contract factories, we were both unprepared and defensive. We didn't have strong relationships with individuals and organizations to whom we could readily turn to for advice. During the following seven years we began to incorporate CR [corporate responsibility] in our business practices, starting with our environmental program ... Our goal [now] is to create strong multi-stakeholder alliances that in turn will help us deliver flagship programs that have both a positive impact on Nike and on some of the big issues in the world we live in today.

While some may view Nike as simply establishing partnerships the company claims it has made a deliberate move away from bilateral engagement towards establishing and working within networks. We suggest that Nike and other leading companies are developing new relationships and new ways of engaging with networks of stakeholders that are both different and much more likely to lead to whole system change. In conceptual terms they are moving out of the centre of the hub and spoke set of bilateral relationships to become active members or convenors of stakeholder networks.

This chapter describes the activities involved in convening stakeholder networks, which are defined as webs of groups, organizations and/or individuals who come together to address a cross-boundary problem, issue or opportunity. As we see it, the role of the convenor is to help a multi-stakeholder network to tap its latent energy, resources and intelligence in order to generate novel solutions and whole system innovations that no one member could achieve on its own.

The role of network convenor is new for most companies. This role involves different ways of thinking, being and engaging beyond managing bilateral stakeholder relationships. We describe this process as 'cocreative engagement' involving three phases of activity: (1) network outreach, (2) collective learning and (3) joint action/innovation. Trust building takes place throughout the three phases.

Our model of cocreative engagement is based on interviews with network members and convenors, as well as on theories and on research into complex adaptive systems, social capital, and societal learning and change. The model is grounded in a dynamic systems view of corporate–stakeholder relationships.

Why are stakeholder networks becoming more important?

Why are some companies moving towards deeper, network-based forms of engagement? Some companies are gravitating towards more collaborative relationships because they realize that in order to address corporate responsibility issues effectively the input and support of external stakeholders is needed. Others recognize that participation in stakeholder networks is appropriate and necessary given the changing context. This next section examines some of the factors behind the growing trend towards network-based engagement.

Relationships: a key to innovation and business success

Networks of relationships are vitally important to financial success today. We live in a networked world where individuals are connected to others who share common interests and activities via informal links or weak ties (Granovetter, 1985). Social networks and the relationships they embody allow people to share ideas and knowledge. In a knowledge-based economy, collaboration and information sharing across and within networks are essential to innovation and profitability. For example, by building a network of external relationships employees can access necessary resources and new ideas, thereby stimulating creativity and enhancing the firm's ability to bring new solutions to the market.

Management theorist Manual Castells (2000) suggests that technology and globalization are making networks of relationships a decisive business asset. In much the same way as the Ford Motor Company's assembly line was the icon of the industrial age, Castells argues, the globally networked business model is the vanguard of the information age. Kelly (2000, p. 7) reinforces this view with his observation that 'the network economy is founded on technology, but it can only be built on relationships. It starts with chips and ends with trust'.

Greater potential for conflict

Beyond missing out on the potential for innovation, failure to build positive, trust-based stakeholder relationships can also be costly in a networked world, and this new reality has been recognized by numerous companies in industries ranging from mining to pharmaceuticals. Many of them have had first-hand experience of how stakeholder opposition can cause companies to lose millions of dollars when projects are delayed or stopped.

Another challenge is the likelihood of conflict over access to resources or labour. Population growth and economic globalization are contributing to growing social inequality and poverty and the depletion of natural resources. Common resources such as air, water and forests are threatened and citizens are demanding that their use by companies be constrained. Companies that depend on access to natural resources and cheap labour (often in developing countries) are facing increased opposition by local as well as globally interconnected stakeholders. To build or expand new facilities they must be much more connected to and trusted by stakeholders.

Increasing demand for meaningful participation

The values and expectations of consumers and the public have changed. The World Values Survey (Inglehart *et al.*, 1998), a random-sample public opinion survey conducted in over 40 countries in the 1990s found that in Western countries there had been a shift from attention to material well-being and physical security towards more emphasis on the quality of life – values such as freedom, self-expression and self-actualization (Nevitte and Kanji, 1997). This values shift has led to a rise in consumer activism, a decline in deference to institutionalized authority and a broad-based demand for participation by citizens, employees and stakeholder organizations (Nevitte, 1996).

Given the growing demand for participation by an increasingly sophisticated set of stakeholders, it is becoming more difficult for any organization to make and impose unilateral decisions or to proceed with projects without engaging stakeholders in a meaningful way. This rising tide of citizen and stakeholder activism has curtailed the ability of companies to act independently, even when they have the legal right to do so.

Stakeholders become more powerful

In a highly interconnected world, citizens and stakeholder organizations with few resources can become known, share information, influence others and create effective networks in a very short time. Business no longer operates in a vacuum – every action is potentially open to scrutiny by technologically proficient stakeholders who often have links with others, both locally and globally. Advances in computer and web-based technology over the past two decades have enabled non-local, asynchronous communication across the divides of time, place, language, culture and organization. Stakeholders use such networks to put pressure on companies and government agencies. The term 'smart mobs' was recently coined to describe groups that influence public and corporate policy by mobilizing internet-based electronic networks (Rheingold, 2002).

The growing complexity of issues requires input by multiple stakeholders

The issues facing today's company are more complex and interconnected, and many cannot be addressed by the company alone. As the complexity of problems increases there is an increased need for more evolved forms of engagement that can generate holistic solutions. This is especially true when companies are attempting to deal with corporate social responsibility (CSR) issues.

Building a new model of corporate stakeholder relations

A number of academics and business leaders have called for more effective engagement between companies and their stakeholders, recognizing the inherent interconnectedness of companies in a dynamic environment (Post *et al.*, 2002). Andriof and Waddock (2002) argue that, if companies are to cope effectively with the stakeholder issues and relationships that now confront them, they need a better understanding of the dynamics and expectations that are fundamental to living, acting and working in a network of collaborative relationships. Stormer (2003, p. 285) suggests that 'viewing business from an organization-centric perspective does not allow us to deal with the complexity we already know about … nor does it allow us to negotiate problems that are inter-system, universal problems'.

Various academics argue that participating in stakeholder (learning) networks allows companies to attune their values with those of their stakeholders, clarify their social responsibilities, develop new knowledge and innovative solutions to complex problems, enhance mutual understanding and build the trust and commitment required for collaborative action (Gray, 1989; Svendsen, 1998; Swanson, 1999; Calton and Payne, 2003). However, very little theory or research exists on how such stakeholder networks evolve and function. It is for this relatively unexplored topic that we propose a model of cocreative stakeholder engagement.

Complex adaptive systems and stakeholder engagement

The literature on general systems theory and complex adaptive systems provides a useful framework for understanding how stakeholder networks are established and maintained. We have drawn from this literature in the development of our model.

The traditional organization-centric model of corporate–stakeholder relationships reflects the mechanistic world-view that has dominated our thinking since the industrial revolution, one based on the belief that everything can be measured, reduced to its component parts and ultimately managed to achieve specific goals. From this perspective, organizations are like machines, with standardized processes, predictable outcomes and controllable relationships with internal and external stakeholders. In a mechanistic world, organizations behave like closed systems – independent of their environment and able to succeed by managing the 'parts' without much attention to the larger whole in which they operate.

This mechanistic view has influenced the traditional approach to stakeholder relationships, the dominant assumption being that it is possible to predict, manage and control relationships. The term 'stakeholder management' reflects this perspective. From a mechanistic view, a closed system such as a corporation need not be concerned with the long-term consequences of what is 'outside'. This results in mostly short-term, transactional exchanges with stakeholders.

Network- or systems-based model

Our model of cocreative stakeholder engagement is based on a different logic, that of a system or network. A system is a whole whose properties are greater than the sum of its parts. In complex adaptive systems the properties of the whole emerge from the relationship between and interaction of its parts. These properties cannot be predicted from a bit-by-bit examination of the parts. For example, the property of 'mechanized motion' cannot be predicted from the properties of the separate components of an unassembled car, or the property of 'singing' from the separate biological components of a bird. In both these examples the properties and capacity of the whole are greater than the sum of its parts. As Capra (2002, p. 298) states in his book *The Web of Life*, 'understanding ecological interdependence means understanding relationships. It requires the shifts of perception that are characteristic of systems thinking – from parts to the whole, from objects to relationships, from contents to patterns.'

The basic pattern of organization of all living systems is the network. Networks are a fundamental building block of living systems, including ecosystems and social systems. Each network is nested within a complex web of relationships. Within a network, actions taken by one part of the system can cycle round to affect other relationships, until they eventually return to the original source with magnified feedback. Feedback loops are the mechanism in networks that enable both self-regulation and self-organization.

Diversity in networks

Diversity creates a multiplicity of choices and creative responses to disturbances that perturb the equilibrium of a system. In that sense, diversity increases the system's overall resilience and capacity. The benefit of diversity depends on strong links, or feedback loops, between different parts of the system. When such links are weak or non-existent, information cannot travel through the network to activate the potential of the whole network to respond in an optimal way to solve a problem, address an opportunity or adapt to a changing reality. As Capra (2002, p. 303) notes, 'A healthy living system relies on the optimization of a diversity of relationships in its network structure. The more complex the network is, the more complex will be its pattern of interconnections, and the more resilient or "healthy" the system as a whole will be.'

In human networks, when the members of a system are isolated from one another and the flow of information is restricted, distrust and defensive responses diminish the capacity of the system to respond effectively to emergent issues. This characteristic of networks reinforces the importance of links between stakeholders, trust-based relationships and mutual understanding.

Diversity (as in the diversity of views and perspectives of stakeholders) also creates a multiplicity of choices and differences in response, which can in turn lead to conflict. From a systems perspective, however, constructive conflict – that is, the tension between differences – is necessary if the system is to evolve, since creativity and innovation are required to bridge such differences.

The self-organizing capacity of networks

Evolution happens in a network through the forging of new synergistic relationships that build on the strengths and uniqueness of the members (or parts) of the system. Through autopoeisis (self-making – the capacity to bring forth or create), new competences and capacities emerge from the interactions and relationships among system members, representing the unique potential of the system (Maturana and Varela, 1980). These new properties may lead, through self-organization, to novel organizational forms, structures, alliances and solutions. As previously stated, according to the systems view these new properties are properties of the whole, and none of the parts has them. However, for social systems to attain higher levels of organization there must be mutuality of purpose and intent among all the members of the larger community or system where it operates. We suggest that in social systems it is the process of engagement among multiple stakeholders that allows them to innovate and develop new capacities.

Applying systems thinking to stakeholder relationships

Stakeholder networks defined

We have coined the term 'stakeholder network' to refer to a web of groups, organizations and/or individuals who come together to address a shared problem, issue or opportunity. In a stakeholder network the focus shifts from the interests of one organization to the interests of the whole system. Rather than one organization convening its stakeholders, a network of stakeholders is engaged to address a shared problem or opportunity (Figure 9.1).

In the cocreative engagement model the members of the stakeholder network have a stake in the issue by virtue of their being part of the system affected by it. In a stakeholder network participation is voluntary. A network is open to all as long as they have a stake in the issue and agree to follow the rules and norms of the network. Network members develop goals collectively and leadership is distributed; that is, no one organization is in charge. By definition, network engagement involves a cocreative process.

Sometimes networks evolve out of multistakeholder groups that have been set up by a company or government agency to deal with a specific organizational concern. Many networks begin by focusing on one organization's issue, and over time move on to deal with broader systemic problems and opportunities that are often related to sustainability.

Cocreative power

Stakeholder networks, like other complex adaptive systems, can tap collective intelligence in order to self-organize and adapt to a changing environment. In living systems autopoeisis enables networks to develop and evolve, continuously renewing themselves and self-regulating in such a way that the

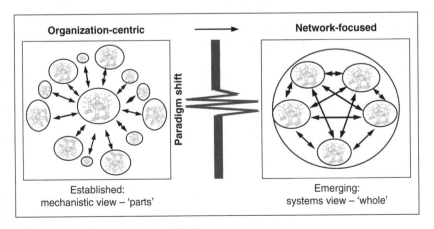

Figure 9.1 The shift to a systems view

integrity of their core identity or structure is maintained. We use the term cocreative power to describe the similar capacity in stakeholder networks to regulate, grow and evolve. In response to emergent issues or opportunities (system shocks), stakeholder networks can develop novel solutions that allow both the members and the system as a whole to succeed.

Cocreative power is the capacity of a stakeholder network to address complex systems issues sustainably. Cocreative engagement, we believe, is an emerging form of systems governance that enables a collective such as a stakeholder network to act coherently to achieve a common goal. Cocreative power taps latent collective energy, resources and intelligence to generate novel solutions and forms of innovation that no one member of the network could achieve on its own. As in other living systems, so-called emergent properties can arise from the interactions and relationships between the members (parts) of the system, including:

- New capacities (for example collective intelligence).
- New complementary relationships that build on the strengths and uniqueness of the members of the network.
- Novel organizational forms, structures and solutions.

These new properties are properties of the whole. They are not available to any individual member acting alone.

Social capital and stakeholder engagement

We shall use the concept of social capital to refine our understanding of stakeholder networks. Social capital has generally been defined as the glue that facilitates collective action. It is 'the stock of active connections among people: the trust, mutual understanding, and shared values and behaviours that bind the members of human networks and communities and make cooperative action possible' (Cohen and Prusak, 2000, pp. 3–4). This definition supports the view in the management literature that social capital has three key dimensions (Nahapiet and Ghoshal, 1998):

- Structural: the structure of the social network.
- Relational: mutual trust and reciprocity.
- Cognitive: mutual understanding and shared goals.

Why is social capital important in stakeholder networks? Research suggests that social capital enables members of a stakeholder network to learn and work together (Svendsen *et al.*, 2003). This is because social capital increases the willingness of the members of a network to share information, follow group norms and rules (for example respect confidentiality, treat others with respect in meetings), put the good of the network ahead of their own short-term interests, cooperate on joint projects and help others to reach their goals (Adler and Kwon, 2002).

Willingness to share information

In a network characterized by high levels of social capital the members understand what kind of information is relevant to others in the network and trust each other with the exchange of more sensitive information. Based on this understanding, they can establish explicit or implicit agreements to become information resources for one another and even grant access to each other's networks of contacts. The information might be on threats or opportunities in the external environment or self-disclosures that open the door to deeper, more mutually rewarding collaboration.

Adherence to norms

Norm adherence involves obeying the formal or informal rules of the group. These can range from rules specified in a formal contract to unspoken rules, such as a tacit agreement to make each other aware of sensitive information before releasing it to outsiders. Solidarity and norm adherence reduce the need for formal controls and therefore can reduce transaction costs.

Acting on behalf of the network

When there is a high level of social capital the members of a network put the good of the group ahead of their own short-term interests. For example, the group members will defend each other's reputations and promote the status of the group vis-à-vis outsiders. They will also be willing to cooperate on joint projects if it is in the interest of the network as a whole.

Willingness to support others

Reciprocity builds social capital. When person A does a favour for B (or acts on his or her behalf), B becomes indebted to A, who can later ask a favour of B. Social capital is a form of credit that is available to the members of the network. When there is a high level of social capital in a network the members will be willing to take action to support others.

Cocreative model of stakeholder engagement

Based on the theory of complex adaptive systems and social capital, plus case study research on a number of stakeholder networks, we have developed a three-stage model of how stakeholder networks form and what it takes for successful whole system innovation. Network outreach is the starting point in our model, the journey is about collective learning, and the prize of engagement is innovation. The capacity of a stakeholder network to innovate depends on a certain amount of social capital existing in the network. Social capital is an emergent property of stakeholder networks that is generated by a cycle of outreach (for example extending membership of the network), collective learning and innovating together for the good of the whole.

Social capital is embedded in networks. Good stakeholder relationships are built up in an ongoing process of interaction and engagement among the members of the network. Based on the theory of complex adaptive systems and social capital, plus the literature mentioned in the preceding section, we make the following assumptions:

- Companies and others outside their boundaries are members of dynamic social networks.
- These networks have some of the properties of complex adaptive systems.
- For a network to function effectively and enable collaboration and innovation its members must develop a certain level of social capital and collective learning.

While there is considerable theory and research on the static components of social capital (for example measures of network structure), little is known of the processes that govern its use, generation and sustainability (White, 2002). There is a need for a more robust model of stakeholder engagement that is based on systems thinking and focuses on processes designed to build social capital in networks of stakeholders.

The three phases in our model of cocreative engagement are illustrated in Figure 9.2 and briefly described below. These phases are not discrete. Networks often go through repeated cycles of outreach, learning and innovation/action. As they move through these cycles, relationships are built and/or strengthened, social capital increases and the members develop a greater willingness to take risks and act for the benefit of the whole network. Eventually power relationships shift and the network, rather than any individual convener, takes ownership of the overall issue or opportunity that brought the members together in the first place.

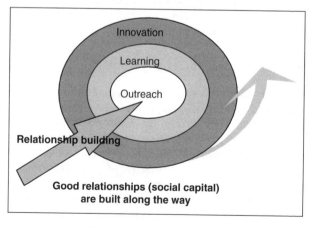

Figure 9.2 The cocreative engagement model

Outreach

> The structure of networks is the key to understanding the complex world around us. Small changes in the typology, affecting only a few nodes or links, can open up hidden doors, allowing new possibilities to emerge. (Barabási, 2002, p. 12)

The purpose of this first phase of cocreative engagement is for a company or small group of stakeholders to build or strengthen a network and, where appropriate, convene the network to address a shared problem, issue or opportunity. The first phase typically involves four tasks:

- Situation analysis.
- Consultation.
- Reframing the issue or question.
- Developing an engagement plan.

When analyzing the situation a manager might clarify the company's reasons for engagement, create a map of internal and external stakeholders, and assess the risks and benefits of moving forward (that is, develop a business case). At this stage the company should keep in mind that if the issue is straightforward, if the company has the authority and power to implement a decision and/or if a decision has already been made, a cocreative form of engagement is likely to be unnecessary or inappropriate. Only when the company needs input and ideas from stakeholders to resolve complex, high-stake, cross-boundary issues is cocreative engagement necessary.

Once the business case has been established the manager should have discussions with potential members of the network to clarify their perspectives, expectations and framing of the issue. It is important to determine whether the key stakeholders think that the issue is important enough for them to participate in the network. The issue, as initially understood by the manager, will probably need to be reframed to incorporate the interests and concerns of other stakeholders.

Identifying and involving diverse participants can be a lengthy and difficult process, especially if two or more stakeholders have been involved in a protracted conflict. For social capital to be built in a stakeholder network its members must develop ways of working together that foster trust and increase mutual understanding. Many successful networks develop a set of written principles. These can include respect, the inclusion of all voices, a valuing of diversity and a commitment to openness, transparency and maximum information sharing.

Once there is general agreement on the framing of the issue or question and on the principles or ground rules for working together, it should be possible to determine the scope and purpose of the engagement as well as to decide who should convene the first meeting. The engagement plan, which can be developed jointly by the members of the network, should provide answers to the following questions:

- What issue/question are we focusing on?
- What kind of engagement is needed, for example virtual or in-person meetings? How often? When? Where?
- What resources will we need, for example a facilitator, space, website?
- What background information do we need to gather?
- What are our roles, responsibilities and success metrics?
- How will we communicate (frequency, method, timing)?
- What principles and values will guide our work?

Collective learning

Inquiry is the focus of the second phase, rather than agreement seeking or problem solving. Learning can be aimed at increasing mutual understanding of relational issues (for example values, perspectives and intentions) and addressing substantive issues such as the root causes of the problem, linkages and patterns. The inquiry will generally need to be supported by quantitative and qualitative data. The collective learning phase allows members of the network to:

- Define the products and outcomes being sought.
- Clarify responsibilities with respect to others, for example what is the larger system; how are we connected to it?
- Develop new knowledge of the issue and larger system.
- Construct shared meanings that allow people to understand each other and work together effectively.
- Build trust and commitment.

When a group learns how to learn together it develops the capacity to tap its collective intelligence. As the inquiry deepens, groups can identify underlying assumptions and the root causes of systemic problems. Collective learning also provides an essential foundation for innovation.

Building a common information base for all members of the stakeholder network enables them to develop a shared understanding of the issue, problem or opportunity. Most low-trust environments are characterized by minimal sharing of information, resulting in many interpretations and perceptions of the same issue by different stakeholders. Sharing information builds trust.

In conflict situations learning involves analysis of the present situation and its probable outcomes. This analysis can promote ownership of the contradictory, confusing, chaotic, fast-moving and often negative present reality.

The process can cause anxiety, pain or confusion, but it is important for the members of a multistakeholder network to grapple with the issue together. Collective ownership of the issue fosters a shift from 'we know what is going on; they are the ones who are confused', to 'no one stakeholder knows fully' (Weisbord and Janoff, 1995).

Another key purpose of the collective learning phase is for members to see the system anew through new insights into cause and effect, recognition of previously invisible or unknown relationships and patterns, and inquiry into assumptions and deeply held beliefs. During this phase the members reflect and think together, and willingly suspend their assumptions in a spirit of inquiry and curiosity.

Achieving a deeply reflective dialogue takes time and practice. Reflective dialogue is a process of delving into underlying causes, rules and assumptions in order to be able to frame old problems in new ways. Generative dialogue can produce unprecedented possibilities and new insights, and thus can spur innovation. The work in this phase involves answering questions such as the following:

- What are the stories and history of the people in the system?
- What do we know about the issue, problem or opportunity that brings us together?
- What external factors, events or potential developments might affect the wellbeing of the network now or in the future?
- What is working or not working in the current situation?
- What root causes, patterns or assumptions underlie this system?
- What is likely to happen if things stay the same? What other scenarios are possible?
- What is the common ground among us? What are our differences in perspective, interests and needs?

Among the many devices that can be effectively used during the learning phase are storytelling and honouring past history. When people share their stories, they share their history and traditions. They speak genuinely about things that are important to them, how they perceive past actions and their present fears and concerns. Stories create connect people to one another as human beings, and to the larger whole of which they are a part. A graphic mapping of past events can help validate elders, acknowledge past grievances and reveal previously unknown cause and effect relationships. By looking back over its history the network can identify those things it wishes to conserve in the future.

Innovation and joint action

When high stakes exist, when stakeholders have recognized their inter-dependence and when the system that connects the issue is understood in depth by all, a shift occurs. People start to take responsibility for the whole. Innovative solutions arise out of the struggle to bridge competing perspectives and needs within the system.

Together the members of a stakeholder network will develop a common vision of their preferred future, articulate shared goals and identify the most fruitful opportunities. Because they have been involved in creating a new direction they will be willing to take action. Groups that are able to innovate collectively to solve small problems are often able to go on to tackle larger systemic problems.

Innovation is not always the end goal for a stakeholder network, but in messy, conflicted situations, innovation is needed to advance the system as a whole to a more effective and sustainable level of functioning. A stakeholder network that has invested in connecting the various parts of the system during the outreach phase, developed a common store of knowledge and understanding during collective learning and built up trust among the members is capable of innovating for the good of the individual members and the whole.

An important assumption in the innovation/joint action phase is that the system must evolve in such a way as to optimize the future prospects of all the members of the system and sustain the system as a whole. In general, stakeholders can be expected to put self-interest ahead of the common good, but enlightened self-interest arises from recognition that interdependence is required for sustainable outcomes, and creates the motivation to overcome competing perspectives and needs in order to make innovation possible. During the innovation phase attention is focused on solutions and actions, as summarized by the following questions:

- What do we yearn for?
- What is our preferred vision of the future?
- What is the common purpose that unites us?
- How can we cocreate the future we all desire?
- What might we do? What will we do?
- How do we organize for action?

The benefits of cocreative network engagement

While engaging stakeholder networks in a cocreative process may take more time and require more resources and greater commitment than organization-centric forms of engagement, it can enable diverse groups to solve highly complex cross-boundary issues and generate new opportunities for social and technical innovation. The benefits of this approach include the following.

First, it improves decision making by systematically bringing together those with knowledge of the issue.

Organizations can develop better long-term solutions that work for the common good by addressing complex problems in a more integrated and comprehensive way. These solutions will be less likely to cause further problems.

Second, it builds up ownership and the commitment to implement solutions. The network can be mobilized to ensure that solutions are sustainable because they are supported by all parts of the system. A process of cocreative engagement will develop the social capital required for continuing collaboration amongst the members of the network.

Third, it allows system-wide innovation. The process of cocreative engagement can lead to coherent, system-wide action by stakeholders to improve the wellbeing and sustainability of a community or ecosystem. Such system-wide change cannot be achieved by any one organization alone.

Fourth, it reduces unproductive conflict. Learning about the perspectives and situations of others can shift the attitude of participants from defensiveness and blame to understanding and openness. Dialogue can generate the reciprocal trust needed to develop a sense of responsibility for others.

Finally, it strengthens communities. Cocreative engagement helps to build up social capital within a community over time. Trust-based relationships support rapid decision making in times of crisis when there is a need for flexibility, adaptability and the capacity to respond quickly to changing conditions.

Conclusions

Organization-centric or managerial relationships with stakeholders are appropriate in certain situations, such as when a company can act unilaterally to achieve its goals, or when issues are relatively straightforward and the company does not need the ideas and support of other stakeholders. However, while an organization-centric approach may have been workable in the past, it is insufficient in a networked world.

For organizations committed not only to a responsive form of corporate social responsibility but also to engaging with their stakeholders in the long term to create sustainable economic, social and environmental value, a new direction is needed. We suggest that engaging in networks for whole system change is a potentially powerful way for companies to advance their sustainability agenda, and in so doing help to create a better world for all.

Notes

1. www.nikeresponsibilitycom, 25 November 2004.
2. Our term stakeholder network is similar to Calton and Payne's (2003) concept of a stakeholder learning network. They define a learning network as an 'interactive field of organizational discourse occupied by all stakeholders who share a complex, interdependent and on-going problem domain and who want/need to talk about it. Within this domain, the corporation is not so much a system within itself as a participant in a larger system that includes other stakeholder citizens' (ibid., p. 7).

References

Adler, P. S. and S. W. Kwon (2002) 'Social capital: Prospects for a new concept', *Academy of Management Review*, 27, pp. 17–40.

Andriof, J. and S. A. Waddock (2002) 'Unfolding stakeholder engagement', in J. Andriof, S. A. Waddock, B. W. Husted and S. S. Rahman (eds), *Unfolding Stakeholder Thinking* (Sheffield: Greenleaf), pp. 1–42.

Barabási, A.-L. (2002) *Linked: The New Science of Networks* (Cambridge, Mass.: Perseus).

Calton, J. M. and S. L. Payne (2003) 'Coping with paradox: Multistakeholder learning dialogue as a pluralist sensemaking process for addressing messy problems', *Business & Society*, 2, pp. 7–42.

Capra, F. (2002) *The Web of Life: A New Scientific Understanding of Living Systems* (New York: Doubleday).

Carroll, A. B. (1979) 'A three-dimensional conceptual model of corporate performance', *Academy of Management Review*, 33, pp. 5–29.

Castells, M. (2000) *The Rise of the Network Society* (Oxford: Blackwell).

Cohen, D. and L. Prusak (2000) *In Good Company: How Social Capital Makes Organizations Work* (Boston, Mass.: Harvard Business School Press).

Freeman, R. E. (1984) *Strategic Management: A Stakeholder Approach* (Boston, Mass.: Pitman).

Granovetter, M. S. (1985) 'Economic action and social structure: The problem of embeddedness', *American Journal of Sociology*, 91, pp. 481–510.

Gray, B. (1989) *Collaborating: Finding Common Ground for Multiparty Problems* (San Francisco, CA: Jossey-Bass).

Inglehart, R., M. Basanez and A. Menendez Moreno (1998) *Human Values and Beliefs: A Cross-Cultural Sourcebook. Political, Religious, Sexual, and Economic Norms in 43 Societies: Findings from the 1990–1993 World Values Survey* (Ann Arbor, Mich.: University of Michigan Press).

Kelly, K. (2000) *New Rules for the New Economy* (New York: Penguin).

Lawrence, A. T. (2002) 'The drivers of stakeholder engagement', *Journal of Corporate Citizenship*, 2 (6), pp. 71–85.

Maturana, H. and F. J. Varela (1980) *Autopoeisis and Cognition: The Realization of the Living* (London: Reidl).

Nahapiet, J. and S. Ghoshal (1998) 'Social capital, intellectual capital, and the organizational advantage', *Academy of Management Review*, 23, pp. 242–66.

Nevitte, N. (1996) *The Decline of Deference: Canadian Value Change in Cross-National Perspective* (Peterborough, Ontario: Broadview Press).

Nevitte, N. and M. Kanji (1997) 'From materialism to postmaterialism: A new set of values for a new century', *Canadian Journal of Marketing Research*, 16, pp. 12–20.

Post, J. E., L. E. Preston and S. Sachs (2002) *Redefining the Corporation: Stakeholder Management and Organizational Wealth* (Stanford, CA: Stanford University Press).

Rheingold, H. (2002) *Smart Mobs: The Next Social Revolution* (New York: Perseus).

Sethi, S. P. (1975) 'Dimensions of corporate social performance: An analytic framework', *California Management Review*, 17 (3), pp. 58–64.

Stormer, F. (2003) 'Making the shift: Moving from ethics pays to an inter-systems model of business', *Journal of Business Ethics*, 44 (4), pp. 279–89.

Svendsen, A. C. (1998) *The Stakeholder Strategy: Profiting from Collaborative Business Relationships* (San Francisco, CA: Berrett-Koehler).

Svendsen, A. C., R. G. Boutilier and D. Wheeler (2003) *Stakeholder Relationships, Social Capital and Business Value Creation* (Toronto: Canadian Institute of Chartered Accountants).

Swanson, D. L. (1999) 'Toward an integrative theory of business and society: A research strategy for corporate social performance', *Academy of Management Review*, 24, pp. 506–21.

Waddell, S. (2005) *Societal Learning and Change* (Sheffield: Greenleaf).

Weisbord, M. R. and S. Janoff (1995) *Future Search: An Action Guide to Finding Common Ground in Organizations and Communities* (San Francisco, CA: Berrett-Koehler).

Wheeler, D., B. Colbert and R. E. Freeman (2003) 'Focusing on value: Reconciling corporate social responsibility, sustainability and a stakeholder approach in a network world', *Journal of General Management*, 28, p. 1.

White, L. (2002) 'Connection matters: Exploring the implications of social capital and social networks for social policy', *Systems Research and Behavioral Science*, 19, pp. 255–69.

10

Learning to be Responsible: Developing Competences for Organization-Wide CSR

*André Nijhof, Theo de Bruijn, Olaf Fisscher, Jan Jonker,
Edgar Karssing and Michiel Schoemaker[1]*

Introduction

The traditional divide between the state and the market is fading. Companies are increasingly, being held accountable for issues such as fair trade, environmental degradation and local or regional socioeconomic matters. They are being required to expand their corporate agenda, and the corporate world realizes that it cannot ignore society is demand for greater responsibility. It also recognizes that companies can themselves benefit from corporate social responsibility (CSR). When developing CSR the organization takes into account additional values and long-term responsibilities in order to meet the expectations and address the critical viewpoints of all parties involved. Implementing CSR requires a company's perspective to be reoriented so that new relationships can be formed, new values defined and new strategies developed. This is more than just another business project. Ultimately, it involves revisiting the very core of the organization, and this poses some difficult challenges for organizations.

The question we address in this chapter is how can an organization become competent in terms of CSR? We argue that CSR is both process and content: companies learn in a, step by step how to strengthen CSR competences such as integrity, loyalty and quality. Individuals alone cannot meet the challenges of CSR. Rather certain competences are required at the collective level and have to be developed throughout the organization.

The structure of the chapter is as follows. In the next section CSR is presented as a strategic challenge it is argued that an organization needs new competences in order to develop CSR. The reason why these competences have to be developed into collective competences is the topic of the third section and in the fourth at model for doing so is proposed. Building on case study research in Dutch firms, the fifth section identifies strategies, mechanisms and instruments that organizations can use to develop collective competences.

CSR as an organizational challenge

The company as a social actor

Consideration of social factors is not a new phenomenon in private firms. Industrialists have long looked at broader issues than profits, be it housing for employees, the cultural development of the latter or employment in general. At the beginning of the twentieth century Henry Ford paid wages that were above the going rate, although one of the purposes of this was for his workers to earn enough to buy his products. In the Netherlands a famous example is Philips. In the city of Eindhoven, where this multinational company was founded, there are still numerous embodiments of the company's social values: residential areas originally built for its workers, sports facilities, college grants for the children of employees, concert halls and so on. In Britain businesses built towns, schools and libraries for families and workers as early as the eighteenth century. What is new to today is (1) the intensity and breadth of the efforts made by private firms (partly or mainly in response to increasingly strong social demands) to behave in a more ethical and responsible way, and the (2) complexity and dynamics of the networks of stakeholders with which companies have to interact. The social agenda has become of much greater strategic value for companies. It is no longer a strictly voluntary effort by a few companies with a strong sense of responsibility instilled by the founder of the organization. Rather companies are increasingly paying attention to issues that are not automatically on their agenda and may become a factor in their long-term survival or give them a competitive edge (Cohen and Prusak, 2001).

The growing attention to CSR during the last two decades has coincided with the development of the concept of sustainable development. During the 1970s governments produced material-specific legislation based mainly on permit systems (direct regulation), but they soon realized that these policies were insufficiently effective. In the direct regulation model, governments retained sole responsibility for the quality of the environment. They gave form and meaning to this responsibility by defining strict limits within which companies must act. Compliance to regulation was, however, not enough to achieve sustainability. Rather environmental policy had to focus on how to use the creativity of all the actors involved beyond the level required by command-and-control strategies. The result was an international trend in environmental policies towards dialogue and consultation, collaboration and the formation of new partnerships (Hartman *et al.*, 2000; De Bruijn and Tukker, 2002). Over the past decade governments throughout the world have recognized that industry is not only a key contributor to environmental degradation but also can be part of the solution through the development of new processes, technologies and products. There is a visible trend away from direct regulation towards coregulation, whereby governments and industry share responsibility (under ISO 14001) (Lévêque, 1996).

The role of companies in society is therefore changing and the traditional divide between state and market is fading. Private firms realize that they cannot ignore social and governmental demands for greater responsibility, and that they might benefit from meeting these demands. A similar development has taken place in the social policy of many companies: their responsibility no longer ends at the gate and they are paying increased attention to the chains and networks in which they operate. Many now condemn child labour, are active in the local community and so on. This is not only because of pressure from consumer organizations and NGOs but also because of value changes within the companies themselves. They have changed from being a political and social factor into a political and social actor.

Defining CSR

The increased attention to the corporate social and environmental agenda has led to a host of activities, mostly by trailblazers, and consequently there are many different definitions of CSR in different fields. At the global level CSR means taking care of social, environmental and economic issues (Elkington, 1999). More specifically, it means attending to such issues as human rights, working conditions, environmental protection, consumer protection and fighting corruption. A well-known definition of CSR is that by the World Business Council on Sustainable Development (Holme and Watts, 1999): 'the continuing commitment by business to behave ethically and contribute to economic development while improving the quality of life of the workforce and their families as well as the local community and society at large'. The WBCSD emphasizes that CSR is a continuous process that is based on ethics and concerns the workforce as well as local and global communities. It also makes a clear link between economic performance and CSR. Hence CSR goes beyond philanthropy. It is essentially based on responsibilities related to the products, services and primary processes of an organization (SER, 2001). It is about the challenge of taking account of additional values and responsibilities. Following this line of reasoning, Karssing (2000) proposes that responsible behaviour can be strengthened along four dimensions:

- *Broader*, with more values being respected in order to take account of the interests of additional parties, as well as other perspectives and alternatives.
- *Deeper*, with the past and long-term consequences being taken more fully into account.
- *Richer*, with additional arguments being used to underpin decisions.
- *More defendable*, with behaviour being increasingly based on sound reasoning that takes account of the expectations of others involved.

This view of responsible behaviour allows us to reformulate and clarify our definition of competences for CSR: an organization is more CSR competent when it can legitimately defend its behaviour towards those with justifiable and reasonable expectations of the functioning of the organization by making broader, deeper and richer decisions.

A central element in the above definitions of CSR is a readiness to respond to the reasonable expectations of stakeholders, coupled with close interaction with a broad range of stakeholders. The expectations and demands of stakeholders to a certain extent define the actions that should be taken by an organization and the nature of its responsibilities. Stakeholder relationships are thus a crucial element of CSR (Donaldson and Preston, 1995). Only through dialogue with society at large (employees, governments, customers, NGOs and so on) can an organization establish a balance between its corporate governance and public governance. But how does this readiness to respond arise, and how is responsible behaviour embedded in organizational practices? Employees are important participants in this process; they have to learn what CSR means and how it can be incorporated into their everyday behaviour.

Competences for CSR

Learning to become more responsible requires new competences. In this regard Jonker and Schoemaker (2004) depict CSR as an organizational capability, as a way of operating with CSR as an embedded value. Working on CSR requires the development of appropriate capacities and skills to make decisions and behaviour broader, deeper, richer and more defendable. As managing CSR is an organization-wide process it has to be embedded in the behaviour of individual employees, departments and so on, and it requires certain competences at the organizational level. In line with the resource-based view of the firm, an organizational competence can be defined as 'a firm's capacity to deploy resources, usually in combination, using organisational processes, to ... [achieve] a desired end' (Amit and Schoemaker, 1993, p. 35). The ability to coordinate and deploy the resources required to perform tasks is therefore a key competence, and dealing with the demands of CSR requires new combinations of competences.

Competence management matches the talents of employees to the work to be done. By drawing up competence profiles the organization can identity which competences are needed to function successfully. Competence profiles are used to select, appraise, develop and (sometimes) reward employees (Schoemaker, 2003a) and to make human resource management more competence-based. In this way the organization's strategy is connected, through the management of organizational processes, to the talents of its employees (Van der Heijden and Nijhof, 2004).

Although competence management is valuable for CSR it also raises some difficult questions, such as what kind of behaviour is CSR-specific? One way of ascertaining this is to analyze the existing competences in order to identify those which are specific to CSR. In this regard the set of competences suggested by Hoekstra and van Sluijs (2003) is useful. The set consists of about 40 competences, including integrity, communication, learning orientation and initiative. However, it does not provide CSR-specific competences. For instance, in the case of the competence of communication, equally strong arguments can be made for and against it being CSR-specific. Competences such as initiative, independence, entrepreneurship, communication, reliability, cooperation, empathy and adaptability lie in a somewhat grey area, while planning, organizing ability, presentation, listening and creativity are not, in our view, CSR-related at all.

In his study of the ethical qualities of organizations Kaptein (1998) identifies seven components:

- *Clarity*: the degree to which the organization's expectations of the moral conduct of employees are accurate, concrete and complete.
- *Consistency*: the degree to which the organization's expectations of the moral conduct of employees are coherent, unambiguous and compatible.
- *Sanctionability*: the degree to which negative or positive sanctions can be applied in the case of irresponsible or responsible conduct.
- *Achievability*: the degree to which responsibilities can be carried out.
- *Supportability*: the degree of support given to employees for the proper use of corporate assets, to close cooperation with coworkers and supervisors, and to realization of the interests of stakeholders.
- *Visibility*: the degree to which the conduct of employees and the effects of this can be observed.
- *Discussability*: the degree to which responsibilities are open to discussion.

Some of the above are relevant to becoming more responsible as an organization, and are therefore more CSR-specific than the general competences outlined by Hoekstra and Van Sluijs (2003). Nevertheless, the question of which competences are CSR-specific has not been fully answered. The companies in our research project also found it difficult to identify CSR-specific competences. They recognized that certain competences became more relevant when working on CSR, but most of the ones they mentioned were more process-based than those distinguished by Kaptein (1998). Moreover, the competence management methods adopted were primarily oriented at individuals. Many organizations had engaged in competence management over the previous five to ten years, but this had been based on the use of competence profiles to appraise individuals and assess individual behaviour, and on the use of so-called personal development plans. Linking these instruments to collective competences was rare (Schoemaker, 2003b).

Mainstream competence management can thus be seen as being oriented towards the individual. However, becoming a responsible organization requires the development of collective competences, and we shall consider this in the next section.

From individual to collective competences

Being competent in terms of CSR concerns every part of the organization. Although the commitment of individuals is essential to the successful implementation of CSR it is not sufficient. Organizations need to develop shared values and coordinated behaviour. Weick and Roberts (1993) highlight the importance of collective thinking in situations that require continuous operational reliability. In such situations cooperation among individuals is necessary to prevent accidents arising from unexpected incidents. Such cooperation develops during the process of association among the members of a group. Associating within groups consists of contributing, representing and subordination; that is, the group members determine their actions (contribute) in the light of the joint task (representation) and their subservience to it (subordination). As Asch (1952, pp. 251–2) puts it:

> There are group actions that are possible only when each participant has a representation that includes the actions of others and their relations. The respective actions converge relevantly, assist and supplement each other only when the joint situation is represented in each and when the representations are structurally similar. Only when these conditions are given can individuals subordinate themselves to the requirements of joint action. These representations, and the actions that they initiate, bring group facts into existence and produce the phenomenal solidity of group process.

The consequence of contribution, representation, and subordination is that the team members act as though they were one. In other words, collective mind' develops and individual actions converge to meet the overall interest. Sandelands and Stablein (1987) suggest that connections between actions are much more important for the emergence of a collective mind than connections between people. Based on joint experiences, shared history and other forms of interrelationship, an understanding arises of the organizational social system and the actions that should be taken by the group. There are four requirements for the building of collective competences for CSR, as discussed below.

CSR must be anchored in a specific organizational identity

The initial requirement when making CSR a collective competence is a strong organizational identity. Whereas organizational reputation relates to the image that outsiders have of an organization, organizational identity relates to the image that employees, managers and other stakeholders have of their own organization. It is about who they are and what is central in terms of values, norms and behaviour. Organizational identity defines an organization and distinguishes it from other organizations. It fosters the development of a community of work and serves as a guideline for employees in their day-to-day activities. It is at the heart of the social capital that employees and managers constitute: 'Social capital consists of the stock of active connections among people: the trust, mutual understanding, and shared values and behaviours that bind the members of human networks and communities and make cooperative action possible' (Cohen and Prusak, 2001, p. 4).

As with other values, CSR should be discussed throughout the organization in order to define the responsibilities of and establish guidelines for managers and employees. As a value anchored in the organizational identity, CSR gives meaning to the functioning of everyone in the organization (Schoemaker and Jonker, 2004). 'We care for our environment' and 'A world without child labour' are examples of company statements that reflect core values. Core values should fit the traditions of the organization and the personal values of its employees. If there is no fit between the organizational values and personal values employees might seek new opportunities outside the organization. Since organizational identity guides collective behaviour, a strong organizational identity and the identification of CSR-specific values can create a sound basis for collective competences in CSR.

CSR requires cooperation at all levels

Another reason for organizing CSR at the collective level is that many responsibilities and functions can only be fulfilled by joint action by several departments, especially in functionally organized organizations with a high degree of task division. For example, when an organization wants to introduce a product innovation with less environmental impact it needs input not only from the R&D department but also from sales, purchasing and production. This connectedness between departments makes it necessary to have a joint understanding of the meaning of CSR throughout the organization.

Cooperation often even goes beyond the confines of the company. Only if there is cooperation and close interaction among the various parties involved in a commercial chain is it possible to engage in responsible chain management. One initiative to encourage responsible chain management is the Forest Stewardship Council (FSC), an international non-profit organization founded in 1993 to support environmentally appropriate, socially beneficial and economically viable management of the world's forests. Timber and goods with an FSC certificate have been checked at each stage of the chain, from forest to retailer.

The connectedness between the various parties involved raises questions about the scope of CSR. When it is a collective competence it is obvious that it should encompass all departments in an organization; but to what extent should it also encompass external parties such as suppliers and customers? Although this is essential to responsible chain management, many organizations are reluctant to force their view of moral responsibility onto others. This will be addressed later when strategies for CSR are presented.

Individual actions constitute organizational actions

The third reason for making CSR a collective competence is that individual actions take place in an organizational context and affect organizational actions. Every action by an individual employee, and every interaction between an individual employee and another stakeholder reflect what the organization is. This is especially true in the service industry, where employees interact with customers and other stakeholders every day.

Employees are representatives of their organization and the actions of one employee can affect all the other employees because they all represent the same organization. For example, if one employee accepts bribes the others will not be believed if they claim that the organization has a strict antibribery policy. Conversely if the organization has a strong reputation for not being open to bribery the employees will not be approached by potential bribers since the latter will know it is useless.

The connectedness between individual and collective actions raises the question of whether an abstract entity such as an organization can bear responsibility. An organization has no feelings, no conscience and cannot act by itself. Only the decision makers can act and evaluate the values involved. Thus Werhane (1985) argues that organizations can act only in a secondary sense. People in an organization are the primary actors, although they are acting on behalf of the organization and the reasons for acting are determined by the organization and authorized by its charter, goals and directives (ibid.) In this regard French (1984) emphasizes the importance of a formal decision-making structure and associated procedures. This structure focuses on the organization's interests, and therefore the organization's intentions may be distinct from the intentions of the individual employees.

This connectedness between individual and collective action makes it impossible for CSR to be organized on a strictly individual basis. It requires the organization as a whole to be moral actor with social, environmental and economic responsibilities. It also requires a collective learning process.

Corporate accountability requires corporate responsibility

The final reason for making CSR a collective competence is that corporate accountability is accompanied by corporate responsibility. When something goes wrong in an organization it is not just the employees who are directly involved who are called to account. First and foremost, the organization itself is called to account: this can include a liability to pay compensation and accept moral accountability for accidents. This second point was addressed above when we explored the interdependence between individual and organizational actions. Here it is important to note that corporate accountability requires the organization, as a collective entity, to be prepared to bear corporate responsibility.

In order to examine the links between accountability and responsibility it is useful to reflect upon the necessary preconditions for bearing responsibility. Bovens (1990) argues that accountability means acting in a responsible way. Lenk (1992) reinforces this position when he asserts that freedom to act and responsibility are indivisible. The degree of responsibility that an individual can reasonably bear is limited by the opportunities to fulfil the accompanying obligations: 'ought implies can'. There are four preconditions for the ability to get in a responsible way (see also De Leede *et al.*, 1999).

First, freedom to determine the reasons for acting, to be an intentional actor, is an essential part of having to bear responsibility (French, 1984; Wempe, 1998). This emphasizes the distinction between responsibility and responsiveness. Being responsive merely involves reacting to external stimuli, while acting in a responsible way requires a conscious evaluation of the values, objectives and consequences of potential actions. The latter is the second precondition, or what Thompson (1988) calls the ability to foresee. It extends the condition of internationality by adding responsibility for consequences that were not intended but could have been envisaged. Thompson puts this in terms of an advisor: 'An advisor is responsible for the consequences of decisions based on his advice insofar as he could reasonably be expected to foresee that they would follow from his advice' (ibid., p. 556). Jonas (1984) builds on this in his analysis of the imperative of responsibility. If it is not possible to exclude the possibility of adverse consequences, however, small they might be, then responsible actors should refrain from acting.

The third precondition relates to the situation in question. The situation should include options: if an actor has no possibility of meeting the expectations that accompany responsibility then responsibility cannot be given to that actor. In other words, in order to take responsibility it is necessary for there to be options available to enable the actor to act in a responsible way. Finally, responsibility requires the actor to have certain capabilities. In this regard the ability to make a balanced evaluation of the various options is especially important. If an actor is not able to make such an evaluation then it is not possible to give that actor full responsibility.

As noted earlier, corporate accountability requires an organization – as a collective entity – to be prepared to bear corporate responsibility. The above preconditions suggest the types of measure that are necessary to function proactively in this regard (Table 10.1). For example, in a complex and highly departmentalized organization it is likely that no individual will have all the knowledge required to oversee and balance all aspects of important tasks such as assessing the safety of a plant or the possible environmental impacts that will occur during the life cycle of a product. In order to address these issues in an informed and balanced way it is necessary to set up information

Table 10.1   Preconditions for responsible actions

Aspect	Preconditions	Associated organizational measures
Intention-related	Freedom to determine the reasons for acting	Procedures for decision making, division of formal authority
Information-related	Foresight	Information and monitoring systems
Situation-related	Options to enable responsible acting	Availability of options, resource allocation
Person-related	Ability to make a balanced evaluation	Dilemma training, dialogue with colleagues

and monitoring systems. Only when these organizational arrangements are in place will it be possible to make responsible choices.

Developing collective competences for CSR

CSR implies a continuous learning process, with organizations learning how to deal with increasingly complex issues in cooperation with growing range of stakeholders. They must ascertain how far they need to extend their responsibilities, what issues to take up, how to give meaning to those issues and how to combine economic, social and environmental strategies. Each phase will require new combinations of competences. According to Roome (2001, p. 3), 'moving up the innovation hierarchy increases the complexity of the issues, the numbers of actors involved in change, and the number of linked, multiple technological and social options, the innovations and new practices that need to be undertaken and the uncertainties that have to be considered'. Whereas companies once interacted primarily with shareholders, customers and local regulators, CSR requires the involvement of a much more extensive range of actors, and probably from beyond the companies' usual production and consumption systems. This is not a move that companies can make in one step; they must gradually learn how to cope with the increasingly they issues. They need to rediscover their role and responsibilities in conjunction with their stakeholders, and to develop activities that are in line with this new perspective. However, most of all they should redirect the organizational processes so that CSR acquires a concrete meaning in every part of the company and for every employee.

A process model for CSR

Based on the above analysis, we argue that collectivizing competences for CSR is a strategic process. It is strategic because individuals' actions have to be anchored in specific organizational values and transformed into collective action. It is a process because learning to be responsible is the core of all individual and collective actions, and this learning (as a process) consists of a complex set of activities. Internal and external stakeholders will evaluate these activities positively, or negatively, depending on the way in which the starting points for the CSR policy are discussed with stakeholders, how this is integrated into actual behaviour, the results of this and whether these results are made transparent to the stakeholders. In this way the evaluation by and the associated reactions of the stakeholders are intertwined with processes taking place in the organization. Based on this line of reasoning we propose a CSR model that consists of four sequential processes (Nijhof and Fisscher, 2001):

- *The consultation process*: balancing the organizational identity and associated values with the claims and expectations of all stakeholders in order to determine the social responsibilities of the organization.
- *The integration process*: integrating and anchoring attention to social responsibilities in the primary and secondary processes of the organization.
- *The justification process*: justifying the choices and actions of the organization to the stakeholders, based on monitoring and reporting actual corporate behaviour in relation to the organization's social responsibilities.
- *The evaluation process*: based on the other processes, all stakeholders can evaluate the organization's behaviour and judge whether it is responsible or irresponsible.

In order to develop competences for CSR, coherence between these processes is essential. For example, if the representatives of an organization have agreed upon certain responsibilities with its stakeholders and integrated these into corporate behaviour but neglected to communicate and justify the outcomes to the relevant stakeholder groups they should expect, despite their good intentions and efforts, a negative judgement from the stakeholders. Similarly, it would be a mistake to agree upon certain responsibilities but to report upon other, less sensitive ones. The relative coherence of the consultation, integration and justification processes will determine whether stakeholders make a positive or negative judgement (Nijhof, 1999). These processes are cyclical in nature and new issues will gradually emerge, some placed on the agenda by new stakeholder groups. The interconnectedness of these processes is illustrated in Figure 10.1.

Clearly the model involves a continuous learning process. It exceeds the preconditions for responsible actions listed in Table 10.1 in respect of the consultation and integration processes, which are designed to facilitate responsible behaviour, and of making the results available for scrutiny and judgement.

The model is normative rather than descriptive. Organizations are not expected to go through the different processes sequentially, but rather to work on the various elements simultaneously. In our empirical work we used

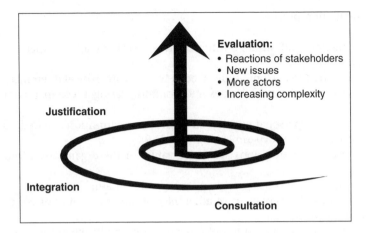

Figure 10.1   The strategic process of learning to be responsible

the model to give the case study organizations a framework for reflecting on their CSR-related activities to date.

Identifying collective competences

Given that an organization has to develop collective competences to achieve CSR the question now is, how can that be done? If learning to be responsible is a strategic process, as suggested in above, then what activities are needed in each stage to develop collective competences? The model highlights the interdependence of two crucial elements in the acquisition of CSR competences: the interaction with stakeholders, and translating the resulting agenda into tasks, responsibilities and actions for all members of the organization. As balancing the shared values that make up the identity of the organization with readiness to respond to the legitimate expectations of stakeholders is at the heart of CSR, the organization has to be capable of engaging in dialogue with its stakeholders and of acting on the outcomes of this dialogue. CSR is a continuous process and learning to be responsible requires the organization to have some of the process competences listed below to enable them to complete the four processes discussed above.

The consultation process:

- defining which stakeholders are important;
- listening to the expectations and demands of external stakeholders;
- defining the relevant ethical dilemmas and issues;
- defining the business case for CSR in the organization;
- defining the norms and values through bottom-up processes in such a way that they are relevant to organization and its stakeholders;
- creating top-management commitment to CSR.

The integration process:

- putting the CSR strategy into concrete terms for all members of the organization;
- developing the personal skills needed to deal with ethical dilemmas;
- internalizing the basic values and communicating these in a committed way;
- developing a personal position based on the organization's shared values;
- creating space for experimenting with CSR;
- cementing the ambitions and basic values of the organization into the core processes;
- making the CSR strategy relevant to the value chain;
- monitoring the behaviour of all employees and rewarding or correcting them accordingly;
- resisting the temptation to opt for short-term results when these conflict with the basic values of the organization.

The justification process:

- monitoring the results of responses to economic, social and environmental issues;
- acting effectively in the event of errors;
- providing the information that stakeholders want;
- creating trust through transparency.

The evaluation process:

- gaining knowledge of the responses of stakeholders;
- learning from those responses;
- adjusting policies and actions;
- remaining alert to new issues and risks.

This is a fairly comprehensive list of all possible competences and whether they are all relevant for a specific organization will depend on its view and definition of CSR. In practice, there is no one model of CSR and therefore different competences will be relevant for different organizations. This also fits with our idea of CSR as a learning process. The development of new competences can be based on the changes that an organization has already undertaken and the challenges it is currently facing.

The question remains as to what extent competences are CSR-specific. Some of the process competences are obviously so, for instance the competence to identify ethical dilemmas and issues. Others, such as the competence to create top-management commitment, are important for all organizational change processes. In between are competences that are not strictly CSR-specific but are essential to CSR. An example is listening to external stakeholders. To some extent all organizations already communicate with external stakeholders such as clients, but CSR requires them to engage with new types of stakeholder (for example NGOs) and to add moral and ethical issues to their exchanges.

From model to practice

The competences listed above are derived from a theoretical analysis. In order to obtain a deeper insight into the relevance of the process model, case study research was carried out in four Dutch organizations. This section discusses the instruments that these organizations were using to develop collective CSR competences.

Methodology and the case study organizations

The aim of the research was to gain insights into the process of developing collective CSR competences. For our research model we chose the critical incident method proposed by Plessner. Although the method was developed for a totally different context, it is well suited to situations in which an interviewee wishes to gain a better understanding of the meaning of CSR for the organization. An important assumption in this research methodology is that the need for collective competences is most obvious to the employees of an organization during attention-grabbing actions or situations. These could be incidents such as criticism by an NGO or an accident that causes casualties, or more positive situations such as a key speech by a new CEO or a customer's demand for environmentally friendly products. Therefore, we prefer to use the more neutral term critical event method rather than the more common critical incident method. For each critical event revealed we investigated all aspects of it and its effects. The validity of the results was improved by the use of methods such as data triangulation, checking the results with members of the organization and having a theoretical basis for the selection of the case study organizations (Eisenhardt, 1989).

The case studies were conducted between October 2003 and June 2004. In each of the four organizations between five and ten employees were interviewed, and relevant documents were analyzed. Followup meetings were held to discuss the findings. The organizations were as follows:

- Coloplast NL is a fully owned subsidiary of the Danish holding company Coloplast A/S. Coloplast develops, produces and sells colostomy and incontinence products, dressings and skincare items. About 60 employees are engaged in marketing, selling and delivering of Coloplast products produced elsewhere.
- HEMA is part of KBB Vendex and is the largest non-food retailer in the Netherlands. It sells about 30000 different products produced

in 40 countries, mainly in Europe and Asia. The company has about 300 shops in the Netherlands, Germany and Belgium.

- Achmea Pension Funds is part of the Achmea Group. This group was created in 1995 as a result of the merger of several insurance companies and is linked to the European Eureko alliance. The Achmea Group has about 13000 employees, about 1500 of whom work in the Achmea Pension Funds business unit. The main activities of the business unit are the administration of pension rights and payments, plus the governance of trust funds and other insurance products in this area.
- Achmea Facility Management is part of the same group as Achmea Pension Funds. It functions as a service unit working for the business units of the Achmea Group. Its main activities are the management of buildings, car parks and gardens, and the purchase of office equipment.

Instruments used to develop collective competences

At all the case study organizations the critical events that has caused employees to change their understanding of and commitment to CSR were recorded. We explored not only the more traditional instruments for developing CSR, such as codes of conduct, dilemma training and auditing but also other activities that the interviewees perceived to have stimulated collective CSR competences. These instruments were then divided into five categories: awareness activities, demands by external stakeholders, policy instruments for CSR, HR-related instruments, and the actual deployment of CSR.

Awareness activities

Some of the critical events mentioned in the interviews had primarily focused on raising awareness of the meaning of CSR for the organization. A review of these activities revealed the importance of the following:

- Holding an introductory meeting on the subject of CSR gives a clear signal to all employees that the management team wants to do something about CSR and is looking for ideas and initiatives.
- Regularly including CSR-related topics in unexpected events and places, such as product presentations, brochures and meetings, keeps the topic alive and stimulates new initiatives in the field of CSR.
- Placing articles about CSR on the intranet and in the company magazine increases awareness of CSR.
- Using games to discuss topics related to the core values of the organization facilitates discussions of dilemmas that are not normally addressed.
- The effects of attempts to raise awareness of the organizational values by giving every employee a printed copy of the values and conducting a poster campaign are limited because they do not require a response by the employees.

- The organization's commitment to CSR should be made visible by organizing projects such as the construction of a school in a developing country, participating in social projects, or asking employees to vote on which projects the company should support with donations.

Demands by external stakeholders

According to the literature an important catalyst for the adoption of CSR by an organization is being publicly accused of unacceptable behaviour by an external party, generally an NGO. Notably only one such incident had touched on the CSR process in the case study organizations. A national TV station had shown a documentary on the working conditions at a number of the companies that supplied one of the organizations. However, this programme has had almost no effect on employees' CSR awareness, possibly because a manager from the organization had appeared in the documentary and presented seemingly sound arguments on the actions that had already been taken by the organization.

Policy instruments for CSR

During any strategic change, process instruments that focus on policy development and implementation can be used. The case study organizations had achieved the results they required by the following means:

- Making CSR an explicit topic on the strategy card. The latter was used as part of the annual planning and control cycle.
- Strategically reorientating of the core of the company so that relationships with society became crucial to the survival of the organization.
- Setting up a project group or working group to develop activities to bring about organizational and cultural change. Employees from different departments and levels were involved so that a widespread feeling of ownership would develop in the organization.
- Making CSR a fixed topic on the agenda for management meetings, and appointing a CSR ambassador in every organizational unit. Without these measures CSR could easily become overshadowed by the urgency of everyday issues.
- Describing all CSR activities and their results in an annual report. This provoked reactions such as, 'Wow, I didn't know that we did so many things in this area'.

HR-related instruments

With the need to develop competences the use of human resource instruments might be expected to have been important in the case study organizations. However, the number of instruments mentioned in this regard was fairly limited:

- Discussions of the importance of CSR and the related values were included in the interviews with potential employees. This was designed to identity which applicants would fit in with the way the organization conducted its business.
- Goals and concrete activities were included in personal development plans or in the annual plans drawn up by the CSR ambassadors.
- Organizational values were included in the guidelines used for the evaluation and appraisal discussions between managers and employees.
- Visits were organized to enable employees to see certain facets of the organization's operations in real life. For example, new senior managers might be sent to visit a major supplier in a developing country. This was intended to stimulate their ability to empathize and put things into perspective.

Actual deployment of CSR

The deployment of CSR practices proved to be a powerful way of developing competences throughout the organization:

- Choices were based on the principles of the organization: for example one manager refused to accept a reorganization of his department because of the effects it would have on the staff. However, if the employees were not aware of concrete choices being made this could result in a feeling that CSR was nothing more than nice words.
- Exemplary behaviour by managers was crucial, ideally linked to obvious ambition and an eagerness to work on CSR. Actions by managers that were perceived as unfair or irresponsible could frustrate the process of developing CSR competences.

CSR as an irreversible process

An important question that we discussed with the case study interviewees was the extent to which the process of learning to be responsible should be regarded as irreversible. Although it was difficult to obtain a definite answer, the interviewees felt that embedding the will to act in a responsible way in the culture, structure, and environment of the organization was crucial in this respect. For instance, as soon as CSR was made a fixed topic at meetings (embedded in the structure), stories about CSR were consistently told (embedded in the culture) and intentions and actions were made transparent (embedded in the environment) it became much more difficult for companies to withdraw. By installing mechanisms to strengthen CSR internally and externally, CSR became a collective competence and one that could not easily be removed.

Challenges for the further development of CSR

CSR is a continuous learning process, in the course which organizations are faced with new challenges. Analyzing such challenges gives further insight into the way in which the case study organizations were trying to develop collective CSR competences. The challenges mentioned here are related to the four processes described in the section on developing collective competences.

The consultation process

One of the core issues in CSR is determining the limits of the responsibility of the organization. Several of the case study organizations were still struggling with this question, and especially in respect of external stakeholders. They wanted to increase the involvement of, for example, interest groups and the consumers of their products, but were unsure about who to consult and how to start.

Another challenge being faced by the case study organizations, where CSR was more or less a top-down process, was to impact the real meaning and added value of CSR to the various organizational units. Until their understanding of these was internalized there could be no feeling of ownership or any desire to make progress with CSR.

The integration process

Almost all the case study organizations had difficulty in establishing the concrete implications of their CSR strategy for all employees and processes. Naturally, motivated people were taking the lead, but it was unclear how the meaning of CSR could be instilled in all employees. Another challenge was to encourage employees to make an active contribution. In this regard, the message of those who were communicating CSR to the employees should have been 'look what has been done' or 'this might be an opportunity for you'.

Functional departments were working on CSR-related issues within their business scope. However, cooperation between departments would have resulted in more possibilities and might have produced better results. For example, in one of the organizations the internal cleansing department was separating different types of waste, but the benefit to the environment would have been much greater if the purchasing department had been consulted and asked to consider the materials bought in.

In one organization, there was a cynical attitude towards anything that hinted of CSR because there has been prior incidents of irresponsible behaviour. Emphasizing good intentions did not help in this situation and the challenge was to make concrete examples of corporate responsible behaviour known throughout the organization.

The justification process

Challenges in the justification process included the following:

- Increasing the visibility of good results in the area of CSR, to increase employees' enthusiasm for it.
- Improving the governance of suppliers. Because this was such a complex issue, one organization was trying to deal with the challenge by cooperating with competitors in several European countries.
- Measuring and evaluating the results of CSR policies. A difficulty here was to find good indicators because some policies involved intangible practices such as respecting each other.

The evaluation process

In one organization, for some employees CSR was related to social management and the way in which they were treated (the internal effects of CSR), while for others CSR was related to customers' health and welfare and to supplier relationships (the external effects of CSR). Improving the links between the two could strengthen CSR practices throughout the organization.

Although many issues were already integrated into the CSR policy of one of the organizations new issues kept arising. Therefore an important challenge was to remain alert to new societal issues and develop the standpoint of the organization according to these issues over time.

In another organization CSR followed two distinct courses. One was aimed at increasing people's awareness of the organizational values, but this had had limited concrete results. The other focused on relatively easy goals such as the use of green energy and the recycling of waste. Both an awareness of values and concrete results were needed to progress with CSR, but these needed to be linked to each other.

Reflections on the challenges

According to the interviewees these challenges were key to the further development of CSR in their organizations, but they were unclear about how to proceed. In this chapter we have suggested some interventions, but these will have to be applied before we can ascertain whether they are able to make the expected contribution to the development of collective competences for CSR.

It is noteworthy that only one of the organizations considered that its main challenges lay in the processes of justification and evaluation. The other three were still focusing on challenges relating to the consultation and integration processes. The fact that all the companies had faced specific challenges in developing CSR competences underlines the point that being responsible is not an either/or issue. It is a continuous learning process where various activities can help organizations to become more responsible without ever reaching the ultimate stage of total excellence.

Towards an integrated framework for developing competences for CSR

Based on the empirical findings and the conceptual model presented earlier, we looked for patterns that would allow us to construct an integrated framework for developing collective competences for CSR. Our finding that the competences actually developed depended on the definition of CSR adopted provided an important anchoring point. In our empirical work we identified companies that had developed competences for CSR based on their desire to strengthen their organizational identity and associated core values. For such organizations dialogue with external stakeholders was of minor importance in respect of CSR. Other companies, some of which were taking part in associated projects in the same research programme, focused much more on identifying risks to their operations by closely monitoring external demands and communicating with NGOs. Clearly in their case competences related to dialogue with external stakeholders were of relevance. A third group of companies concentrated on the role of the various parties in the overall production and consumption chain when developing their competences for CSR (Jonker and Roome, 2005). Thus companies with an orientation towards their own identity or potential risks focused on the organization itself as the primary actor, while companies in the third category adopted a systems orientation, including a focus on the roles and responsibilities of suppliers, consumers and governments. In this sense the third group had adopted an integrated strategy while the other groups were following an inside-out and an outside-in strategy respectively:

- Inside-out identity strategy: with this strategy CSR achieves meaning through the organization's own identity. Strengthening the level of pride in and loyalty and commitment to the organization are important goals in this strategy.
- Outside-in risk strategy: with this strategy CSR achieves meaning by identifying, monitoring and controlling risks in order to prevent reputation damage or other costs.
- Integrated, open system strategy: with this strategy CSR achieves meaning by the reflecting on the role and function of the organization in the overall production and consumption chain. Reducing environmental damage, social inequality and other socially undesirable situations are important goals in this strategy.

While it is theoretically possible for organizations to follow all three strategies simultaneously, in practice most seem to adopt just one. Depending on the strategy chosen, certain competences will be more or less relevant to each of the CSR processes. Some examples of competences that correspond to specific CSR processes and strategies are shown in Table 10.2.

Table 10.2   Competences associated with CSR processes and strategies

Strategy process	Risk orientation (outside-in)	Identity orientation (inside-out)	Open system orientation (integrated)
Consultation	Issue-based dialogue to ascertain to the expectations and demands of external stakeholders	Internal dialogue to define the relevant ethical dilemmas and issues	Stakeholder dialogue to discuss the roles and responsibilities of all the parties involved
Integration	Initiating and maintaining projects related to the identified risks, even when this conflicts with short-term goals	Active involvement all employees to make CSR concrete for all functions in the organization	Integrating values in the core processes to make the CSR strategy relevant for the whole value chain
Justification	Acting and communicating effectively in the event of transgressions	Use of personal stories and experiences to strengthen employees' pride and commitment	Monitoring success according to economic, social and environmental criteria throughout the value chain

The identification of different strategies for CSR offers alternatives to the cyclical process presented in Figure 10.1. This has important implications for the development of collective CSR competences: in order to stay in line with changing stakeholder demands and business requirements the composition and quality of the organization's resources and competences must be constantly monitored and existing competences realigned with newly required ones (Teece *et al.*, 1997). In the case study companies, CSR required the redirection of certain competences that already existed in the company. This should be taken into account by managers when developing an agenda for CSR. Based on the above points we propose a six-step model for the development of collective competences for CSR:

- *Step 1: determine the importance of the individual CSR strategies.* This step focuses on the relevance of the three strategies for CSR: a risk orientation, an identity orientation and an open-system orientation. Most organizations have one dominant strategy but the others may be appropriate in certain parts of the organization or for certain issues.
- *Step 2: identify the competences developed during the consultation, integration and justification process.* The list of competences presented in the subsection on identifying collective competences can function as a checklist for this step.
- *Step 3: determine which new competences should be prioritized.* CSR is subject to external changes that affect many parts of the organization. Therefore, the development of CSR competences can best be viewed as a continuous learning process during which gradual improvements are made. Although

there may be many new challenges only a limited number of competences can be prioritized.

- *Step 4: evaluate performance against stakeholders' reactions.* In this step the actions of the organization are evaluated to see whether they have produced in the desired reactions from stakeholders. Depending on the strategy adopted these stakeholders may be internal, external or present in the entire production and consumption chain.
- *Step 5: adjust, strengthen and anchor the competences developed.* In order to preserve the developed competences they should be anchored in the structure, culture and environment of the organization. In this way, the development of CSR can become irreversible.
- *Step 6: periodically evaluate whether more emphasis should be placed on one other CSR strategy.* In line with social and organizational developments, new stakeholders and stakeholder issues will emerge over time. Therefore it might become necessary for an organization to change from an identity orientation to a risk or open system orientation. If this is the case, then new competences will become important and must be addressed, as in steps 2 to 5.

Final remarks

Throughout this chapter we have emphasized that learning to become socially responsible is a strategic process that requires fundamental organizational changes. It requires a willingness to move beyond the borders of the organization in order to engage in new relationships, to be alert to new issues that might lie outside the production and consumption chain, and to design new strategies and deploy them in day-to-day operations. All this cannot be accomplished in one step, which is why the focus of this chapter has been on the gradual of the development of the competences required to face emerging challenges.

Although the competences needed for CSR are ultimately based on individual actions, we have stressed that the learning process requires collective competences because:

- CSR is anchored in a specific organizational identity.
- Organizational units have to cooperate in order to become more responsible.
- Individuals have to be aware that their actions constitute organizational actions.
- Corporate accountability requires an organization, as a collective entity, to be willing to bear corporate responsibility.

These four requirements lie at the heart the strategic process of developing CSR competences and diffusing them throughout the organization. As it can be difficult for organizations to make their way through this learning process. We have offered a process model and a list of relevant competences. Our empirical research has shown that this list is reasonably comprehensive, but depending on the organization's orientation towards CSR and the stage of development of the organization, certain process competences will at times be more relevant than others.

Another topic addressed in this chapter is whether competence management, which nowadays is used as a management tool in many organizations, is of value when developing collective CSR competences. We conclude that competence management can be of some use in learning to become responsible because it can link strategic choices to individual tasks. However, if organizations wish to use competence management for CSR purposes the existing competences should be expanded to include CSR-specific competences based on the defining organizational values.

Furthermore, competence management should never be used as the sole instrument for developing collective CSR competences. Besides establishing links between strategic choices and individual tasks, organization-wide CSR requires action in other areas, such as developing a shared understanding of the identity of the organization, fulfilling the necessary preconditions for responsible behaviour in the respect of information exchange, the allocation of suitable resources and an appropriate division of tasks, formal responsibilities and areas of authority.

Collective competences can be developed by means of appropriate instruments. Our empirical research has shown that organizations use a variety approaches, instruments and tools to develop process competences for CSR. Further research could be conducted to identity specific configurations of instruments that would be suitable for tackling the ongoing challenge of learning to be more responsible.

Note

1. This chapter stems from a project that is currently being conducted by a consortium of researchers from the University of Twente, the University of Nijmegen and Nyenrode University (all in the Netherlands). It is part of a research programme on CSR by the Dutch Ministry of Economic Affairs. The purpose of the project is to identify strategies, mechanisms and instruments that organizations can employ to develop CSR. Particular attention is paid to the question of how organizations can ensure that CSR is not a one-off endeavour, but becomes relevant throughout the organization. The empirical part of the research consists of in-depth case studies of four Dutch companies. The knowledge gathered from these companies and the theoretical debate among the researchers have guided the writing of this chapter.

References

Amit, R. and P. J. H. Schoemaker (1993) 'Strategic assets and organisational rent', *Strategic Management Journal*, 14, pp. 33–46.

Asch, S. E. (1952) *Social Psychology* (Englewood Cliffs, NJ: Prentice-Hall).

Bovens, M. A. P. (1990) *Verantwoordelijkheid en Organisatie; beschouwingen over Aansprakelijkheid, Institutioneel Burgerschap en Ambtelijke Ongehoorzaamheid* (Zwolle: Tjeenk Willink).

Cohen, D. and L. Prusak (2001) *In Good Company. How Social Capital Makes Organisations Work* (Boston, Mass.: Harvard Business School Press).

De Bruijn, T. and A. Nijhof (2004) *Partnerships for CSR: Dream Wish or Necessity?* (Hong Kong: Greening of Industries Network).

De Bruijn, T. and A. Tukker (2002) *Partnership and Leadership* (Dordrecht: Kluwer).

De Leede, J., A. H. J. Nijhof and O. A. M. Fisscher (1999) 'The myth of self-managing teams: a reflection on the allocation of responsibilities between individuals, teams and the organisation; *Journal of Business Ethics*, 21, pp. 203–15.

Donaldson, T. J. and L. Preston (1995) 'The stakeholder theory of the corporation: Concepts, evidence, and implications', *Academy of Management Review*, 20, pp. 65–91.

Dreyfus, L. and S. E. Dreyfus (1992) 'What is Moral Maturity? Towards a Phenomology of Ethical Expertise', in Ogilvy, J. (ed.), *Revisioning Philosophy* (New York: State University of New York Press).

Eisenhardt, K. M. (1989) 'Building Theories from Case-Study Research', *Academy of Management Review*, 14, pp. 532–50.

Elkington, J. (1999) *'Cannibals with Forks: The Triple Bottom Line of 21st Century Business* (Oxford: Capstone).

French, P. A. (1984) *Collective and Corporate Responsibility* (New York: Columbia University Press).

Hartman, C. L., E. R. Stafford and M. J. Polonsky (2000) 'Environmental NGO–Business collaboration and strategic bridging: a case, analysis of the Greenpeace–foron alliance, *Business Strategy and Environment*, March/April, pp. 122–35.

Hoekstra, H. and E. van Sluijs (2003) *Competence Management* (Assen: van Gorcum).

Holmes, R. and P. Watts (1999) *Corporate Social Responsibility: Meeting Changing Expectations* (Geneva: WBCSD).

Jonas, H. (1984) *The Imperative of Responsibility: In search of an Ethics for the Technological Age* (London: Chicago Press).

Jonker, J. and M. Schoemaker (2004) *Developing CSR as an Organisational Value* (Nijmegen: Radboud University).

Kaptein, M. (1998) *Ethics Management: Auditing and Developing the Ethical Content of Organisations* (Dordrecht: Kluwer).

Karssing, E. (2000) *Morele Competentie in Organisaties* (Assen: van Gorcum).

Lenk, H. (1992) *Zwischen Wissenschaft und Ethik* (Frankfurt am Main: Suhrkamp Verlag).

Lévêque, F. (ed.) (1996) *Environmental Policy in Europe: Industry, Competition and the Policy Process*, (Cheltenham: Brookfield).

Nijhof, A. (1999) *Met zorg besluiten* (*Decision Making with Care*) (Enschede: University Press).

Nijhof, A. and O. Fisscher (2001) 'Unravelling morally responsible behaviour; A process model for developing ethics programs', paper presented at the Production and Environmental Management Conference, Nijmegen.

Roome, N. (2001) 'Policies and Conditions for Environmental Innovation and Management in Industry', paper presented at the International Conference on Environmental Innovation Systems, Garmisch-Partenkirchen, 27–9 September.

Sandelands, L. E. and R. E. Stablein (1987) 'The Concept of Organisation Mind', in S. Bacharach and N. DiTomaso (eds), *Research in the Sociology of Organisations* (Greenwich, CT: JAI Press), pp. 135–61.

Schoemaker, M. (2003a) 'Identity in Flexible Organisations: Experiences in Dutch Organisations', *Creativity and Innovation Management*, 12 (4), pp. 191–201.

Schoemaker, M. (ed.) (2003b) *Jaarboek Personeelsmanagement 2004* (Alphen a/d Rijn: Kluwer).

Schoemaker, M. and J. Jonker (2004) 'Managing intangible assets', *Journal of Management Development*.

SER (2001) *Corporate Social Responsibility: A Dutch Approach* (Assen: van Gorcum).

Teece, D. J., G. Pisano and A. Schven (1997) 'Dynamic Capabilities and Strategic Management', *Strategic Management Journal*, 18(7), pp. 509–33.

Thompson, D. (1988) 'Ascribing Responsibility to Advisors in Government', in *Ethical Issues in Professional Life* (New York: Oxford University Press).

Van der Heijden, B. I. J. M. (1998) *The Measurement and Development of Professional Expertise throughout the Career. A Retrospective Study among Higher Level Dutch Professionals'* (Enschede: PrintPartners Ipskamp).

Van der Heijden, B. I. J. M. and A. Nijhof (2004) 'The value of subjectivity; problems and prospects for 360-degree appraisal systems', *International Journal of Human Resource Management*, 15, pp. 493–511.

Van Riel, C. (1995) *Principles of Corporate Communication* (Harlow: Prentice-Hall).

World Business Council for Sustainable Development (WBCSD) (2001) *Sustainability through the Market: Seven Keys to Success* (Geneva: WBCSD).

Weaver, G. R., L. K. Trevino and P. L. Cochran (1999) 'Corporate Ethics Programs as Control Systems: Influences of Executive Commitment and Environmental Factors', *Academy of Management Journal*, pp. 41–57.

Weick, K. E. and K. H. Roberts (1993) 'Collective Mind in Organisations; Heedful inter-relating on Flight Decks', *Administrative Science Quarterly*, 38pp.

Wempe, J. (1998) 'Market and Morality: Business Ethics and the Dirty and Many Hands Dilemma', unpublished thesis, Erasmus University, Rotterdam.

Werhane, P. H. (1985) *Persons, Rights and Corporations* (Englewood Cliffs, NJ: Prentice-Hall).

11

Standards for Corporate Social Responsibility

Math Göbbels

Introduction

Since the Second World War organizations have increasingly been subject to strong social pressure to account for the adverse consequences of their activities as profit-seeking corporations. This development, *inter alia* referred to as corporate social responsibility (CSR), has resulted in organizations and industries being held directly responsible for their actions and any damage caused to society. Because of these developments many organizations have been compelled to consider a more socially acceptable way of doing business. Against the background of the less prescriptive role of national governments, society and its international representatives – governmental organizations such as the UN and non-governmental organizations such as Greenpeace and Oxfam – are urging corporations to take action.

The growing attention to CSR and the parallel emergence of numerous institutions specializing in the matter have resulted in a considerable number of diverse initiatives. Codes of conduct, education and training, stakeholder dialogue and sustainability reporting are amongst the many examples of what is offered in the CSR field. This chapter deals with the emergence of one specific type of CSR initiative that is generally referred to as CSR standards. Recent examples include SA8000, AA1000, ISO 14001, the Global Reporting Initiative, the United Nation's Global Compact and SIGMA. Earlier initiatives were the Caux Roundtable Principles for Business, the OECD Guidelines for Multinational Enterprises and the ILO's Fundamental Principles and Rights at Work. Based on several studies (OECD, 1999; Urminsky, 2000) the number of initiatives related to the standardization of CSR may – depending on the definition, term or scope used – amount to more than 300.

Although the standardization of CSR is a rather recent phenomenon, standards in general have existed for a long time and are widely accepted in today's society. Relics from ancient civilizations such as Babylon and early Egypt provide evidence that standardization was applied as many as seven thousand years ago. Some of the first forms of standardization were physical standards for weights and measures. Throughout the centuries more and more agreements were reached on measurements, symbols, signals, means of payment, trials and conduct. By the turn of the twentieth century standardization was flourishing, and it has now developed to the point where it is intrinsic to the workings of society. It has extended far beyond its original industrial focus and now includes areas such as consumer safety, occupational health and a myriad of others, all of which serve to improve the quality and comfort of everyday life.

According to Standards Australia (2002), standardization and standards have, in part due to globalization and the related need for additional arrangements, become an integral part of economic, social and legal systems. Brunsson and Jacobsson (2000, p. 21) note that 'without standardisation the world would look quite different, and co-ordination would be much more difficult. Standards facilitate contact, co-operation, and trade over large areas and even throughout the world'. As de Vries (1999, p. 3) puts it, standardization functions 'a lubricant for modern industrial society'. Its role is so taken for granted and deeply rooted in our daily life that we tend to forget its significance for the development of, for example, telecommunications and the internet. According to Brunsson and Jacobsson (2000) standards flourish for common activities such as playing football, withdrawing money from an ATM machine, using a personal computer and a variety of other activities that need rules to facilitate convenience in one way or another. Nowadays not only technical and tangible objects are standardized but also organizations and the way they are expected to behave. Examples include the standards laid down by the International Standards Organization (ISO) for quality and environmental management systems (ISO 9001/14001). CSR can be regarded as the latest area in which an attempt is being made to set general standards.

The neglected debate

As is the case with the development of CSR as a phenomenon, the debate on CSR standards is characterized by a normative emphasis on their importance for organizations. Absent, however, is a substantive debate on the assumptions that underlie the standardization of CSR. In this section these assumptions are introduced and briefly discussed. The factors associated with these assumptions can be viewed as taken-for-granted ideas about the nature of CSR standards and therefore will not be elaborated upon in this chapter.

Assumption 1: definitions of CSR standards are taken for granted

In addition to the sources mentioned above, various publications provide extensive lists of CSR standardization initiatives (Goodell, 1999; BSR, 2000; Williams, 2000; Jamal, 2001; COPOLCO, 2002; European Commission, 2003; Leipziger, 2003; WBCSD and AccountAbility, 2004; Abrahams, 2004;

see also Appendix 11.1). Many of these examples are often presented or interpreted as CSR standards, which implies that it is clear what a CSR standard is. However, it is questionable whether this is correct since there are also, in addition to the term 'standard', references to norms, rules, agreements, guidelines and codes. Intuitively, many of the abovementioned lists include not only CSR standards but also instruments, tools, techniques and frameworks related to CSR.

Despite the assertion that the definitional aspect has been neglected in the debate on CSR standards, many of the classical definitions of a standard seem to provide evidence of some commonality. In his study of standardization processes de Vries (1999, pp. 143–63) reviews many of these definitions and refers to a standard as a 'limited set of solutions to actual or potential matching problems, directed at benefits for the party or parties involved, balancing their needs and intending and expecting that these solutions will be repeatedly or continuously used, over a certain period, by a substantial number of the parties for whom they are meant'. A little differently, Standards Australia (2000, p. 2) defines a standard as a 'published document, which sets out specifications and procedures designed to ensure that a material, product, method or service is fit for its purpose and consistently performs the way it was intended to'. A standard is often regarded as something laid down in a document, produced by one or more parties with the objective of regulating something that is thought to need regulating. The problem is that the term standard is often used interchangeably with terms such as guideline, code, code of conduct, principle, statement and approach. For example Urminsky's (2000) definition of a code of conduct actually refers to a business code of conduct, while his list of codes should intuitively be seen as CSR standards. Leipziger (2003, p. 35) uses the collective term 'voluntary corporate responsibility instruments', which include 'principles, codes of conduct, standards, norms, guidelines and framework agreements'. She notes that there are still more types of instrument but her concern is only with 'documents that guide behaviour'. The term standard is also confused with the term 'standardization', which refer to the process that results in a standard, and with the verb to standardize or to make objects or activities of the same type have the same features or qualities.

Despite some degree of commonality in respect of what a standard is the application of classical definitions to the notion of CSR remains a problem. While most of the definitions refer to rather technical objects that can be standardized in a uniform way, the question is whether the same can be applied to rather diffuse and evolving notion such as CSR. For the purpose of this chapter, instead of talking in terms of a CSR standard it would be better to use the term CSR standardization initiative to refer to the variety of initiatives that are usually presented as a CSR standard. However, both terms will be used interchangeably.

Assumption 2: CSR can be standardized

In the CSR debate few people seem to question the combining of CSR with standardization; as the two notions seem to be reconcilable with each other. However, can a phenomenon such as CSR, which by definition varies in different situations due to the diversity of organizations and their stakeholders, be standardized at all? According to Leipziger (2003, p. 37) 'the term "standard" implies that companies can and should achieve a uniform output.... Given the significant differences between companies, arising from sectoral, regional, cultural and historical differences, it is unlikely that standardisation is possible or even desirable.' Theoretically it is rather doubtful that CSR can be standardized in the traditional sense of establishing uniformity. Given the contingent nature of CSR, which is always dependent on its context it does not seem to lend itself to standardization. Perhaps the standardization of CSR should be seen in terms of providing organizations with appropriate guidance on practically and instrumentally dealing with CSR or aspects of it. No one standard, with the exception of technical standards, is able to cover the broad range of social and stakeholder issues and how to deal with them. Therefore the attempt by the ISO to develop a world standard for corporate social responsibility is doomed to failure because it will generate a document that is so generic that individual organizations, while agreeing with it, will not be able to use it for practical purposes.

Assumption 3: CSR standards are actually used

According to Brunsson and Jacobsson (2000, p. 6) standardization 'is based on the hope that some organisations ... will adhere to the standards concerned, or will at least consider doing so'. In addition the proliferation of standardization initiatives in the field of CSR gives the impression that these initiatives anticipate the needs and expectations of various stakeholders. Although the available figures show that CSR standards such as the Global Reporting Initiative and the Global Compact have been adopted and adhered to by many companies, they fail to provide clear evidence of which standards are actually used by organizations. Therefore further research is necessary to obtain empirical evidence of the actual use of CSR standards by organizations.

Assumption 4: CSR standards are desirable and useful for organizations

This chapter focuses on the final assumption in the debate on CSR standards, namely that CSR standards are desirable and useful. As far as desirability is concerned, it is notable that most CSR standards are produced by organizations that appear to be convinced that the corporate world is standing in line for their standardization initiatives. According to Leipziger (2003, p. 2) 'there are millions of pages and web pages written on codes and standards, but most of it is "spin" put out by organisations punting to sell their code or standard'.

Just because proposed CSR standards are quickly distributed throughout the business world, this does not necessarily mean that they meet the requirements of the corporations at which they are primarily targeted. It is still not clear whether standardization institutions produce their standards with the demands and expectations of future users in mind.

Most works on standardization portray it as providing various advantages for companies. According to Leipziger, however, 'many of the best code of conduct and standards ... are not well known and ... some corporate responsibility instruments that are well disseminated are not terribly effective' (ibid., p. 20). Although some studies have been conducted in this field (for example Williams, 2000), there is little information on the extent to which CSR standardization initiatives are useful in terms of providing practical solutions. The findings so far are not encouraging. The experience of organizations that use ISO 9001:2000 as the basis of their quality management system shows that such standards are often counterproductive. Leipziger refers to this as the code paradox: 'that it is possible to have comprehensive codes of conduct that achieve nothing and quite vague codes of conduct that are well embedded in the organisation and that foster innovation and change' (ibid.)

Criteria for CSR standards

In this section the main focus is on the assumption that CSR standards are useful for organizations. In order to analyze this assumption it is necessary to ascertain companies' criteria for using a CSR standard. Such criteria have been partially identified by researchers, and others emerged from multistakeholder discussions during a conference held by the International Standards Organization (ISO) in June 2004 on the question of whether it was feasible to develop a world standard for social responsibility. Representatives from labour, industry, consumer groups, governments and NGOs took part in several discussions on whether or not to proceed with the development of a new CSR standard. When drawing up a list of criteria that would meet the requirements and expectations of organizations the focus was primarily on industry.

Two categories of criteria for CSR standards have been defined. The first concerns the aspects of CSR that should fall within the scope of CSR standards and therefore form part of their content:

- Assessment of CSR risks: a CSR standard should deal with the notion of risk, especially when it concerns CSR.*
- Stakeholders: a CSR standard should deal with the identification of and dialogue with stakeholders.
- Determination of (relevant) CSR activities: A CSR standard should deal with the question of which measures an organization should employ to deal with CSR.*

- Establishment of support for and awareness of CSR: a CSR standard should deal with the question of how support for and awareness of CSR can be brought about an organization.*
- Implementation of CSR: a CSR standard should deal with the question of how to implement CSR.*
- Accountability mechanisms: a CSR standard should deal with accountability mechanisms such as measuring, monitoring, evaluating, reporting and external verification.
- External comparison/benchmarking of CSR performance: a CSR standard should deal with the possibility of benchmarking the CSR performance of individual companies or across sectors and industries.
- Continuous improvement of CSR: a CSR standard should deal with the continuous improvement of CSR.
- Information on the meaning of CSR: a CSR standard should provide background information on the notion of CSR, its rationale and relevance for an organization.*
- Context-specificity: a CSR standard should allow room for a context-specific approach to CSR. That is, the standard should allow for differences in size, life cycle, sector, national culture and so on.*

The aspects marked with an asterisk emerged from the multistakeholder discussions during the ISO Conference in 2004. The others derive from the vast body of literature on the contemporary meaning of CSR.

The second category deals with the types of CSR standard required by organizations in respect of regulating the aspects of CSR listed above. The multistakeholder discussions revealed that organizations wish to have some degree of freedom. In some areas an organization only requires general guidance, but in others a more prescriptive standard may be required. This conforms to Robin *et al.*'s (1989) concept of different forms of code design. According to Post (2000, pp. 113–14) 'codes vary in terms of the type of guidance provided (rule-based or value-based) and the degree of guidance (low specificity to high specificity) regarding conduct'. Organizations' preferences depend on the nature of their business, and – more specifically on their competitive and institutional interests.

Based on Robin *et al.*'s (1989) framework and the results of the multistakeholder discussions, the following ways of regulating CSR through a standard appear to be relevant:

- The CSR aspect is mentioned but a standard is not prescribed.
- The CSR aspect is mentioned and a standard is prescribed, but in a limited way (descriptive or explanatory).
- The CSR aspect is only covered by general guidelines and there is room for discretion by organizations.
- The CSR aspect is covered by guidelines on and requirements for processes followed when implementing CSR.

- The CSR aspect is covered by guidelines on and requirements for a suitable management system. This often consists of mechanisms for the PDCA cycle: plan (policy and objectives), do (operational processes), check (measuring, monitoring or auditing) and act (continuous improvement).
- Practical tools and techniques are provided for the CSR aspect in terms of organizing and implementing CSR or aspects of it, for example stakeholder dialogue.
- Prescriptive requirements are set for the CSR aspect, including what an organization must do when dealing with CSR. There is limited room for manoeuvre.
- Performance requirements are set for the CSR aspect in respect of output.

Other criteria for CSR standards, such as the structure and consistency of language, are not included here as they would have required additional research that beyond the scope of the project.

Research results

The study consisted of content research and it was therefore necessary to operationalize the various criteria and develop a method of scoring. Details of this can be found in Appendix 11.1.

From the total number of CSR standardization initiatives (Appendix 11.2) ten were selected for detailed study. The main criteria for selection were their explicit reference as a CSR standard and its assumed familiarity in the business world. Both known ones and less familiar ones were chosen. Appendix 11.3 provides a short description of each of these.

Table 11.1 shows the quantitative results of the analysis. These relate to the extent to which each of the CSR standardization initiatives complies with the criteria listed in the previous section 3. Ideally Table 11.1 should be read in conjunction with Appendix 11.1, which also explains the scoring. In essence a standard can be deemed good it covers all the CSR aspects presented above. However, much depends on the specific purpose of using the standard so there will be variations among companies. The same goes for the way in which a standard is used to regulate the various CSR aspects. Some companies prefer it to be strict or practical, while others prefer general guidelines with considerable room for discretion.

AccountAbility 1000:1999 Framework (AA1000:1999)

AA1000:1999 is the only initiative that meets all the criteria. Most of the standards are more than general guidelines, provide more than just a framework and are elaborated in terms of processes for CSR. The identification of stakeholders and the implementation of CSR require practical methods and techniques, but CSR can be adjusted to the context in question.

Table 11.1 The quantitative results of the study

Aspect of CSR	AA1000: 1999	AA1000: 2002	ECS 2000	ECSF	GRI	OECD	Q-RES	SA8000	SIGMA	UN Global Compact
Assessment of CSR risks	4	1	1	–	3	1	3	–	4/5/6	1
Identification of and dialogue with stakeholders	3/4/6	1/3	1	1	3	1	3	2	4/5/6	1
Determination of (relevant) CSR activities	3/4	–	2	2	3	–	3	–	4/5/6	–
Establishment of support for and awareness for CSR	2	–	3	1	–	1	3	3	4/5/6	1
Implementation of CSR	4/6	–	5	6	6	3	4	5/7	4/5/6	–
Accountability mechanisms	3/4	3	1/3	1/6	5	1/3	3/4	2/3	4/5/6	1
External comparison/ benchmarking of CSR performance	3/4	1	–	–	1	–	–	–	–	–
Continuous improvement of CSR performance	3/4	–	2	–	1	2	3	2	4/5/6	–
Information on the meaning of CSR	2	2	–	3	3	1	3	2	3	3
Context-specificity	3	2	2	1	2	1	2	2	3	1

Notes: The scores in table refer to the following:
1: the CSR aspect is mentioned but a standard is not prescribed.
2: the CSR aspect is mentioned and a limited standard is prescribed in (descriptive or explanatory).
3: guidelines with room for discretion are provided for the CSR aspect.
4: guidelines/requirements are provided for CSR processes.
5: guidelines/requirements are provided for a management system for the CSR aspect.
6: practical tools and techniques are provided for the CSR aspect.
7: prescriptive requirements are set for the CSR aspect.
8: performance requirements are set for the CSR aspect.

AccountAbility 1000:2002 Assurance Standard (AA1000:2002)

AA1000:2002 is the successor to AA1000:1999 but it meets fewer criteria and cannot be viewed as an improvement. No attention is paid to the processes of establishing and implementing a CSR strategy. The standards take the form of general guidelines and for some of the criteria these lack detail: assessment of CSR risks, is identification of stakeholders and (external) comparison of CSR performance. Moreover, it pays limited attention to context-specificity.

Ethics Compliance Standard 2000 (ECS2000)

ECS2000 covers most of the CRS aspects and the implementation of CSR is covered in detail. The identification of stakeholders is not mentioned but dialogue with stakeholders is. This is odd as the latter implies the former. One of the objectives of ECS2000 is continuous improvement, but this is not covered in detail. The same applies to context-specificity.

European Corporate Sustainability Framework (ECSF)

Three of the CRS aspects are not mentioned in the ECSF of those which are, not all are covered in detail. A positive point is the ECSF's attention to the identification of CSR activities and their implementation. The measurement and monitoring of CSR performance (accountability mechanism) also receive a lot of attention. However, stakeholder engagement and reporting, are almost ignored and there is only slight attention to organizations being of different size or from different sectors.

Global Reporting Initiative (GRI)

The name Global Reporting Initiative implies that only reporting and accounting are covered, but many other aspects are included, such as the design and implementation of CSR. It provides a general outline of CSR and its underlying trends and drivers, although attention is paid to continuous improvement by only mentioning the term and to the creation of awareness of CSR. Most of the CRS aspects are covered in detail. Interesting by GRI explicitly refers to the following:

The guidelines do not:

- provide instructions for designing an organisation's internal data management and reporting systems; or
- offer instruction on methodologies for preparing reports, or on performance monitoring and verification practices.

Therefore the GRI, does not give instructions for the monitoring and verification of reporting applications but instead concentrates on concrete reporting systems.

OECD Guidelines

At first glance the OECD Guidelines look good, but closer examination shows that most of the CRS aspects are sparsely covered. Exceptions are the implementation and reporting of CSR, but even these are not subject to strict standards. There is no elaboration of aspects such as stakeholder involvement, CSR risks and awareness of CSR. Because there are no explicit guidelines for organizing and implementing CSR, the OECD Guidelines can best be used to evaluate the importance given to CSR key organizations.

Quality of the Social and Ethical Responsibility of Corporations (Q-RES)

Q-RES is one of the most comprehensive initiatives. Eight of the CRS aspects are covered by requirements or guidelines in respect of CSR processes and systems, as well as related tools and techniques Most of the aspects are distinctly defined and there are standards for function, content, development methodology, auditing evidence and excellence criteria. The external benchmarking of CSR performance, however, receives no attention. Central to Q-RES is continuous improvement, for which general guidelines are provided but no practical tools or techniques.

Social Accountability 8000 (SA8000)

SA8000 is a limited initiative in terms of size and content. Many of the CRS aspects are mentioned but only briefly discussed. The only aspect that is covered in detail is the implementation of CSR, for which requirements and guidelines for a management system are provided.

Sustainability Integrated Guidelines for Management (SIGMA)

SIGMA seems to be top of the bill, although two of the CRS aspects are not addressed: external benchmarking of CSR performance and accountability mechanisms. All the other aspects are covered in detail. The instruments provided with sigma the so-called 'SIGMA toolkit', add value to the guidelines and requirements by and offering practical tools and techniques.

UN Global Compact

It is difficult to assess the objective of the UN Global Compact. It is really only useful to those who wish to gain an insight into the nature of CSR because detailed information is provided on the meaning of CSR. The other aspects are barely mentioned. Various sector-specific documents with specific guidance on CSR implementation have been added to the Global Compact, but these were not available at the time of this assessment.

Conclusions

CSR initiatives come in many shapes and sizes and vary in purpose, target groups and issues. Most of the documents that are referred to as CSR standards, such as the Global Sullivan Principles and the Caux Round Table Principles, cannot be regarded as offering regulatory frameworks as they merely tell organizations that it is important to deal with CSR or aspects of it.

Of the CSR standardization initiatives that were researched for this chapter only four meet the criteria for CSR standards: AA1000:1999, ECS2000, Q-RES and SIGMA. These can be called true CSR standards as they contain clear methodological principles and subsequent translation of these principles into practical elements. They also pay attention to the design and organization of CSR and the need for interaction with stakeholders, both of which are important elements of today's conception of CSR. There are differences between the initiatives however. For example, AA1000 mainly focuses on processes that are important when organizing and implementing CSR, while SIGMA provides practical tools and techniques for CSR.

Overall, it can be concluded that the familiar names in the world of CSR standards are failing to meet the requirements and expectation of organizations.

Appendix 11.1   Operationalization of criteria for CSR standards

Criteria for CSR standardization initiatives	Operationalization on the basis of synonyms/search terms
Assessment of CSR risks	Risk assessment Risk analysis Risk management
Identification of and dialogue with stakeholders	Recognize Track Identify Understand Inclusivity, inclusiveness Stakeholder(s), interested party(ies) Respond to the aspirations and needs of stakeholders Respond to stakeholder concerns Stakeholder engagement Stakeholder commitment Stakeholder involvement Stakeholder consultation Dialogue Communication Participation Inform Respond to Stakeholder dialogue Views of stakeholders
Determination of (relevant) CSR activities	CSR targets CSR strategy CSR vision CSR process CSR approach

Continued

Appendix 11.1   Continued

Criteria for CSR standardization initiatives	Operationalization on the basis of synonyms/search terms
Establishment of support for and awareness of CSR	Creating trust
	Creating understanding
	Awareness
	Training
Implementation of CSR	Use
	Apply
	Implement
	Activities
	Enforce
Accountability mechanisms	Evaluation
	Auditing
	Monitoring
	Indicators
	Parameters
	Criteria
	Parameters
	Targets
	Indicators
	Conformity assessment
	CSR performance
	Reporting
	Inform
	External communication
	Records
	External reporting
	To account for
	Accountability
	Demonstrate
	Evidence
	External verification
External comparison/benchmarking of CSR performance	Quantification
	Benchmarking
	Comparability (against)
	Comparability (over time/against)
Continuous improvement of CSR performance performance	Continuous improvement
	Internal auditing
	Evaluation
	Monitoring
Information on the meaning of CSR	Definition of CSR
	Scope of the standard
	Background and origins of CSR
	The 'business case' behind CSR (motives and drivers, both positive and negative)
Context-specificity	Context-specific (country, social background, geography, culture, issue etc.)

Continued

Appendix 11.1   Continued

Criteria for CSR standardization initiatives	Operationalization on the basis of synonyms/search terms
	Sector-specific (chemical, toys, clothing etc.) Organization-specific Organization size Organizational life cycle Depending on: level of, if relevant, if any

Notes: The scores awarded for the first nine criteria are as follows:

1: the CSR aspect is mentioned but a standard is not prescribed.

2: the CSR aspect is mentioned and a limited standard prescribed (by definition, description or explanation).

3: general guidelines with room for discretion are provided for the CSR aspect.

4: guidelines/requirements are provided for CSR processes.

5: guidelines/requirements are provided for a CSR management system (PDCA cycle).

6: practical tools and techniques (or references to these) are provided for the CSR aspect.

7: prescriptive requirements are set for the CSR aspect.

8: performance requirements (output requirements in general or output requirements with a minimum level) are set for the CSR aspect.

The scores of the final criterion are as follows:

1: the CSR aspect is implicitly dealt with.

2: the CSR aspect is dealt with but only a limited standard is prescribed.

3: the CSR aspect is dealt with and a clear standard is prescribed.

Appendix 11.2   CSR standardization initiatives

AA1000	EFQM Model
AENOR, Draft Standards, Management System	EOA ISO Business Conduct Management Systems
BNQ's CSR-Human Resources, Donations, Sponsorship- Certification Protocol	FTSE4, Good UK Corporate Responsibility Investment Index Series
BR, Table Principles of Corporate Governance	Global Reporting Initiative (GRI) Global Sullivan Principles
Caux Principles	Greenhouse Gas Protocol
CERES Principles	Guidelines for Environmental Records Management
Corporate Environmental Reporting	
CSR Europe, Communicating CSR	ICC, Business Charter for Sustainable Development
Draft Australian Standard 03025	
Draft Australian Standard 03026	ICC, Rules of Conduct to Combat Extortion and Bribery
Draft Australian Standard 03027	
Draft Australian Standard 03028	ICCR, Principles for Global Corporate Responsibility
Draft Australian Standard 03029	
Dutch Quality Award Model	ICCR, Global Codes of Conduct
ECS 2000, Ethical Compliance Management	ICFTU, Basic Code of Labour Practice
Ecumenical Council, Standard for Corporate Responsibility	IFPMM, Ethical Code

Continued

Appendix 11.2   Continued

ILO, Conventions on Core Labour Standards	Principles for Global Corporate Responsibility
INEM, Sustainability Reporting Guidelines	Q-Res Codes of Ethics
Investors in People	Responsible Business Initiative
ISO 9001:2000	SA8000
ISO 9004:2000	SI 10000
ISO 14001	SIGMA Project –
ISO 14063	Social Venture Network
ISO 19011 – Guidelines	Standards on CSR
OECD, Principles for Corporate Governance	Stakeholder Alliance Sunshine Standards
OHSAS 18001:1999 – Occupational Health and Safety	Sustainable Development Reporting, (New Zealand)
OHSAS 18001	TR Q0005
Principles for Global Corporate Responsibility, Benchmarks	UNCTAD Principles for the Control of Business Practices
	UN Global Compact
	World Bank, Group Corporate Governance Principles

Appendix 11.3   Description of selected CSR standardization initiatives

AccountAbility1000:1999 and AccountAbility1000:2002 (AA1000)

The London-based Institute of Social and Ethical Accountability (Account-Ability) developed AA1000, a set of principles for processing social and ethical accountability. It also provides guidelines for accountability processes such as planning, stakeholder engagement, auditing and reporting, and a guide to performing an audit on the use of child labour, corruption, charity and the testing of new products.

Ethics Compliance Standard 2000 (ECS2000)

The objective of ECS2000 is to enable organizations to identify illegal and unfair practices in their operations without the help of external systems or third parties. The ECS2000 is aimed at the establishing and documenting a system for legal compliance (also referred to as mechanisms of compliance). This system is used to identify and evaluate the legal requirements to which an organization must comply, and to establish an internal system for gathering the opinions and ideas of stakeholders in order to formulate internal norms and values and facilitate continuous improvement (also referred to as the mechanisms of enhancement).

European Corporate Sustainability Framework (ECSF)

The ECSF emerged from an international research project that took place between December 2001 and February 2004. It includes a model for the identification and implementation of complex management issues in the areas of sustainability, corporate responsibility and societal change.

Global Reporting Initiative (GRI)

The Global Reporting Initiative was founded by the United Nations Environmental Programme and CERES, a coalition of investment funds, environmental organizations and public groups. The goal of the GRI is to improve the quality, comparability and practicability of sustainability reporting. It brings together standards for sustainability reporting in a framework for economic, social and environmental reporting and is mainly targeted at large organizations. The primary objective of this reporting is to facilitate a continuous stakeholder dialogue, in which stakeholders are kept informed and behaviour and decisions are influenced. The GRI primarily is about guidelines for reporting and secondarily about interacting with stakeholders, based on the report.

Organization for Economic Cooperation and Development (OECD) Guidelines

The OECD Guidelines provide organizations with CSR recommendations that are in line with existing legislation. The OECD has three objectives:

- To establish the highest possible sustainable economic growth and employment in order to help the development of the world economy.
- To contribute to the economic development of both members and non-members.
- To contribute to the extension of world trade on a multilateral, non-discriminatory basis in line with international regulations.

Quality of the Social and Ethical Responsibility of Corporations (Q-RES)

Q-RES is an initiative by the Centre for Ethics, Law and Economics and is operated in association with business organizations, NGOs, the European Commision and SIGMA. Q-RES is a consequence of the need for the social and ethical performance of organizations to be made more credible. The initiative is based on a management system that derives from the relationship between organizations and their stakeholders. The central aim is to develop a process of continuous improvement, resulting in the establishment and implementation of instruments for corporate social responsibility within the organization. The focus is on:

- A corporate ethical vision.
- An ethical code of conduct.
- Training in ethics.
- Organizational systems for implementation and monitoring.
- A social and ethical accountability process.
- Independent verification.

Social Accountability 8000 (SA 8000)

The SA8000, initiated by the Council on Economic Priorities Accreditation Agency (CEPAA), is based on international agreements on human rights and labour laws, as defined in the ILO Conventions and the UN Universal Declaration of Human Rights. The SA8000 is a universal standard aimed at safeguarding the fundamental (social) rights of workers and employees worldwide. The standard requires the development of a management system that includes policies on and procedures for issues such as human rights. The standard is designed in such a way that adjustment to local laws and requirements is possible. The SA8000 includes a 'social management system' to facilitate compliance with requirements and make continuous improvement possible. This system covers processes such as planning, implementation and auditing.

Sustainability Integrated Guidelines for Management (SIGMA)

The SIGMA project was established by Forum for the Future, AccountAbility and the British Standards Institute. SIGMA provides guidelines for organizations that wish to operate sustainably. It consists of three parts:

- A set of guiding principles.
- A management framework for integrating sustainability into the core functions of the company.
- A toolkit.

The guiding principles are aimed at supporting organizations in their effort to deal with corporate responsibility and accountability. The management framework is based on the principle of continuous improvement and is aimed at embedding the SIGMA guidelines into the organization. The toolkit comprises a number of instruments and guidelines for implementing the guiding principles and for the support of more general aspects of CSR. The instruments specifically developed for SIGMA include stakeholder dialogue.

An important aspect of this initiative is integrating social, economic and environmental issues into the process of becoming a sustainable organization. The SIGMA project has drawn on a large number of other CSR standardization initiatives such as the GRI, the UN Global Compact, the OECD

Guidelines and the ISO standards. It has integrated agreements, guidelines and principles from these initiatives without excluding adaptation to an organization's context and specific situation. SIGMA can also be used to evaluate an organization's performance on sustainability and social accountability.

UN Global Compact

The UN Global Compact, an initiative by the United Nations, is targeted at human rights and labour issues. It consists of nine principles that are based on the Universal Declaration of Human Rights and the International Labour Organization's Fundamental Principles of Rights at Work. The aim of the Global Compact is to raise awareness of the implications of globalization and the related need for corporate responsibility and accountability. The initiative claims to be universally applicable and usable in a variety of situations.

References

Abrahams, D. (2004) *Regulating Corporations. A Resource Guide* (Geneva: UNRISD).

AccountAbility (1999) *AccountAbility 1000 (AA1000) Framework* (London: AccountAbility).

AccountAbility (2003) *Assurance Standard AA1000* (London: AccountAbility).

Brunsson, N. and B. Jacobsson (2000) *A World of Standards* (Oxford: Oxford University Press).

BSR (2000) *Comparison of Selected Corporate Social Responsibility-Related Standards* (San Francisco: BSR).

Centre for Ethics, Law and Economics (CELE) (2002) *The Q-RES Project. The Quality of the Social and Ethical Responsibility of Corporations. Guidelines for Management* (www.qres.it).

CEPAA (2001) *Social Accountability SA8000* (New York: CEPAA).

COPOLCO (2002) *The Desirability and Feasibility of ISO Corporate Social Responsibility Standards* (www.iso.org/wqsr).

ECSF (2004) *The European Corporate Sustainability Framework* (www.ecsf.info).

Egyedi, T. (1996) *Shaping Standardization. A Study of Standards Processes and Standards Policies in the Field of Telematic Services* (Delft: Delft University Press).

European Commission (2003) *Mapping Instruments for Corporate Social Responsibility* (Brussels: European Commission).

Goodell, E. (ed.) (1999) *Standards of Corporate Social Responsibility* (San Fransisco, CA: Social Venture Network).

GRI (2002) *Sustainability Reporting Guidelines. Boston: Global Reporting Initiative* (www.globalreporting.org).

Jamal, R. (2001) *USCIB Compendium of Corporate Responsibility Initiatives* (New York: Corporate Responsibility Working Group).

Jenkins, R. (2001) 'Corporate Codes of Conduct. Self-Regulation in a Global Economy', Technology, Business and Society Programme Paper, No. 2, April, United Nations Research Institute for Social Development.

Krechmer, K. (2000) 'The Fundamental Nature of Standards: Technical Perspective', *IEEE Comunications Magazine*, 38 (6), p. 7.

Leipziger, D. (2003) *The Corporate Responsibility Code Book* (Sheffield: Greenleaf).

OECD (1999) *Codes of Corporate conduct: An Inventory* (Paris: OECD).

OECD (2000) *The OECD Guidelines for Multinational Enterprises (revision 2000)* (Paris: OECD).

Post, J. E. (2000) 'Global Codes of Conduct: Activists, Lawyers and Managers in Search of a Solution', in O. F. Williams (ed.), *Global Codes of Conduct: An Idea whose Time Has Come* (Notre Dame, Ind.: University of Notre Dame Press).

Reitaku University (1999) *ECS2000. Ethics Compliance Standard 2000* (Kikarigaoka, Kashiwa (Japan): Reitaku Centre for Economic Studies).

Robin, D., M. Giallourakis, F. R. David and Th. E. Moritz (1989) 'A Different Look at Codes of Ethics', *Business Horizons*, Jan.–Feb., pp. 66–73.

Sigma Project (2003) *The Sigma Guidelines. Putting Sustainable Development into Practice – A Guide for Organizations* (www.projectsigma.com).

Standards Australia (2000) *Standards and Standardisation* (Sydney: Focus Press).

United Nations (2003) *Global Compact* (www.unglobalcompact.org).

Urminsky, M. (ed.) (2000) *Self-Regulation in the Workplace: Codes of Conduct, Social Labelling and Socially Responsible Investment* (Geneva: ILO).

Vries, H. de (1999) 'Standards for the Nation. Analysis of National Standardization Organizations', PhD dissertation, Erasmus University, Rotterdam, The Netherlands.

WBCSD and AccountAbility (2004) *Strategic Challenges for Business in the Use of Corporate Responsibility Codes, Standards, and Frameworks* (Geneva: WBCSD).

Williams, O. F. (ed.) (2000) *Global Codes of Conduct. An Idea Whose Time has Come* (Notre Dame, Ind.: University of Notre Dame Press).

Part III
Change and CSR

12

Implementing CSR: The Challenge of Change

Malcolm Higgs

Introduction

Previous chapters have explored the different lenses through which CSR can be viewed – that is, the philanthropical, compliance, structural and sense-making approaches. In this chapter we shall not revisit the discourses on these approaches. However, it is evident that if CSR is taken seriously by a business there will have to be fundamental and transformational changes to its core paradigms. What is increasingly evident is that CSR is a somewhat ill-defined and 'fuzzy' concept. It is a complex phenomenon and one that often emerges at the boundary of the business enterprise – that is, where the organization interacts with its stakeholders. It is also clear that the changes an emergent CSR agenda implies are difficult to manage, and there is growing evidence that a fundamental shift in the business paradigm cannot occur without a significant commitment by the leadership and a change in the focus and behaviour of leaders (Williams, 2002; Edelman, 2004). Given this it is important to reflect on how change can be implemented most effectively and the consequences for leaders.

Research has shown, that it is difficult successfully to effect change in organizations, and that many of the prescriptions for and approaches to change fail to deliver the required results. However, recent research (explored in this chapter) indicates that there are alternative ways of thinking about and approaching change, and that these frequently lead to more successful outcomes.

This chapter explores a range of approaches to change that those involved in introducing CSR in a systems or sense-making way may wish to consider. The intention is not to present a 'formula for success' or to be prescriptive. Rather it is to provide a framework for thinking about change that will enable leaders to make informed choices about their approach to introducing CSR as a business issue and in a way that embeds change in the business.

The chapter begins with a general review of thinking on and frameworks for change. It then explores leadership behaviours and the relative success of differing change and leadership approaches in a range of contexts. It concludes with a consideration of the implications of these issues when introducing CSR.

What we know about change

According to many authors, up to 70 per cent of change initiatives fail (Hammer and Champy, 1993; Kotter, 1998; Higgs and Rowland, 2000). However, there is a growing need for organizations to implement major change in order to respond to a business environment that is increasingly volatile and complex (Buchannan and Boddy, 1992). So what are the reasons for consistent failure, and what leads to success? This chapter explores these questions and presents empirical evidence on approaches to change that appear to be successful. It also examines the leadership behaviours that contribute to this success.

The failure to manage change is illustrated by Buchanan *et al.* (1999), who report the results of a survey that show that managers have neither the expertise nor the capacity to implement change successfully and that managing change according to textbook theory is difficult. Stacey (1996) argues that the prevailing theoretical paradigms are based on three assumptions: managers can choose successful mutations in advance of environmental changes; change is a linear process; and organizations are systems that tend towards a state of stable equilibrium. This paradigm has a long history, perhaps beginning with Lewin (1941), who proposed the classic three-stage model of the change process: unfreeze, mobilize, refreeze. The centrality of this 'mental model' is illustrated in Kotter's (1998) study of reasons for the failure of major transformational initiatives.

This view of change encompasses the assumptions that change, because of its linearity, is a relatively straightforward process and that it can (and should) be driven from the top of the organization and be implemented uniformly according to a detailed plan (Beckhard, 1969; Kotter, 1998; Hammer and Champy, 1999; Duck, 2000). Stacey (1996) challenges the assumption of linearity and suggests that change may in reality be a more complex process. This view is shared by others, whose approaches entail educating managers in a range of change theories and involving them more actively in the change process by equipping them with practical tools (Senge, 1997; Conner, 1999; Beer and Nohria, 2000). Although they see change as a more complex process, the scholars in this school retain the assumption that change can be implemented uniformly throughout the organization. However, this 'one look' approach has been widely challenged (see for example McGhanan and Porter, 1997) Empirical research has shown that strategic intent-led change programmes often have unpredictable outcomes that are generated by interactions within the network. Similarly, in the context of change to organizational culture Harris and Ogebonna (2002) present empirical evidence of the failure of top-down change and the impact of unexpected or unintended outcomes that result from interactions within the system.

Some have responded to this view by proposing an approach that, whilst retaining the assumption of linearity, recognizes the need for a more distributed view of the nature of change. Here the general direction of change is set at the top of the organization and agents throughout the organization are equipped with a range of 'change tools to use in pursuit of the overall goal' (Buchanan and Boddy, 1992; Senge, 1997; Pascale, 1999).

A framework for viewing change

From the above it is evident that the assumptions underlying change can be depicted as lying on two axes, one of which is concerned with the complexity of change and the other with the extent to which change can be effected on a uniform basis or is more widely distributed as an activity. Figure 12.1 summarizes the way in which the various streams of literature map onto these dimensions.

A detailed analysis of the work of these authors allows the development of a model of approaches to change (Figure 12.2). The present author, working with colleagues from a change consulting firm, has undertaken qualitative research at seven organizations to explore the relevance and applicability of

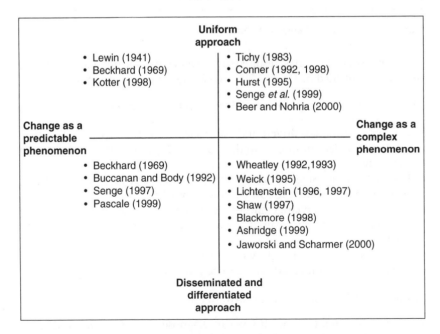

Figure 12.1   Map of the approaches to change in the literature

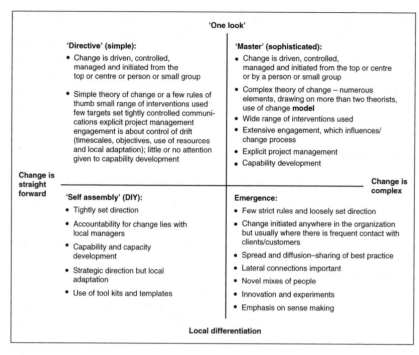

Figure 12.2 The RFLC change quadrant

this framework. This has resulted in a somewhat clearer picture of the approaches outlined in Figure 12.2 and can be summarized as follows:

Directive: change is straightforward and can be managed ('one look'):

- Change is initiated, driven and controlled from the top or centre by a small group (determining both the 'what' and the 'how'); the information flow is mainly one way.
- Leadership is decisive and unwavering; the leaders believe that they know best and others should follow ('you're in or you're out').
- Simple theories of change/chosen 'recipes' with predictable programmed phases and check lists are used; it is assumed that change is sequential and predictable.
- Project management is tightly controlled to avoid 'drift'.
- Little attention is focused on organizational capability development.

Self-assembly: change is straightforward and needs local differentiation:

- Change is straightforward if you can diagnose what is needed and select the best tool and processes to implement it.

- Tightly set central strategic change direction (the 'what'); local managers accountable for implementation; flexibility and adaptation are encouraged.
- Developing the capability to understand and apply the change work is important, but not difficult.
- Extensive use of toolkits and templates/manuals for change implementation.
- Fixes 'parts' and 'bits' of the organization; a fragmented approach and not necessarily systemic.

Master: change is complex but can be managed ('one look'):

- Change is seen not as a linear and predictable process but as complex and difficult to implement.
- It is believed that 'the solution is within us' so there is use of dialogue and engagement; open to shifts based on input; resistance is to be expected and managed.
- Initiated, driven and controlled from the top or centre by a small group; conducted as a programme of managed activity with monitoring and diagnosis.
- Pilots are conducted and then expanded throughout the system; delays occur as learning takes place, often guided by change theory/models/ frameworks.
- Capability development is important for those involved in implementation.

Emergence: change is complex and locally differentiated:

- Change is both complex and unpredictable; you cannot 'direct' but only 'disturb' an organization and then let collective intelligence find the answer.
- The environment is important: there are a few basic rules and direction is loosely set; there is no central programmatic framework.
- Can be initiated anywhere but often happens at the front line; enables rapid diffusion of knowledge and sharing of best practice.
- Involves informal lateral connections and novel mixes of people.
- Starts small and builds momentum; trials and experiments conducted; goes step by step.
- The leaders respond to and work with the tensions, develop sense-making and dialogue skills, reflect back patterns and help make meaning out of what is going on.

Leadership and change

It is beyond the scope of this chapter to explore the vast body of literature on leadership. However, there is clear and growing evidence that the part played by leaders in the change process has a significant impact on the success of change (Conner, 1992, 1999; Kotter, 1998; Higgs and Rowland, 2001, 2003; Higgs, 2003). The beliefs and mind-sets of leaders have been shown to influence their choices and approaches to problem solving (Hambrick and

Brandon, 1988; Finklestein and Hambrick, 1996). Thus it can be deduced that leaders' behaviour will influence their approach to change and its implementation. It has been suggested that there has been insufficient empirical research on the role and behaviour of leaders in a change context (Higgs and Rowland, 2000). However, the transformational leadership model developed by Bass (1985) has been the subject of much empirical investigation. This primarily quantitative research demonstrates clear links between leadership behaviour and a variety of 'follower' behaviours and performance measures (Alimo-Metcalfe, 1995; Higgs, 2003), but it fails to make direct links with change. It has also been suggested that it fails to provide insights into the actual behaviour of leaders (Kets de Vries, 1995; House, 1995; Kouzes and Posner, 1998). Those studies which have investigated this topic tend to conclude that for effective leadership there are a relatively small number of behaviours, and these are executed in somewhat different ways according to the personality of the leader (Kouzes and Posner, 1998; Goffee and Jones, 2000; Higgs, 2003).

When examining leaders' role and behaviour in the change process few studies have moved beyond generic descriptions. Exceptions to this are those by Higgs and Rowland (2000, 2001), who specifically link leadership behaviours to activities involved in implementing change. However, the basis of this is rooted in the view of change that falls into the 'master' quadrant in Figure 12.2. Some have questioned the efficacy of such a view of leadership in a change context (Wheatley, 1992, 1993; Wheatley and Rogers, 1996; Senge, 1997; Giglio *et al.*, 1998). In particular, it is argued that a different perspective on leadership arises in the context of a complex and distributed view of change (Senge, 1997; Wheatley, 2000; Jaworski, 2001). If change is perceived as complex and emergent, then according to Wheatley (2000) there is a need to bring leaders to a transformational edge so that they can work differently. However, beyond such theoretical conjecture there has been little research on the broader relationship between leadership and differing approaches to change. The study described by Higgs and Rowland (2003) is an exception to this. In this study some 40 change leaders were interviewed and from these interviews some 70 change stories were identified. When reviewing the interview transcripts for evidence of leadership behaviours, it became clear that a very leader-centric approach – with the leader driving the change through personal involvement, persuasion and influence – was not the cause of success in any of the contexts. Instead it appeared to mitigate against success. In contrast success does seem to be related to leadership that is facilitative and enabling (Higgs, 2003), with the leader building a 'container for change' (Lichtenstein, 1997) and fostering the capacity to change in others (Conner, 1998). It is also evident from the analysis of the transcripts that differing approaches to change appear to place differing emphasis on the types of leadership behaviours involved (Higgs and Rowland, 2003).

To explore the leadership behaviours the transcripts were analyzed to identify themes relating to leadership (Denzin and Lincoln, 2000). Nine behavioural categories were identified:

- What leaders say and do (the communications and actions of leaders are directly related to the change).
- Making others accountable.
- Thinking about change.
- Using an individual focus.
- Establishing 'starting points' for change.
- Designing and managing the change journey.
- Communicating guiding principles.
- Creating individual and organizational capabilities.
- Communicating and creating connections.

These were then divided into three groups:

- Shaping behaviour: what leaders say and do; making others accountable, thinking about change, using an individual focus. Here the focus is on personal leadership and consideration is taken of the behaviour of leaders, how their personal presence can affect change situations and how they can shape the leadership practices of others. Their beliefs about and theories of change are also taken into account.
- Framing change: establishing starting points for change, designing and managing the change journey; communicating guiding principles. Framing the change involves establishing the starting points for and the setting up of the change, followed by a focus on the more strategic aspects of the change in terms of direction. It also gives consideration to the environment and how that can affect the implementation of the change. In a sense it creates an overall framework or container for the change.
- Creating capacity: creating individual and organizational capabilities, communicating and creating connections. An important consideration here is the development of skills to work with change, through coaching and other means, in order to strengthen the organization's ability to implement change. An important factor in capacity building is the power and significance of informal networks that allow understanding of the value and importance of the need to have the capability in place. Both formal and informal communications have a role in raising awareness of both the micro and the macro aspects of the change process.

Research study

From the above it is clear that it is difficult to implement change successfully (Kotter, 1998; Higgs and Rowland, 2000, 2001). Moreover, there is relatively little empirical research on what does lead to successful change. Kotter's (1990) seminal study was based on the assumption that change is linear and driven from the top. However, in the literature this assumption is challenged and a more comprehensive way of categorizing and examining change is proposed. Much of the literature in question is, however, theoretical and derivative (for example Lichtenstein, 1996; Aldrich, 1999). Moreover, few researchers have explored the link between leadership behaviour, change models and the effectiveness of change. These two points give rise to the following questions:

- What approach to change management is likely to be the most effective in today's business environment?
- What leadership behaviours tend to be associated with effective change management?
- Are leadership behaviours related to the assumptions underlying different approaches to change?

The empirical study described in this section was designed to explore these questions.

Methodology and design of the study

When searching for an appropriate methodology to explore the above questions it was important to address two issues. First, it was necessary to identify unintended or unplanned consequences of interventions. This suggested a case study approach, particularly as a number of the areas of investigation were predominantly theoretical with limited empirical evidence. The second issue was prompted by Lichtenstein (1997), who had highlighted the conflict between the academic logic of change and the intuitive or practical experiences of agents of change.

In light of the above it was decided to use a collaborative research model (Huff and Jenkins, 2002) employing case studies. Seven organizations agreed to participate in the study. Each selected a number of employees to take part in one-to-one interviews to explore their experiences of the change process. In total some 40 participants were interviewed, all of whom were in leadership roles. All the interviews were recorded and full transcripts were produced. Within the interview framework the participants were encouraged to relate more than one change story. Thus the unit of analysis was the change story and the interviews produced some 70 stories.

The overall design of the stages of the study was informed by the participants' issues, concerns and questions (Eden and Huxham, 1996). Whilst the methodology was designed to be predominantly qualitative the participants unexpectedly raised questions that required answers of a more quantitative nature. Employing an approach that enabled quantitative analysis of qualitative data (Parry and Meidl, 2002) allowed the team to respond to the participants' enquiries (full details of the methodology can be found in Higgs and Rowland, 2003).

Results of the study

The initial analysis was designed to establish the extent to which the model of change (Figure 12.2) reflected the reality of the different practices in the organizations. The transcripts were reviewed holistically and for each change story the dominant approach to change was examined and categorized according to that model. The stories from the informants were then mapped on to the overall model. The results of this analysis are shown in Figure 12.3.

It was evident that the stories indicated a move away from directive change and towards a more emergent approach. Furthermore, the analysis suggested that the relatively simplistic model, based on two axes, was too limited to capture the complexity and diversity of the ways in which changed happened in practice. They felt that exploring this model would provide data that would enable them to encourage leaders in their organizations to think differently about change.

When discussing the framework and possible relationships to success it became apparent that the context in which the change was set was a significant factor. When reviewing our original findings, based on our own experience and conversations with our interviewees, we found that changes occur in a variety of contextual settings. Our reflections, conversations and an analysis of the data revealed a range of contextual variables that would

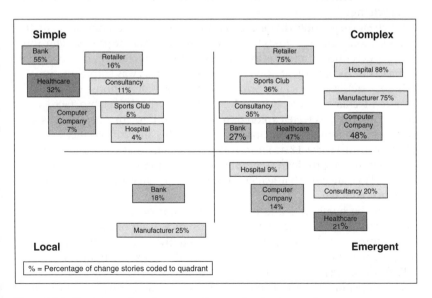

Figure 12.3 Participants' stories mapped on to the change quadrant

help us to analyze the leadership factors and change approaches discussed above in different contextual environments.

More detailed content analyses of the data, using differing contexts, provided some evidence of a pattern in the relationship between change approaches and success, as well as illustrations of the way in which approaches within the model occur in practice. In general the style labelled 'directive' was evident in many of the stories of unsuccessful change implementation in all contexts. Some interviewees spoke of an underlying assumption that fast and fundamental change required a rapid, top-down and relatively simplistic approach. The more complex 'master' approach and its higher degree of involvement was seen by the interviewees as more successful, particularly if the change time scale was relatively long and the organization had a history of implementing many changes.

The idea that change can be implemented on a linear and relatively simple basis by providing change agents with 'tool kits' is referred to as the self-assembly approach to change. However, when this approach has been employed it has ultimately proved unsuccessful.

In reviewing the initial change stories it was evident that the stories indicated a trend away from 'Directive' change and towards a more emergent approach. Furthermore, analyses of the stories suggested that the relatively simplistic model, based on two axes, provided too limited a way of capturing the complexity and diversity of the ways in which changed happened in practice. They felt that exploring this model would provide data to enable them to encourage leaders within their organizations to think differently about change.

Much of the complexity and evolutionary theory literature suggests that organizational change should be viewed as an emergent process. Our interviewees described numerous examples of successful changes that contained elements of the emergent approach. However, what was surprising was that this approach was associated with success in relatively short-term as well as long-term change. The relationships between the leadership factors and change approaches were explored in order to address the question raised by participants about relationships (see above). This analysis produced the profile shown in Figure 12.4. From this it is evident that each approach produces a different profile in terms of the relative dominance of the leadership factors. This suggests that leaders should modify their behaviour to suit the approach adopted.

When the qualitative and quantitative findings were reviewed together there appeared to be a great deal of consistency. Each of the main quantitative findings could be matched to qualitative data in the transcripts. Bringing together all the analyses produced the following findings.

First, in the case of high-magnitude change (that is, change that affects a large number of people and entails changes to numerous parts of the system) the most effective approach is the emergent one (emergent change accounted

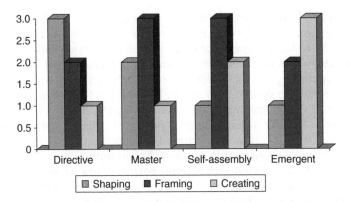

Figure 12.4   The relationship between leadership factors and change approaches

for 32 per cent of variance in success in our study). The leadership factor that accounts for the highest variance in success in this context is framing change (accounting for some 52 per cent of the variance).

Second, the case of short-term change (change that is implemented in 12 months or less) that affects a large number of people in the organization leadership behaviours are crucial to success. The set of behaviours encompassed within the factor framing change appear to be the most likely to lead to successful implementation (in our analysis framing accounted for 42 per cent of the variance of success).

Third, change is a complex activity. The approaches at the simple end of the simple – complex axis in Figure 12.2 (directive change and self-assembly change) are less effective in most situations than those which take account of the underlying complexity of the phenomenon (the master and emergent approaches). Indeed our analysis suggests there is a negative relationship between both the directive and the self-assembly approach and success in most contexts.

Fourth, the emergent approach to change appears to be more successful than any of the other three approaches in most situations. However, our interviewees often described the emergent approach from an intuitive rather than a theoretically informed perspective. From the interviews it was apparent that the emergent approach was used when the change framework was planned and structured. It is therefore feasible to propose that the emergent approach describes how change actually happens as opposed to how change is articulated.

Fifth, leadership behaviours that centre on the position, role and power of leaders and their abilities (that is, those behaviours captured by the factor shaping behaviour) appear to be negatively related to the success of a change.

In long-term change initiatives (those with a time horizon of more than 18 months) and in organizations undergoing continuous change, the master approach and leadership behaviours that are captured in the factor creating capacity appear to be effective. Evidence from our interviews points to the importance, in these contexts, of creating an overall framework for change and developing both the individual and the organizational capacity for change. According to the results of our analysis the master approach accounts for 21 per cent of the variance in success in long-term change and the leadership factor framing change accounts for 45 per cent of the variance in success in long-term change and 27 per cent in change contexts with a long history (that is continuous change and adaptation).

Finally, there is a relationship between change approaches and leadership behaviours. However, it is one of differing balances rather than absolutes. All the leadership factors were mentioned by our interviewees in relation to each change approach. However, their dominance varied. This was supported by our quantitative data, the analysis of which produced different profiles for each of the three leadership factors in each of the four change approaches.

Implications of new thinking on change and leadership

Overall the findings from our study provide empirical support for many of the theories and conjectures in the literature. The view that top-down pro-grammatic change does not work (Senge, 1997; Pascale, 1999; Buchanan *et al.*, 1999) is endorsed to some extent. Certainly the findings show that the directive approach to change is ineffective in most situations. However, the master approach (which is planned and requires uniform implementa-tion) is effective for long-term initiatives in an environment of continuous change. It is perhaps the underlying mindset of the master approach, which recognizes the complexity associated with change, that explains this. Our study has produced clear evidence to support the view that recog-nition of the complexity of change is important to the formulation of effective change strategies (Wheatley, 1992; Lichtenstein, 1996; Stacey, 1996; Balogum *et al.*, 2003) and that unintended consequences (often neg-ative) are associated with change approaches that are linear and relatively simplistic, although it is difficult to predict outcomes in complex environ-ments (Pascal, 1999; Buchanan *et al.*, 1999; Sammut-Bonnici and Wensley, 2002).

A somewhat surprising finding is that the emergent approach appears to be strongly related to success in so many contexts. In particular its apparent effectiveness in the case relatively short-term change is surprising as many have asserted that a more emergent approach to change takes longer to deliver results (Weick, 1995; Shaw, 1997; Robichaud, 1999; Alimo-Metcalfe *et al.*, 2000). However, is our interviews the approaches to change that were categorized as emergent were not articulated as such or based on any theoretical model or framework. In many cases the stories told by the interviewees were of somewhat unstructured and 'messy' activities and interventions. This is in line with Shaw's (1997) observation that change becomes very 'messy' when moving from a planned approach to a complex adaptive systems perspective. Although the stories on the emergent approach were not structured the interviews revealed a number of similarities in terms of the following.

- Micro-level interventions.
- Interventions involving individuals or small groups outside the mainstream of the organization.
- Explicit experimentation.
- Establishing unusual connections in order to share learning and transfer new behaviours.
- Working through informal networks and alliances.

These similarities endorse much of the writing of those who use complexity and evolutionary theory as a means of understanding organizational change (Wheatley, 1992, 1993; Depew and Weber, 1995; Lichtenstein, 1996; Shaw, 1997; Metcalfe *et al.*, 2000).

What was notable about many of the emergent change stories was that emergent behaviours and activities frequently occurred in the context of, or in response to, a more structured and planned change initiative that was floundering or going off course. Frequently a specific event or outcome triggered a different approach, behaviour or experiment. It may well be that the experiences of the initial change process provided the 'container for change' and basis for building relationships, with the 'floundering' events indicating the 'threshold at the edge of linear logic' referred to by Lichtenstein (1996).

Our findings certainly give weight to the complexity and evolutionary perceptions of change. However, following this line is unlikely to produce a new theory of change *per se* but it could, as proposed by Sammut-Bonnici and Wensley (2002), provide a powerful tool for understanding the change process. Indeed, if the finding of our study are supported by future research we should not seek a prescriptive theory of change but rather, in the spirit of complexity theory, we should look for a broad general direction and a small number of simple guiding rules (Reynolds, 1987; Wheatley, 1992, 1993). To an extent, therefore, our model of change approaches (Figure 12.2) should not be seen as definitive but more as a lens through which to try to make sense of the change process (Weick, 1995).

Turning now to leadership behaviours, our study again challenges some of the more traditional thinking on change leadership (Kotter, 1998). However, our findings are not unique in this regard. Higgs (2003) points to evidence that leadership effectiveness is moving away from leader-centric and top-down models. Similarly, Alimo-Metcalfe (1995) notes that a more supportive model of leadership is necessary in a transformational context. Therefore our finding that the leadership behaviours within the 'shaping behaviour' factor are not correlated with successful change is not surprising. The apparent success of the cluster 'creating capacity' in more complex change contexts is supported by Conner (1999), who highlights the importance of leaders' ability to build the capacity for change and to embed this in the organization. Similarly, other leadership researchers have highlighted leaders' crucial role in developing individual capabilities (Kouzes and Posner, 1998; Higgs and Rowland, 2000, 2001, 2003; Goffee and Jones, 2000). In a change-specific context Higgs and Rowland (2000, 2001) have identified a cluster of change leadership competences in the area of coaching and developing others. However, the 'creating capacity' leadership factor encompasses behaviours that go beyond building individual capabilities to include the enhancement organizational capacity. This can be seen as closely aligned to Conner's (1999) view of capability building.

The third of the leadership factors identified in our study (framing change) has fewer parallels in the literature than the other two. Whilst its non-directive and facilitating nature does find some support in the literature (Alimo-Metcalfe, 1995; Kouzes and Posner, 1998; Collins, 2001; Higgs, 2003) the change-focused behaviours (including journey design) are more specific. The change leadership competence model described by Higgs and Rowland (2000, 2001) does include journey design and a competence associated with making the case for change (see also Kotter, 1998). However, the 'framing change' factor goes beyond this to include the establishment of boundary conditions, thereby in a sense creating what Lichtenstein (1997) refers to as a 'container for change'. Perhaps this behavioural cluster also captures the role of the leader as sense maker (Weick, 1995). In this context the leader is concerned with the creation of meaning, and therefore is a sense giver as well as a sense maker.

Overall our study provides evidence to support the claim in the literature that centrally planned changes based on assumptions of linearity fail to achieve their aims (Stacey, 1996; Senge, 1997; Sammut-Bonnici and Wensley, 2002; Harris & Ogbonna, 2002) and the view that complexity and evolutionary theories provide a useful framework for understanding the process of change (Depew and Weber, 1995; Lichtenstein, 1996, 1997; Aldrich, 1999). However, the latter presents a dilemma for organizations. These theories are rooted in views of the unplanned nature of change and the consequent challenges for leadership and management of the process. The broad principles of complexity outlined by Reynolds (1987) constitute a form of 'container' for the change with a general direction. Adopting such an approach may prove difficult for organizations that are rooted in rational Weberian mindsets associated with planning, direction and control (Johnson, 2001).

Implications for the implementation of CSR

Our findings clearly have implications for organizations and those with leadership roles. If these findings are corroborated by further research and practitioner experience, then organizations might well have to reconsider their assumptions about change and its implementation. A more emergent approach requires less centralization and the creation of an environment in which emergence can function. In addition leaders will have to be helped to understand their role in this context.

What is clear is that in the twenty-first century a company's ability to stand out will be defined more by its relationships with the world at large than by its quarterly figures and financial strength. In addressing this change it is essential to rethink the nature of the role and behaviours of leaders. It is not simply a case of moving towards 'quiet leadership' (Edelman, 2004), but also of leading in a different way. Leaders will have to lead less and change more. They will have to engage with a wider range of communities and to willing to face challenges and accept that they are not heroic champions who have all the answers. They will have to forge relationships in a different way, based on continuous and open communication, with a view to being a facilitator rather than a director of change (ibid.) The focus of leaders will be on building relationships and creating capabilities. As Lord Browne of BP has observed, access to capital was a key differentiator in the 1990s but relationships will be the key differentiator in the twenty-first century (ibid.)

Leaders will have to focus on developing values and aligning behaviours in a 'responsible' organization. Thus CSR will increasingly become a core business issue. According to Maria Eitel, the CEO of Nike, 'As long as companies perceive CSR as something "on the side", away from the main business decisions, they will continue to be vulnerable' (Williams, 2002). This implies that leaders should position CSR at the heart of the business. When so doing they must approach change in a different way and learn to behave differently.

In this regard a linear directive approach implemented in a leader-centric way is unlikely to be effective. However, the study described in this chapter has found no single formula for success, in terms either of the approach to change or of the behaviours of the leader. In essence the findings suggest that when planning a significant or transformational change the leader must be in a position to make an informed choice about the approach to be adopted. For example, if CSR involves a systems change then a master approach may be most effective, while a sense-making approach to CSR may lend itself more to an emergent approach. The leader should also reflect on the leadership behaviours required for the introduction of change. Here too there is no single formula for success. When introducing business-centred CSR the leader may need to begin in the sense-making arena, using emergent principles to develop an understanding of current realities before moving to an overall systemic change (using a master approach) or continuing an emergent approach. Whatever the approach chosen, it will have to be anchored in the context of the business and based on an informed understanding of the business and the dynamics of change.

The message is clear: simplistic linear models do not work in change situations that are complex and messy. The leader must obtain a clear grasp of the context in which the change is being introduced, and then make an informed choice about how best to approach the implementation of the change. Pilot projects and experiments are useful means of ascertaining the appropriateness of any approach. Viewing CSR as a core business issue offers significant long-term benefits, and it is important to invest time and effort in ensuring that these are not lost as a result of inappropriate or ineffective approaches to the change process.

References

Aldrich, H. (1999) *Organisations Evolving* (Thousand Oaks, CA: Sage).

Alimo-Metcalfe, B. (1995) 'An investigation of female and male constructs of leadership', *Women in Management Review* (Bradford: MCB).

Balogum, J., A. S. Huff and P. Johnson (2003) 'Three responses to the methodological challenges of studying strategizing', *Journal of Management Studies*, 40 (1), pp. 197–224.

Bass, B. M. (1995) *Leadership and Performance Beyond Expectations* (New York: Harper & Row).

Beckhard, R. (1969) *Organisational Development: Strategies and Models* (Reading, Mass.: Addison-Wesley).

Beer, M. (1980) *Organisational Change and Development: A Systems View* (Santa Monica, CA: Goodyear).

Beer, M. and N. Nohria (2000) *Breaking The Code Of Change* (Boston, Mass.: Harvard Business School Press).

Blackmore, S. (1998) *The Meme Machine* (Oxford: Oxford University Press).

Buchanan, D. and D. Boddy (1992) *The Expertise of the Change Agent* (London: Prentice-Hall).

Buchanan, D., T. Claydon and M. Doyle (1999) 'Organisation Development and Change: The Legacy of the Nineties', *Human Resource Management Journal*, 9 (2), pp. 20–37.

Collins, J. (2001). 'Level 5 Leadership. The triumph of humility and fierce resolve', *Harvard Business Review*, Jan.–Feb., pp. 67–76.

Conner, D. (1990) *Managing at the Speed Of Change* (New York: John Wiley).

Conner, D. (1999) *Leading at the Edge of Chaos* (New York: John Wiley).

Dawkins, R. (1976) *The Selfish Gene* (Oxford: Oxford University Press).

Denzin, N. K. and Y. S. Lincoln (2000) *Handbook of Qualitative Research*, 2nd edn (Thousand Oaks, CA: Sage).

Depew, D. J. and B. H. Weber (1995) *Darwinism Evolving: Systems Dynamics and the Genealogy of Natural Selection* (Cambridge, Mass.: MIT Press).

Duck, D. J. (2001) *The Change Monster: The Human Forces that Foil or Fuel Corporate Transformation and Change* (New York: Crown).

Edelman, R. (2004) 'Managing corporate risk and reputation', *Global Agenda*, 2, pp. 127–8.

Eden, C. and C. Huxham (1996) 'Action Research for the Study Of Organizations', in
S. R. Clegg, C. Hardy and W. R. Nord (eds), *Handbook Of Organisational Studies*
(London: Sage).

Finkelstein, S. and D. Hambrick (1996) *Strategic Leadership – Top Executives and Their
Influence on Organisations* (St. Paul, Min.: West).

Giglio, L., T. Diamante, and J. M. Urban (1998) 'Coaching A Leader: Leveraging
Change At The Top', *Journal of Management Development*, 17 (2), pp. 93–105.

Goffee, R. and G. Jones (2000) 'Why Should Anyone be Led by You?', *Harvard Business
Review*, Sept.–Oct. pp. 63–70.

Hambrick, D. C. and G. L. Brandon (1988) 'Executive Values', in D. C. Hambrick (ed.),
Executive Effectiveness: Concepts and Methods for Studying Top Mangers (Greenwich, CT:
JAI Press).

Hammer, M. and J. Champy (1993) *Reengineering the Corporation: A Manifesto for
Business Revolution* (New York: HarperCollins).

Harris, L. C. and E. Ogbonna (2002) 'The Unintended Consequences of Culture
Interventions: A Study of Unexpected Outcomes', *British Journal of Management*, 13,
pp. 31–49.

Higgs, M. J. (2003) 'Developments in Leadership Thinking', *Journal of Organisational
Development and Leadership*, 24 (5), pp. 273–84.

Higgs, M. J., and D. Rowland (2000) 'Building Change Leadership Capability: 'The
Quest for Change Competence', *Journal of Change Management*, 1 (2), pp. 116–31.

Higgs, M. J. and D. Rowland (2001) 'Developing Change Leaders: Assessing the impact
of a development programme', *Change Management Journal* 2 (1).

Higgs M. J., and D. Rowland (2003) *Is Change Changing?*, Henley Working Paper Series
HWP0313 (Henley: Henley Management College).

House, J. (1995) 'Leadership in the Twenty-First Century: A Speculative Inquiry', in
A. Howard (ed.), *The Changing Nature Of Work* (San Francisco, CA: Jossey-Bass),
pp. 411–50.

Huff, A. S., and M. Jenkins (2002) *Mapping Strategic Knowledge* (London: Sage).

Hurst, D. (1995) *Crisis and Renewal: Meeting the Challenge of Organisational Change*
(Boston, Mass.: Harvard Business School Press).

Jaworski, J. (2000) *Synchronicity* (New York: Berrett-Koehler).

Jaworski, J. and C. O. Scharmer (2000) *Leadership in the New Economy: Sensing and
Actualising Emerging Futures* (Cambridge: Society for Organisational Learning).

Johnson, S. (2001) *Emergence* (London: Penguin).

Kets de Vries, M. (1995) *Life and Death in the Executive Fast Lane* (San Francisco, CA:
Jossey-Bass).

Kotter, J. P. (1998) 'Leading Change: Why Transformation Efforts Fail', *Harvard
Business Review*, May–June, pp. 11–16.

Kouzes, J. R. and B. F. Posner (1998) *Encouraging the Heart* (San Francisco, CA: Jossey-
Bass).

Lewin, K. (1941) *Field Theory in Social Science* (New York: Harper & Row).

Lichtenstein, B. M. (1996) 'Evolution or Transformation: A Critique and Alternative to
Punctuated Equilibrium', in D. Moore (ed.), *Academy of Management Best Paper
Proceedings* (Vancouver: Academy of Management), pp. 291–5.

Lichtenstein, B. M. (1997) 'Grace, Magic And Miracles: A "Chaotic Logic" Of
Organisational Transformation', *Journal of Organisational Change Management*, 10
(5), pp. 393–411.

McGhahan, A. M., and M. E. Porter (1997) 'How Much Does Industry Matter Really?',
Strategic Management Journal, 18, pp. 15–30.

Parry, K. W., and J. R. Meindl (2002) *Grounding Leadership Theory and Research* (Greenwich: CT: Information Age).

Pascale, R. (1999) *Managing on the Edge: How Successful Companies Use Conflict to Stay Ahead* (London: Viking).

Reynolds, C. W. (1987) 'Flocks, Herds and Schools: A Distributed Behavioural Model', *Computer Graphics*, 21 (4), pp. 25–34.

Robichaud, D. (1999) 'Textualisation and Organising: Illustrations From a Public Discussion Process', *Communication Review*, 3 (2), pp. 103–25.

Sammut-Bonnici, R. and R. Wensley (2002) 'Darwinism, Probability and Complexity: Market-based organisational transformation and change explained through the theories of evolution', *International Journal of Management Reviews*, 4 (3), pp. 291–315.

Senge, P. M. (1997) 'Communities of Leaders and Learners', *Harvard Business Review*, 75 (5), pp. 30–1.

Shaw, P. (1997) 'Intervening in the Shadow Systems of Organisations: Consulting From a Complexity Perspective', *Journal of Organisational Change Management*, 10 (3), pp. 235–50.

Stacey, R. (1996) 'Management and the Science of Complexity: If Organisational Life is Non-Linear, Can Business Strategies Prevail?', *Research and Technology Management*, 39 (3), pp. 2–5.

Tichy, N. M. (1983) *Managing Strategic Change: Technical, Political and Cultural Dynamics* (New York: John Wiley).

Weick, K. E. (1995) *Sense-making in Organisations* (Thousand Oaks, CA: Sage).

Wheatley, M. (1992) *Leadership and the New Science* (San Francisco, CA: Berrett-Koehler).

Wheatley, M. (1993) *Leadership and the New Science* (San Francisco, CA: Berrett-Koehler).

Wheatley, M. (2000) *Turning to One Another* (San Francisco, CA: Berrett-Koehler).

Wheatley, M. and M. Kellner Rogers (1996) *A Simpler Way* (San Francisco, CA: Berrett-Koehler).

Williams, D. (2002) 'Weaving ethics into corporate culture', *Communication World*, 19 (4), pp. 38–40.

13
Corporate Social Responsibility as a Tailor-Made Search Process

Jacqueline Cramer and Angela van der Heijden[1]

Introduction

Corporate social responsibility (CSR) is becoming a key issue in business. It involves companies consciously orienting their activities towards value creation along three dimensions – people (the establishment of wellbeing within and outside the organization), planet (ecological stewardship) and profit maximization – while maintaining an open and communicative relationship with diverse stakeholders. How companies can properly respond to this endeavour cannot be addressed by adopting a single approach, strategy or scenario. The starting point here is that CSR can only be anchored in the organization if those involved can make sense of the concept.

In recent years various companies have started the process of implementing CSR. In this chapter examples are taken from a group of 18 companies that participated in the 'From financial to sustainable profit' programme organized by the Dutch National Initiative for Sustainable Development (NIDO). The latter was a temporary initiative (1999–2004) aimed at promoting sustainable development. The key questions addressed in the chapter as follows:

- How does the process of giving meaning to CSR at the company level evolve?
- Can specific patterns be identified that characterize the ways in which companies deal with the process of implementing CSR?

The theoretical concept of sense making is based here on the study of sense making by Weick (1979, 1995) and studies that partly built on that work (Thomas *et al.*, 1993; Drazin *et al.*, 1999; Craig-Lees, 2001; Moss, 2001; De Weerd, 2001; Calton and Payne, 2003). According to Weick (1995, p. 6): 'sense making is about such things as placement of items into a framework, comprehending, redressing surprise, constructing meaning, interacting in pursuit of mutual understanding, and patterning'. His 'placement of items in a framework' and 'constructing meaning' are particularly relevant here. CSR is usually a new concept for most people who become involved and they try to make sense of it by creating their own frame of reference and constructing meaning. As De Weerd (2001, p. 129), puts it:

> Sense making occurs when people cannot cope with reality on the basis of existing routines and schemes and cannot construct reality in a meaningful way anymore. This happens, for example, when there is a lot of complicated and conflicting information. In such cases, new meaning has to be created.

Employees and other stakeholders in a company may be uncertain about the nature and consequences of CSR because they know little about it or, conversely, are overloaded with information (Weick, 1995).

According to Weick, the process of sense making starts with mutual interaction. People constantly react to each other and in doing so they 'play an active and defining role in the production of their own reality' (De Weerd, 2001, p.). As a result of this interaction they come to see their shared environment in a similar way. They share their beliefs and consequently they collectivize meaning. Weick (1995) distinguishes two types of collective sense making: belief driven and action driven. If people make sense of CSR in a belief-driven way they share their ideas on and opinions of CSR with others. People who engage in action-driven sense making develop collective activities in order to generate a shared meaning of CSR.

Weick divides each of these into two processes of creating and collectivizing meaning. The two belief-driven processes are arguing (convincing each other through arguments) and expecting (interactions between people on the basis of self-fulfilling prophecies). The two action-driven processes are committing (carrying out activities aimed at nurturing involvement) and manipulating (carrying out activities aimed at changing the situation within and outside the company to correspond with its own insights and wishes). This chapter focuses on the ways in which the companies in the research group created and collectivized their meaning of CSR.

In the following sections we first outline the methodology used, in our study and how the 18 companies in question started their CSR search process. Next we focus on four companies that have proceeded further down the road to CSR. This analysis provides information on the ways in which companies deal with the process of implementing CSR and enables us to expand our theoretical framework.

Sample and methodology

The sample consisted of 18 Dutch companies that had been practicing CSR for several years.[2] Three of the companies operated mainly in the Netherlands or the other Benelux countries and employed 4000–9500 people: Holding AVR (waste management), Ordina (information and communication technology) and Nuon (water and energy distribution). The Dutch food company Dumeco (specializing in meat) operated at the European level and had about 5000 employees. The PAP Egg Group (boiled and peeled eggs) employed about 40 people and also operated at the European level. Peeze Coffee (coffee roasting and associated machinery) and Ouwehands Zoo mainly catered to the domestic market and had 40–60 employees. Rabobank, KLM (the Dutch airline) and DSM (a chemical company) operated all over the world and employed about 58000, 30000 and 20000 personnel respectively.

The other companies were Dutch subsidiaries of international parent companies: StoraEnso Fine Paper Berghuizer Mill (a paper mill), Coca-Cola Enterprises Netherlands, Interface (a carpet manufacturer), Perfetti Van Melle (a confectionery company), Sodexho Nederland (a caterer), Ytong Nederland (a supplier of autoclaved concrete bricks) and Uniqema (an oil and chemical company). Sodexho Nederland employed roughly 7000 people and the other companies had a staff of 400–800. All 18 companies had taken part in the NIDO 'From financial to sustainable profit' programme from May 2000 to September 2002 (Cramer, 2002, 2003). The representatives of the companies that had participated in the programme were usually the CSR change agents in their organization and therefore had an important role to play. One of the members of our research team had also managed the NIDO programme and had established a relationship of trust with the companies. The latter were, therefore, willing to be interviewed and to provide extensive information, including confidential data. Moreover, the earlier cooperation with these companies had produced a considerable amount of data on their structure, culture and history and the manner in which CSR had originally been handled. Finally, every company had carried out an assessment of the current status of their CSR practices using a sustainability score card. This too provided information for the research.

The research was qualitative in nature and used a social-constructivist approach in which people constructed their everyday world on the basis of social-symbolic (inter)actions. The study was split into three phases. The first consisted of a systematic content analysis of the data from the NIDO programme, plus annual reports and policy documents from the 18 sample companies. The second phase comprised semistructured interviews with the participants to obtain information on their CSR implementation process and ascertain why they made sense of CSR in a particular way. The interviews were guided by a protocol that focused on the evolution of CSR in the companies and covered five key issues: the use of language, the themes addressed, the systems put in place, the activities carried out and the change drivers. The participants were also asked about their rationale for taking part in the NIDO.

After analyzing the results of these interviews, four companies were selected for more detailed study in the third phase. The companies in question were selected because they appeared to be the most advanced in the implementation of CSR. At each company a group session with four to five representatives was held to reconstruct the implementation process. All those who took part had played a key role in this process. During each session the group members jointly recounted the way in which their understanding of the meaning of CSR had evolved, the actions that had been taken and the factors that had influenced the process.

The group sessions adhered to a set procedure. The participants were first asked to discuss their current understanding of CSR and the understanding they had had at the start of the process four to five years previously. The meanings of CSR formulated by the individual group members were compared with each another during the session. These exercises provided valuable information on the degree to which a shared meaning had gradually emerged and why. Subsequently the participants jointly reconstructed the process of sense making in their company. Every important step in the process was discussed in terms of objectives, activities, actors, effects and determining factors. The results were interpreted during the session according to Weick's four ways of sense making: arguing, expecting, committing and manipulating. The data gathered during the initial interviews and the four group sessions form the empirical basis of the following analysis.

The process of sense making

Our analysis shows that CSR approaches vary strongly from company to company, although a general pattern can be recognized in the approaches to sense making. The mental implementation process of CSR starts with a diffuse sensitivity for CSR. There is increased awareness of the importance of CSR for the organization. A particular reason or set of reasons forms the starting point for companies to take up the issue in their own specific manner. As one interviewer explained, 'We have a central place in society through our product and therefore many parties want to get involved. A lot of emotion concerning the image of our product has to do with the visible position we have in society'. When CSR has been placed on the internal business agenda one or a few individuals develop ideas about the most appropriate form of CSR for the organization and then search for ways to convert their ideas into concrete actions.

Our research suggests that when a company seriously takes up the issue of CSR at least one change agent is appointed internally to coordinate the activities. Change agents function as initiators and catalysts. They start with small projects and communicate the CSR concept in various ways. This leads to an iterative process of value creation in which a consensus is gradually reached on the rather fuzzy notion of CSR. Initially the actions are based on ideas formed by a small group of people; this is characteristic of a belief-driven process. Each company tries to translate the general concept of CSR into a form that is compatible with its organizational culture. This is illustrated by the following quotations from three of the change agents in our study: 'It is important to make a translation to the way it works in practice, to find a practical application.' 'It is a mental shift in communication; being transparent, including customers.' 'It is about searching for a reason to do something: what is our own advantage? What are we doing and what suits us?'

The change agent can be regarded as a broker who continuously translates the general concept of CSR into language that fits the organization and/or specific departments in the organization. As one of the change agents in our study stated, 'I try to explain the concept in such a way that everybody can comprehend its meaning in their particular situation.' They also use a special terminology, derived from the general concept of CSR. For instance, some companies use their own unique term instead of CSR, such as 'Coca-Cola Cares'. Another company adds the Ps of 'product' and 'processes' to the three Ps of people, planet and profit. During this process the change agents tend to become aware that there is a need to increase support for CSR in their organization. This requires reflection on the part of the change agents about their role and the roles of others. In the course of this process of collectivization there is a shift away from individual interpretations of CSR to ones shared by an inner circle of people. In a few of the 18 companies studied this shift was already evident. The next step – an interpretation shared by all people in the organization, whether implicitly or explicitly – had not yet been achieved in any of the companies involved.

To increase support for CSR the change agents develop concrete activities and involve more and more people in the process. In turn the CSR beliefs of the organization are shaped by the input of a growing number of people. The nature of the approach becomes action-driven: beliefs are created and/or anchored as a result of actions. The companies studied put different emphases on their CSR activities. For instance, some were concentrating on environment-related issues and others on societal issues. One had set up programmes for schools and printed a simple brochure for the purpose. According to one interviewee, in personal terms this had brought the concept a live: 'Previously one was quite sceptical [about CSR], but through such a brochure [the concept] has started to become visible.' Two other companies had set up an energy mirror in their main entrance hall to show employees and visitors the energy consumption over the last months and to create environmental awareness.

In summary, every company develops its own meaning (or configuration of meanings) of CSR, as well as activities and terminology to make sense of it.

Analysis

As noted earlier, four companies were selected for a more detailed analysis of the process of implementing CSR. These companies were relatively well advanced in this process. All were Dutch branches of multinational organizations. Company A produced a food product, companies B and C manufactured non-food products and company D was a service provider. Every significant step in the evolution of their CSR programme was investigated in respect of objective, activities, actors, consequences and determining factors.

Company A

Company A had started with a very pragmatic perspective that was in line with the company's culture, but since 2000 CSR activities had become increasingly important. The catalysts had been NGO criticism of the company's packaging and social opposition to the proposed expansion of one of its plants. These stakeholder objections had made the company aware that it would become increasingly subject to societal pressure and therefore action had to be taken. Although the company had been involved in community initiatives, it was clear that CSR, had to, put into a broader perspective. As a result the management decided to develop a clear strategy and implementation plan for CSR. The initial focus was on developing an environmental policy that was embedded in the strategy of the company. 'We began with the environmental dimension ... and selected a number of crucial issues. Then we looked at the people dimension. This topic was so tremendously complex that it is easy to get stuck.'

Of the possible target groups it was decided to focus on schools first. In order to ascertain its chance of success in this area it started with a number of small pilot projects. If these proved successful it would consider implementing a similar approach for other target groups. A growing number of people became involved, including individuals from management, commercial affairs, sales and external affairs, plus regional managers. The programme was subsequented extended along similar lines. According to one interviewee the main reasons for success were 'the pragmatic approach, attuned to the culture of the organization, the personal convictions of key figures (including members of the board), momentum [a sense of urgency] and some luck'.

In the course of the process contextual beliefs about CSR were formed and partially collectivized, but ongoing efforts had to be made to gain full support for the ideas associated. The four participants in the group session admitted that their view of CSR had changed over time. Four years previously they had associated CSR with issues such as sponsorship or specific environmental measures. However, they saw it now as a core organizational activity. Broadly speaking, they all had the same interpretation of the concept. Key objectives were to ensure the company's survival in the long term, to provide added value for the company and society, to treat CSR as a continuous improvement process and to build on the collective mental awareness it was producing.

Company B

Company B took up CSR in a different way. It adopted a pragmatic approach that reflected procedures laid down for its quality and management systems. In 2000 a change agent was appointed to lead the process. An additional spur was provided by NIDO's request that the company take part in its programme. Placing its quality and management systems and other activities into the CSR framework was quite a challenge for the company. The change agent initiated the first steps, which were aimed at creating a consensus on the company's beliefs about and intentions for CSR. His first initiative was to fill in a sustainability scorecard with the nine members of the management team and discuss the results. Next the management team set up a multidisciplinary working group to prepare for implementation of the measures derived from this exercises. The group's efforts were successful and a second working group, consisting of a new participants, was established to set up and report on a sustainability target. As expected, this target was reached after one year. At the time of the study the management was deliberating about what to do next. The main factors in the success of the venture so far were, according to the interviewees, the commitment of the management, the competent middle managers, the structured manner of working, the introduction of mechanisms to ensure that everybody in the company cooperated, and the establishment of a structure to integrate the new ways of working into the system.

The people participating in the group session had a shared meaning of CSR. This was not surprising as they had all participated in the CSR process from the start. Prior to that they had had different conceptions of CSR one had related it to the continuity of the company, another to specific environmental issues and another had confused sustainability with durability. A key issue for them now was balancing the three Ps with stakeholder dialogues. The participants commented that the absorption of CSR into the organization as a whole was taking time.

Company C

Company C had been actively engaged in CSR since its CEO proclaimed in the mid 1990s that the issue should be made a core element of the overall strategy of the company. The concept of CSR was embraced at the top level and then diffused downwards. The corporate sustainability programme had clear targets, based on policies developed at the US headquarters.

Implementation in the Netherlands began with an extensive sustainability programme specifically focused on operations. As one interviewee working in operations explained:

This was a kind of awareness programme using standardized terminology. Its purpose was to encourage everybody in the organization to come up with ideas to help prevent waste, emissions and the depletion of resources. What we did here in the Netherlands, was to organize annual company-wide activities and working groups to generate ideas. Ideas were collected and presented; some of them were accepted, others were not. We also identified and reported on those areas where resources were being wasted.

The results of this endeavour had not been as hoped, in that it was proving

difficult to consolidate and constantly re-energize the initiative. It takes quite some effort to maintain a high level of awareness. This is primarily due to the fact that the results of the endeavour were presented by means of a financial reporting system, using specific indicators. What we are doing now – for we want to revitalize the issue – is to look at how the indicators can be related to existing processes. How we can translate the results into local indicators that are still comprehensible for the people and ... are within the individual's sphere of influence.

The interviewees' interpretations of CSR varied. As one of them stated, 'I believe that as a company we have one corporate vision, but individual interpretations of this vision may vary.' Despite these differences two key objectives were shared: the need for innovation and the need to communicate what had been achieved to others.

Company D

Company D shaped CSR via changes to its service provision and operations and by means of goal-oriented policy adaptations. The company's approach to CSR, initiated in the 1990s, was inspired by the CEO's vision of CSR and directors' strategies. In the early 1990s the company took its first taken steps in the environmental area. It appointed a small group of specialist coordinators and personnel to elaborate its vision of sustainability. This group was inspired by the CEO's vision of this issue. The environmental efforts consisted of adopting an internal environmental policy and engaging in dialogues with clients about potential environmental risks. The first reports, issued in 1997 and 1998, were intended to create internal support for environmental measures and explore the most appropriate content of the report.

The focus on the environment was soon extended to the broader concept of sustainable development. This led to the introduction of new niche products and innovations in existing markets. According to one of the participants in the group session, the publication of the first external sustainability report in 1999 'put the issue of sustainability on the agenda. By publishing a separate sustainability report under the auspices of the Board of Management the importance of the subject had become clear for the people inside and outside the company.

As CSR gradually spread throughout the organization some of the initiatives undertaken by different departments tended to overlap. Consequently in 2000, in order better to coordinate the efforts, it was decided to set up a new department for the purpose. This consisted of 30 people, including the members of the original sustainable development staff group (established in 1998). Since then all CSR activities have been efficiently structured. A central element of employees' shared view of sustainable development is the alignment of social responsibility with the company's core activities and operations. Transparency is improving and sustainable development will remain on the company's policy agenda.

Reflections on CSR sense making

In this section, the following questions are answered, based on the four case studies discussed it the previous section:

- To what degree had a shared meaning emerged and why?
- Which of the four ways of creating meaning, as distinguished by Weick (1995), were used and in what manner?

CSR was successfully developed in three of the four case study companies. During the process a core group of people in each company came to share a common understanding of CSR. The way in which this was achieved differed among the companies. For example, at company A the people involved consulted each other informally – during lunch or in the hallway – about their ideas on and measures for CSR. Company B used more formal methods such as handbooks, meetings and working groups, while company D focused on anchoring CSR into its overall policy. For instance, sustainability was included in the company's mission statement. However, the shared understandings so reached were restricted to the care groups and further effort was required to extend them to all employees.

In each of the three companies where the implementation of CSR was successful, two or more of three methods of sense making were used: arguing, manipulation and commitment. Arguing (convincing each other through arguments) was a particularly popular method during in the first phase of the sense-making process, both at formal meetings and in informal office conversations. At company B working groups consisting of senior staff members were established. During their sessions, according to one of the participants in our study:

we started to find out what is going on inside our company as well as which criteria for social involvement we wanted to formulate. ... That has broadened awareness. Within the working groups a learning process took place. With each other we established a certain picture and a framework of sustainability. ... We started from a theoretical angle, but through conversations with one another the approach became more practical and the thoughts behind it more clearly defined.

During the process more and more people became involved, leading to growing support for CSR. The companies began to adopt action-driven processes aimed at furthering the implementation and shaping CSR of beliefs. These beliefs were adapted from general CSR concepts to notions that were attuned to the characteristics and language of the company. Manipulation was clearly noticeable in company A. Sense making through manipulation consists, according to Weick (1995, p. 165), of 'acting in ways that create an environment that people can then comprehend and manage'. In the case of CSR this can be done by creating an organizational context that functions as a shared framework for people. This is exactly what happened at company A: 'The change that we tried to make was to make it [CSR] tangible by placing it in a frame that matched the company.' The associated programme provided the employees with a platform to develop joint ideas and activities, or in Weick's terminology, 'meaningful structures and environments' (ibid., p. 167).

Companies B and D mainly drew on commitment to collectivize the meaning of CSR. According to Weick, 'The basic idea is that people try hardest to build meaning around those actions to which their commitment is strongest. Once people choose how to justify the action that they chose to perform, they fix the frame within which their beliefs, actions and associations will then make sense' (ibid., p. 164). For instance, company B used commitment as a way to create support by including CSR aspects in the management handbook. The management team obtained the commitment of the employees to cooperate by implementing measures in operating procedures and management and quality systems. As one change agent explained: 'Because it is consciously accepted by the management team, every manager can make sure that his department knows: this is our method of working, so that's the way we do it. And furthermore, everyone is also fully aware of the idea that this is the only right way to work.' According to a member of the management team, 'Of course people try to get around certain requirements, but if the management team has a joint agreement about it and deals with it in the same way, then that road is closed very quickly.'

In company C, where the development of CSR was less successful, the various ways of sense making were not very evident. CSR was being implemented as a top-down measure by the international parent company and creating meaning at the local level was proving difficult as the ideas of people diverged. Their process of sense making was mainly based on what seemed to be expected of them and they developed activities that reflected the beliefs of the parent company. Hence they did not adapt the CEO's beliefs to their local situation and CSR was sometimes regarded as being imposed on them. As Weick states: 'People see things of their own making. They see what they expect' (ibid., p. 148). The approaches developed by the three more successful companies were clearly connected to their own culture or identity. The participants in our study referred to certain properties that they considered as characteristic of their company. During the group conversation at company A, for example, the company's pragmatic organizational culture was referred to on several occasions. Company B, which tied CSR to its quality and management systems, dealt with CSR in a more systems-oriented way.

Conclusions

From the above analysis it can be concluded that creating shared understanding of CSR is a tailor-made process. Despite the context-specific understanding developed by the individual companies in our study, however, a general pattern of sense making can be identified. This consists of three phases: encourage sensitivity to CSR; appoint change agents and prioritize company-specific themes; and increase corporate support for the company's interpretation of CSR. The fourth phase would consist of CSR being embedded in a shared understanding throughout the organization, but none of the companies had reached that stage.

To mobilize the interest of the members of the organization, change agents tend to make their terminology company-specific. That is, use a special vocabulary, derived from the general concept of CSR, that everyone in the company can understand. A sharper understanding of CSR is developed by carrying out activities and then reflecting on their contribution to CSR. In this way CSR acquires a company-specific meaning with emotional, functional or practical value. This meaning determines the (implicit) arguments and (boundary) conditions with which people in the company can agree or not.

Weick's (1995) theory of sense making provides a good basis for the process of embedding CSR in the company. The development of shared values is a vital aspect of organizational change, and Weick clarifies and substantiates the mental process of organisational change towards CSR. Based on the sense making theory and the empirical data, the above analysis answers the key questions in this contribution about the sense making process of CSR at a company level. Also, specific patterns of implementing CSR are identified. In general, the sense making process of CSR starts with belief-driven sense making (based on the beliefs created by a small group of people) and gradually transforms into action-driven sense making. Depending on the particular manner in which CSR is implemented, one or more ways of creating meaning become apparent: arguing, expecting, committing and manipulating. The approaches developed by the three more successful companies were clearly connected to the culture or identity of their organization.

The participants in the conversation referred to certain properties that they considered as characteristic for their company. However, general rules or scenarios are difficult to derive from the current theory on sense making. The theory of sense making does not give enough basis to (1) connect the tailor-made approaches with the factors that determine successful implementation, and (2) distract general scenarios from these connections which can serve as tools for companies to embed CSR. The theory is not suitable for research into the relations and effects of elements that shape the coherence of shared CSR-values. 'Weick does not tell us what constitutes "sense", does not describe its operation, and does not explain how emotions fit into the equation' (Craig-Lees, 2001, p. 515). Despite these shortcomings, Weick's theory provides a valuable framework for the process of making sense of CSR in companies.

Notes

1. We would like to thank Dr Jan Jonker (Radboud Univestity, Nijmegen) for his valuable contribution to this chapter.
2. The research was carried out within the framework of the Dutch National Research Programme on CSR, financed by the Ministry of Economic Affairs, from January 2003 to December 2004.

References

Calton, J. M. and S. L. Payne (2003) 'Coping with Paradox. Multistakeholder Learning Dialogue as a Pluralist Sense Making Process for Addressing Messy Problems', *Business & Society*, 42 (1), pp. 7–42.
Craig-Lees, M. (2001) 'Sense Making: Trojan Horse? Pandora's Box?', *Psychology & Marketing*, 18, pp. 513–26.
Cramer, J. (2002). *Ondememen met Hoofd en Hart. Duurzaam Ondememen: Praktijkervaringen* (Assen: Koninklijke Van Gorcum).
Cramer, J. (2003) *Learning about Corporate Social Responsibility: The Dutch Experience*, (Amsterdam: IOS Press).
H. De Weerd (2001) *Plezier in Werken. Zingevingsaspecten en Waarden op de Werkvloer* (Nieuwstadt: ISGS).
Drazin, R., M. A. Glynn and R. K. Kazanjian (1999) 'Multilevel Theorizing about Creativity in Organizations: A Sense Making Perspective', *Academy of Management Review*, 24, pp. 286–307.
Gioia, D. A. and A. Mehra (1996). 'Sense making in Organizations', *The Academy of Management Review*, 21, pp. 1226–31.
Moss, M. (2001). 'Sense making, Complexity and Organizational Knowledge', *Knowledge and Process Management*, 8, pp. 217–32.
Thomas, J. B., S. M. Clark and D. A. Gioia (1993) 'Strategic sense making and organizational performance. Linkages among scanning, interpretation, action and outcomes', *Academy of Management Journal*, 36, pp. 239–70.
Weick, K. E. (1979) *The Social Psychology of Organizing* (New York: Random House).
Weick, K. E. (1995) *Sense Making in Organizations* (Thousand Oaks, CA: Sage).

14

The Enterprise Strategies of European Leaders in Corporate Social Responsibility

Nigel Roome and Jan Jonker

Introduction

Corporate social responsibility (CSR) in Europe can be viewed as a social movement that includes leading companies, policy makers, advocates, pressure groups, knowledge institutes (universities and consulting companies), business associations and sections of the investment community (see Chapter 6 of this volume). This movement has many roles and functions. Its main concern is to address the position and responsibilities of business in society. It provides an institutional framework to support and legitimize CSR and its relationship to modern business, a means to develop a better understanding of thinking and practice, and a network through which ideas and practices can be diffused. For example, the European Commission (2002) continues to push for the inclusion of CSR as a key factor in the drive for competitiveness by European companies. A number of leading companies and knowledge institutes have begun to address the theory and practice of CSR and growing number of advisory bodies and groups are promoting corporate responsibility, for example the UN Global Compact and the Global Reporting Initiative.

This chapter reports the results of a study of how companies in Europe were reconciling competitiveness and profitability with performance in CSR. The intention was to go beyond recent studies of high profile companies with activities in the field of CSR and to investigate how successful European companies with well-established records in CSR were managing to integrate their performance in CSR with their performance in business.

We assumed that such companies would be characterized by a comprehensive approach to CSR that involved their business principles or core values. CSR would therefore be part of their overall approach to business rather than a separate activity. The expectation was that their historical performance and their identity would have influenced their business propositions and the value chain(s) of their products or services. A further characteristic of such companies would be that their approach was known by stakeholders outside the company. These assumptions guided our choice of companies to take part in the study.

Much of the present debate on CSR focuses on ways that companies can operate responsibly in social, environmental and economic contexts that are increasingly complex, turbulent and demanding while maintaining their capacity for competitiveness and profitability. In this regard CSR is seen as a response to a rapidly changing business context. The ability to combine CSR with conventional competitive activities provides a unique basis for the future development of business. Although conceptual models suggest that CSR and competitiveness can be reconciled, it remains unclear how this can be translated into strategic and operational practices. Our study was designed to help narrow this knowledge gap.

In the following sections we outline the research design and methodology used in our study and briefly describe the drivers and trends that are shaping the context of business and putting pressure on companies to improve their CSR and business performance. We focus on these drivers and trends because while the senior managers in the companies we studied were aware of them, few if any viewed them in their entirety. Instead what they saw were pressures that required strategic, organizational change involving aspects of CSR. The discussion of this is followed by details of our key findings.

Research design, protocol and organizing principles

Research design

For the purposes of our study we required pioneering companies that were successfully combining CSR with good business performance. We expected that such companies might have exceptional strategic and operational approaches to business, involving a unique blend of CSR and competitive practices. In all other respects our study was explorative rather than based on hypothesis testing and our research method was designed to reveal how the companies were addressing the question of CSR. We planned to use a set of case studies to construct a meta-level analysis that would enable us to identify common approaches among the participating companies, even though they might operate in different countries and business sectors.

We used two means to select up to ten companies to take part in the study. The first was to ask European academics who were active in CSR research to suggest companies that they regarded had established good credentials as leaders in CSR. The second was to send an e-mail alert through a wide range of CSR-related list servers. The e-mails invited companies to fill in a questionnaire on their CSR performance and practices at a dedicated web site (www.corporateresponsiblity.nl). In total some 50 000 e-mails were despatched across Europe.

The academic referrals and web questionnaires provided profiles of 120 companies from which to choose. To whittle these down to a short list we reviewed the companies' web sites, discussed the companies with researchers in the companies' countries of origin and, when deemed appropriate, asked the companies themselves for additional information. This exercise was principally informed by the criteria outlined above. The only other selection criterion was that the short list should ideally include companies with head offices in at least five European countries outside the Netherlands.

Next the companies in the short list were asked whether they would be willing to participate in on-site case studies. A number were unable to spare the time required for this phase of the research, but eventually eight companies from seven countries across Europe agreed to participate:

• Beacon Press (printing, UK).
• Betapharm (the marketing of generic drugs, Germany).
• Carillion (construction, UK).
• ITT Flygt (submersible pumps, Sweden).
• Hartmann (packaging, Denmark).
• Rohner (textiles, Switzerland).
• Sabaf (gas burners, hinges and domestic gas appliances, Italy).
• Simon Levelt (coffee and tea importer, Netherlands).

A file on each of the eight companies had been built up during the selection process. These consisted of information that we had obtained from secondary sources and material published by the companies themselves. Our focus then shifted to the collection of primary data through site visits and interviews with key personnel.

The site visits took place between September 2003 and July 2004 and involved three to five days at each company, during which key senior personnel were interviewed and material collected according to a case study protocol. The interviewees were the senior manager responsible for CSR, the company CEO and other senior managers who dealt with strategic and operational issues, such as research and development and operations. The interviews, which were recorded and later transcribed, provided details of the managers' interactions with their colleagues, subordinates, customers and suppliers and the way in which CSR was organized and positioned in the business. Our aim was to develop an authentic record of how CSR was understood and communicated in each company. Each case study was conducted at the company's main premises in the country of origin, rather than at one of their affiliate or operations elsewhere in the world. This was deemed the best possible approach given the time frame, the geographical spread of the companies and the resources available for research.

Research protocol and organizing principles

As discussed above, the research was based on explorative, qualitative, multiple case studies. Case study research is regarded as appropriate for the investigation of questions of how and why, especially when studying phenomena over which the researcher has little or no control and when the boundary between the phenomenon under investigation and its organizational and social context is blurred (Yin, 1994). We anticipated that the latter would be the case in our study as it focused on processes that involved the interaction of the organization with its social context. The companies in the study were likely to be reacting to perceived changes in their context, while their responses were in turn likely to affect both the company and its context. The phenomena being investigated would probably be blurred by the effect of this two-way causality and their own dynamic. We obtained a mixture of qualitative and quantitative information, with an emphasis on the written and spoken word. Given the exploratory nature of the research and our wish to understand how CSR was developed, we did not apply specific analytical techniques to the raw material. However, we corroborated the case material with the companies and discussed it extensively with the research team to identify key themes in the descriptions of practices and processes.

Our selection process and criteria meant that we had little control over factors such as company sector, size, form of ownership and so on. Indeed the final set of companies ranged in size from 30 to 18 000 employees and no two operated in the same sector. Therefore acknowledge that our findings cannot be generalized, but that was not the purpose of the study. Rather it was to gain insights into the integration of CSR, what each company had done in this regard and whether discernible patterns could be found among the companies.

We explored the role of CSR in terms of the formation and implementation of strategies. The research framework viewed CSR as a complex, multifaceted phenomenon arising at the interface of business and society (Roome, 2004). It assumed that social, environmental and economic phenomena were interacting to create a new context for business. It was recognized that the national (local) fabric of society was crucial in setting the agenda and strategy of each company. The interaction of these phenomena is regarded as typical of the postmodern era (Koot *et al.*, 2003). In our study CSR strategy was defined as the response by the sample companies to these phenomena and how their relationships with society were perceived, configured and organized. Thus strategic CSR was the process by which the companies learnt how their context was changing, leading to organizational changes that created new and altered relationships at the interface between the companies and their business environment (Roome, 2004). We sought to capture the main elements of this strategic process by analyzing the changing pattern of responsibilities and relationships between the company and other actors in its business and social context. We considered how CSR affected the companies in three broad spheres: (1) context, or the factors that had given rise to the development of their strategic CSR responses; (2) concept, or the ideas used to formulate and implement their strategic approach to CSR; and (3) content, or the operational outcomes or means by which the companies implemented their strategic approach to CSR.

The research protocol was designed to explore the notion that the companies were learning how to interact and respond to their changing context in ways that were new to them. It was thought that this might involve the generic process advanced by some authors (Jick, 1991; Kotter, 1995; Garvin, 2000; Roome, 2004). This starts with recognition of the need for change and the creation of a shared vision, after which a strategic management process moves the company as a whole towards the chosen vision.

The research protocol was tested in preliminary research on Dutch and German multinational companies. It was found that there was a distinction between the internal and external drivers of CSR, and this had caused the companies to recognize that they needed to interact with new constituencies of actors. Second, the development of a shared vision of CSR in terms of these relationships had been complex, multilayered and dynamic. That is, as the companies were developing their approach to CSR the position of external actors shifted in response to that approach. At the same time the companies were responding to other external events and experiences. The skill set and capabilities of the managers who were determining and implementing the companies unfolding CSR strategy also developed. This dynamic and its outcomes were unique to each company. It contributed to the strategic orientation towards CSR. It seems that the companies developed and organized the content of their CSR in ways that accorded with their competences, business proposition, technological base, business context and social environment.

The preliminary research also revealed that key agents of change (for example owners, managers and CEOs) often played a crucial role in the process of conceptualizing CSR, and that CSR had followed an evolutionary path, often over a long period of time. In particular, differences in context (situation, history and institutional fabric) had led to different visions of the relationship between the company and others, and hence to CSR concepts that were specific to each company. The companies seemed to have adopted specific concepts of CSR with strong symbolic and communicative purposes, which served as a guide to detailed change. The combination of vision, conceptual insights and the drivers of CSR, enabled the companies and their employees to make sense of the complex and dynamic nature of CSR and to contribute ideas.

We also analyzed the content of organizational development and change; that is, the choices made and actions taken to implement the CSR strategy. Although there is no consensus on the actions required for the successful implementation of strategy, Stoner *et al.* (1995) argue that theorists and practitioners share three basic ideas. First, the successful implementation of a strategy depends on the structure of the organization (Chandler, 1962; Mintzberg, 1979). Strategies have to be institutionalized and embedded in the values, norms, roles and routines that govern the behaviour of employees. Third, strategies are operationalized through concrete policies, procedures, rules, management systems and projects.

The research protocol included the gathering of material to provide the basis for the written reports. This material mainly consisted of transcripts interview and company materials obtained during the site visits, but notes had also been taken of the images and language that senior managers had used when describing their company's CSR strategy and practices. Indeed the managers had been explicitly asked to describe how they communicated their CSR approach inside and outside the company. The final draft of each report was sent to the interviewee who had been the key point of contact with the company. Each was asked to confirm the accuracy of the report, to point out any matters that were confidential, and to answer three questions. These questions dealt with the key factors in the success of the company's CSR efforts, the main obstacles that had to be overcome to progress with CSR, and the key lessons that had been learnt during the process of managing CSR. The aim of these questions was to facilitate a qualitative interpretation of the factors that had given rise to the organizational activities of the companies during their successful pioneering venture in CSR.

The preliminary findings from the analysis of all eight companies will be presented later, but one clear finding was that all the companies had developed their CSR approach in response to events in their specific social, environmental and business context. An analysis of this phenomenon is presented in the next section.

Drivers of and patterns in contemporary business

Globalization has been described as the most profound transformation to take place in the twentieth century (Castells, 1996). In his analysis of globalization Roome (2000) distinguishes between 'narrow definition' globalization, arising from the interconnection of financial markets and economic systems, and 'broad definition' globalization, or the interconnection of many parts of the globe. The latter was gradually brought about by three significant developments. The first was growing concern about the environmental and social consequences of development activities in the developing and developed world from the 1970s onwards. The second was the greatly increased trade in goods and capital that followed the global spread of communications technology and computers in the late 1980s and 1990s.The third was the rise in the global movement of people and ideas from the early 1990s. Each of these provoked calls for new forms of governance to mitigate the instability they were causing. Concrete responses to these calls included Agenda 21 (dealing with the environmental and social aspects of development), the Basel Accord (headed by the International Bank of Settlements), the work by the WTO in relation to financial and economic globalization, and new policies on migration and the movement of people. The three waves of globalization now interact to create an even more complex setting for government and business, and result in a growing interconnectedness between public and private institutions in the addressing of common issues, including CSR.

Business is facing pressure on all fronts to integrate social and environmental issues into its financial and economic decisions. It is also being asked to pay greater attention to cultural shifts as the world becomes more multicultural but more separated on ideological grounds. There is a potential for progressively greater turbulence, ambiguity, contests of opinion and disorder. For business the span of management and the speed of change have increased and stakeholders other than shareholders have become increasingly important. Yet who these stakeholders are has become progressively more unclear as societies fragment. At the same time companies' brands and identity have become more global and therefore more valuable. However, companies have also become more vulnerable to criticism, leading to increased emphasis on their values and the way in which these are developed and communicated.

Economic analyses of business options now have to be accompanied by judgments of their political, social and environmental risk and their acceptability in a range of production locations and markets, while taking account of the changing needs and expectations of stakeholders. The same factors that have connected global localities have also facilitated human and organizational interconnection. Many authors have identified organizational designs that incorporate information or knowledge networks (Hastings, 1993; Nohria and Ghoshal, 1997; Schoemaker, 1998; Brenters, 1999; Castells, 2000). Others consider that the development of inter- and intraorganizational networks brought in the move towards a 'systems' world in which some companies will provide the technological, organizational and institutional components of systems while others will become systems organizers (Roome, 2001).

The move towards organizational networks has followed the widespread adoption of digital information, communication and computing technologies. Computer networks, e-mail, mobile phones, the internet and intranets have affected many aspects of work, from control through to innovation. However, rather than a network replacing the classical organization hierarchy, at present line systems and network systems are used in tandem in some organizations. These hybrid organizations have to deal with what Schoemaker (1998) calls the in-built structural dilemma of connecting the innovative and participative aspects of work in networks with the control and organizational aspects of work in hierarchies. What enables these two systems to be combined is the development of a recognizable organizational identity and a commitment by employees to the business values that underpin the relationship of trust between the members of the organization and between them and others (Roome, 2001). This relationship of trust also enables each community of work within an organization to maintain its unique orientation towards its internal and external environment while contributing to the common purpose.

Globalization means that relationships have become more extended, numerous and dynamic. Choices are more contested so options have to be assessed more carefully. There is growing awareness that the opinions and concerns of traditional and new stakeholders have to be taken into account. Shareholders expect assurance and openness in respect of business information. Consumers increasingly want to be informed of the provenance of what they buy. Interest groups and regulators expect their concerns to be heard and taken into account, and explanations to be provided by companies of the actions they take. In addition hybrid interests have developed, such as ethical investors with an interest in both financial performance and social and environmental performance.

With the growing importance of relationships more attention has been paid to trustworthiness. Are individuals and organizations open to scrutiny and accountable for their actions? What are the company's business principles, values, mission and identity? Does it do what it says and say what it does? Do companies and managers accept responsibility and act responsibly? Corporate social responsibility, as a concept, concerns the way in which companies and their managers understand, organize, structure, manage and act out these relationships with others.

In general the companies in our study were aware that the nature and quality of their relationships with other actors (economic or otherwise) were changing and affecting the way they did business. They were having to confront issues that could not be tackled in conventional ways. They were also conscious of the effects of poor or bad relationships and that business opportunities required the alignment of relationships with new values. For whatever reason, all the companies in our study recognized the need to pay strategic attention to their relationships as a core factor in their future operations.

While none of the companies was fully cognisant of the developments discussed above, the CSR practices of all of them had been triggered by an awareness of the growing importance of extended relationships. They recognized that this required internal and external strategic changes to link responsible relationships to business performance. This would also help to protect or add value, either directly through additional turnover, lower costs, higher profitability or improved market position, or indirectly through improved reputation, better risk management or new market opportunities. The companies were also aware that the development of responsible relationships would require the acquisition of new skills and capabilities by employees and that these would contribute to the development of distinct organizational competences.

Case study findings

The final report of each case study amounted to approximately 25 pages, including background material and transcripts of the interviews. This section presents the findings of the meta-analysis of the eight cases. This analysis was intended to identify patterns in the approach taken by the companies as they progressed from awareness of the need to restructure their relationships with other actors to their present integrated approach to CSR and business performance. This meta-analysis is based on the pattern seen to underscore the emergent approach in the case companies. It does not mean that the managers deliberately designed the approaches or processes we describe. While some elements of the approach taken by each company were designed, others were simply instinctive or emerged spontaneously. Indeed there was strong evidence of serendipity. For example, all the companies experienced events that created challenges but also afforded opportunities, and a number of the managers possessed the rare ability to recognize these events as moments of business opportunity and had the skill to act on them.

Despite the differences between the companies in terms of sector, size and country of origin, all but one had what could be described as an innovational structure supported by the management system. A model of this is shown in Figure 14.1. All the companies had a formal management system of one kind or another, the development of which was governed by the company's commitment to good performance in terms of quality, safety and environmental responsibility, which in turn required the measurement and monitoring of performance. The management systems were therefore not seen as ends in themselves but as means to formalize and support the more strategic innovations the companies were introducing.

At all the companies, senior managers or others carried out a series of linked activities to support the process of innovation. The first of these was the construction of a vision for the company that connected responsibility with business operations. This vision was invariably based on the understanding that the company was part of a complex, dynamic system of relationships and that these relationships had to be managed better if the company was to survive and prosper. Recognition of this had often been triggered by some event or combination of events, and/or built on the personal experiences or convictions of the senior manager. The new managements of relationships was based on non-traditional business values that also became key elements of the new business model. Sometimes constructing the vision proved difficult and required the help and input of others.

In some cases the senior manager involved in constructing the vision had access to the resources needed to embed it in the company, but in other cases the support of a sponsor was necessary who could provide these resources. Two particular types of resource were needed: long-term capital and organizational space. Long-term capital was necessary as the innovation process

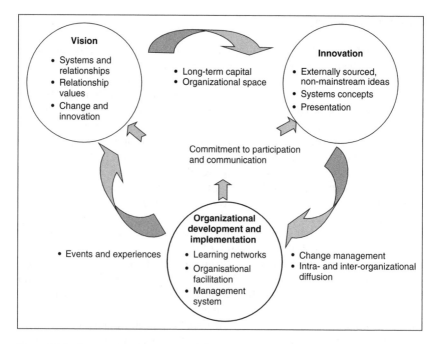

Figure 14.1   Innovational structure of the case study companies

that would follow on from the vision would take time. Organizational space was needed for the development and implementation of the innovations. The way that sponsors and visionary managers connected differed among the companies. In some cases a manager was hired by the sponsor to develop a vision; in others the manager had to convince the sponsor of the need for change and the value of a new vision for the company. Often this was not an easy task, especially as the vision was often a quite radical departure from existing thinking and practice in the company.

The manager invariably oversaw the development of new concept that stemmed from the vision, but in seven of the companies the managers realized that they could not develop their vision without an input of ideas by others. Without exception this involved combining ideas from outside the business with aspects of the company's current business logic. These ideas might come from hired consultants, academics, new employees or non-business organizations. The development of company-specific concepts required the establishment of what might be called an idea-generating space, where ideas were combined, refined and assessed for feasibility. The resulting concepts were then translated into a form that could be communicated to the rest of the company.

These new concepts can best be described as systems concepts as they were generally interrelated rather than discrete and individual. They tended to be highly conceptual and relatively low in detail. They were based either on new approaches to interpersonal relationships (involving factors such as trust, respect and integrity) within the company or with other actors (supply-chain members, customers or institutions), or on new types of interaction between the company and other actors or resources. Irrespective of the nature of the concepts there was a commitment to company-wide learning and the introduction of practices to develop the concepts. Equally there was a high degree of confidence among senior managers that employees would be willing to contribute to the new concepts by offering fresh ideas and/or suggesting actions. Sometimes the process was accompanied by measures to aid employees' understanding of the new participative approach, to which not all were accustomed.

The vision and new concepts had strategic significance and served to guide the further development of the company. Often senior managers, the owners of capital and others with strategic roles in the company were invited to contribute to the final content of the concepts. Once agreed the vision for the company was not debatable, although the concepts were often sufficiently broad to be adapted to new ideas.

The commitment of employees to the implementation of the vision and its supporting concepts was essential. Implementation involved the diffusion and operationalization of the concepts in concert with a process of inter- and intraorganizational development. There were a number of clear elements to this process. The vision and concepts were viewed as providing a strategic framework, but within this framework ideas for changed working practices were sought from employees throughout the company. This fostered a sense of ownership and produced champions to chaperone the process of change. These champions served as a network to connect the vision and concepts with practices in all parts of the company. Often a key individual oversaw this learning or knowledge development network, which was backed up by training programmes, special workshops, publications and so on. The new CSR-based vision and concepts were also communicated outside the company to suppliers, markets, providers of financial capital and potential recruits.

Many of the companies aspired to a learning or quality philosophy based on a very participatory culture. This supported the processes of collaborative learning and change required in moving toward their vision. This was complemented by the development of management systems and structures that created routines and systems for management control. These routines codified the content that arose out of the learning processes, including mission, through policies, resource allocation, training and education, participation, key performance indicators and regular reviews. A key part of these new routines was monitoring, recording and tracking performance in ways tailored to the company and its technologies, products and services.

234 Strategies of European Leaders in CSR

All the companies placed a premium on communication, whether this was to do with presenting their vision and concepts to others or with taking in and adapting ideas. Communication was invariably principled and always respectful of difference. Visual symbols used to communicate often made use of loops, circles and spirals or networks.

The companies exhibited remarkable similarities. In general they, their senior managers and other members of the workforce did not separate doing business from their CSR principles. They rarely saw the need to justify the business case for what they were doing, except when attempting to gain the support of those with capital interests in the company. The business case was developed in one of two ways. The first involved a business analysis to assess the financial implications of the capital investments required to implement the vision and concepts. The second was derived by looking back at the benefits that resulted from the new approach, for example that employees were more motivated and/or productive after the changes, that the costs and risks of doing business were lower, or that the changes boosted trust or led to the creation of new markets. The vision and concepts themselves were rarely subject to a robust business analysis. A possible reason for this is that what the companies envisioned involved a rather radical change to their business model, and therefore a new or altered business proposition. However, all the companies maintained that what they had accomplished had contributed to a clearer identity, better relationships with others and a new business model.

Conclusions

This chapter has described a study of the approaches taken by eight pioneering companies and leading exponents of CSR in Europe. The model we have outlined and our findings can be used as guidelines for other companies that intend to integrate CSR into their business activities.

The companies in our study had confronted a growing array of issues that required them to change the relationships they had with other actors in society and that placed additional demands on their traditional business activities. They chose to address this by developing a new vision for their business. This often included improved relationships with external stakeholders, reduced use of resources and organizational change based on principles of engagement and participation. The process was initially top-down and the concepts developed were based on a clear understanding of the present business and its impacts, and on ideas from external actors to help resolve the deficiencies arising from the present approach. After the concepts had taken shape they were presented throughout the organization and employees were invited to contribute ideas for their implementation. This was often supported by a communication network, new participatory work practices, training programmes and the development of means to measure, monitor and review progress. The new vision, concepts and practices required a revision of the business model and business proposition, and this was duly communicated to external stakeholders in the supply chain and to financial interests and shareholders.

Our findings suggest that the success of these companies was due to the fact that they did not treat the incorporation of CSR as a strictly top-down process. Rather they encouraged the participation of employees in all areas of the company: strategy, communications, human resources, general management, quality control, health and safety product development marketing, sales and so on. Through the capabilities developed during the course of this, CSR was made a central part of the companies' activities.

References

Brenters, M. (1999) *De Organisatie als Netwerk. Hoe Mensen Organisaties Veranderen en Organisaties Mensen* (Alphen aan de Rijn: Samson).

Castells, M. (1996) *The Rise of the Network Society* (Malden: Blackwell).

Castells, M. (2000) 'Materials for an exploratory theory of the network society', *British Journal of Sociology*, 51 (1), pp. 5–24.

Chandler, A. (1962) *Strategy and Structure: Chapters in the History of the Industrial Enterprise* (Cambridge, Mass.: MIT Press).

CSR Europe (2002) *Exploring Business Dynamics: Mainstreaming Corporate Social Responsibility in a Company's Strategy, Management, and Systems* (Brussels: CSR Europe).

European Commission (2002) *Corporate Social Responsibility: A Business Contribution to Sustainable Development, Communication from the Commission* (Brussels: European Union).

Garvin, D. (2000) *Learning in Action: A Guide to Putting the Learning Organization to Work* (Boston, Mass.: Harvard Business School Press).

Hastings, C. (1993) *The New Organization* (New York: McGraw-Hill).

Holliday, C. O., S. Schmidheiny and P. Watts (2002) *Walking the Talk: The Business Case for Sustainable Development* (Sheffield: Greenleaf).

Jick, T. (1991) 'Note on the recipients of change', Note 9-491-039 (Boston, Mass.: Harvard Business School Press).

Johnson, G. and K. Scholes (1999) *Exploring Corporate Strategy* (Englewood Cliffs, NJ: Prentice-Hall).

Kanter, R. M. (2002) 'Managing the Extended Enterprise in a Globally Connected World', *Organizational Dynamics*, 28 (1), pp. 7–23.

Koot, W., P. Leisink and P. Verweel (2003) *Organizational Relationships in the Networking Age: The Dynamics of Identity Formation and Bonding* (Cheltenham: Edward Elgar).

Kotter, J. P. (1995) 'Why Transformation Efforts Fail', *Harvard Business Review*, 74 (2), pp. 59–67.

Maslow, A. (1971) *The Farther Reaches of Human Nature* (London: Arkana).

Mintzberg, H. (1979) *The Structuring of Organisations: A Synthesis of the Research* (Englewood Cliffs, NJ: Prentice-Hall).

Nohria, N. and S. Ghoshal (1997) *The Differentiated Network – Organizing Multinational Corporations for Value Creation* (San Fransisco, CA: Jossey-Bass).

Roome, N. (2000) 'Globalization and Sustainable Development: Toward a Transatlantic Agenda', in C. Bonser (ed.), *Security, Trade, and Environmental Policy: A US/European Union Transatlantic Agenda* (Dordrecht: Kluwer), pp. 161–86.

Roome, N. (2001) 'Metatextual Organizations – Innovation and Adaptation for Global Change, inaugural address, Erasmus Center for Sustainable Development and Management', Erasmus University, Rotterdam.

Roome, N. (2004) 'A pan-European Approach to CSR: Some implications of national agendas for corporate social responsibility', paper delivered at the CSR Discovery Colloquium, Wildbad Kreuth, Bavaria, 29–31 January.

Schoemaker, M. (1998a) *Organiseren van Werk en Contractrelaties; Tussen Slavernij en Anarchie* (Deventer: Kluwer).

Schoemaker, M. (1998b) 'Naar een pluriform personeelsmanagement', *Tijdschrift voor HRM*, 1, pp. 37–62.

Stoner, J., R. E. Freeman and D. Gilbert (1995) *Management* (Englewood Cliffs, NJ: Prentice-Hall).

Yin, R. (1994) *Case Study Research: Design and Methods*, 2nd edn (London: Sage).

15

Conclusion: The Real Challenges of Organizing and Implementing CSR

Jan Jonker and Marco de Witte

Introduction

In response to unprecedented changes in the business and social environment, corporate social responsibility (CSR) has emerged as an important managerial consideration. In recent years companies around the world have introduced CSR, as evidenced by the avalanche of CSR reports, the growth of networks such as BITC, Econsense and Aderse, stakeholder dialogues, reports by the EU and so on. However, companies now have to put the notion of CSR into organizational practice, thus going beyond the relabelling of existing activities.

Stripped to its bare essence, CSR addresses the rights and new responsibilities of companies in a broader social context – be it local or global. It focuses on the nature of the contributions an enterprise makes to society and brings into question many established business practices. As this volume has demonstrated, CSR is above all a 'sensitizing concept': a term that draws attention to a complex range of issues and elements that are all related to the position and functioning of companies in a world in transition. On the one hand it focuses on how issues are or ought to be organized internally, on the other it demonstrates the growing importance and influence of the context in question. The main challenge is to use the capabilities and competences of the company to address social and environmental concerns while at the same time continuing to operate successfully in the traditional business sense. This often demands an innovative vision, one that goes beyond traditional management thinking. Good intentions are, however, not enough. Rather this vision has to be embedded in the company's systems, structures, processes and culture, and in the everyday actions of employees.

It is important to recognize that in its operations a company produces not only private goods but also public goods such as social capital that results in, for instance, a healthier, safer and more prosperous environment. Contributing to the creation of common goods is not a traditional managerial practice. 'Alien' issues therefore have to be introduced and these can result in conflicting demands that can only be handled in an untraditional manner. To address these issues the company often has to find new partners and alliances in order to create the necessary competences to address issues that go beyond the conventional economic scope of the company. At the same time these very issues (for example public health, the conservation of natural resources and social cohesion) are playing an increasingly significant part in the achievement of the key objective of companies: to make a profit. CSR is not only about reducing the negative consequences of companies' activities, but about the manner in which of company can take part in society in a meaningful way. This means that they have to recognize the necessity of making a greater contribution to society and organize themselves accordingly, which places new demands on existing business strategies, systems, policies and plans. These need to be revised if not redesigned in the light of present and future issues. CSR is perhaps also about creating wealth and distributing it to a growing number of stakeholders in a correct and fair manner.

As this volume has shown, managing CSR goes far beyond rhetoric and a number of fundamental managerial questions. These can be viewed as four 'building blocks'. First, in the 'context' stage issues like stakeholder dialogue, partnership management and strategic alliances are established. Second, 'organizational management' focuses on designing the necessary systems, structures, culture and competences. Third, in the 'implementation' stage the CSR vision is incorporated into strategies, plans and daily activities. Finally, the strategy is translated into a 'business proposition', in which CSR plays a central role and is linked to the process of value creation in the value chain. These building blocks are schematically depicted in Figure 15.1. We

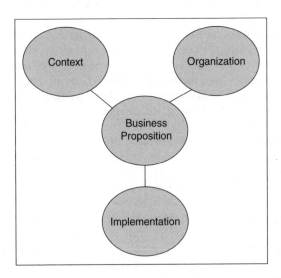

Figure 15.1 The BP-COI model

call this the BP-COI model, where BP stands for business proposition and COI for context, organization and implementation. The model will be used to summarize the issues discussed in this volume.

Contributions to the CSR debate

What should have become apparent when reading the previous chapters is that the debate on CSR is very lively. It is taking place both inside and outside organizations, is sometimes difficult to conceptualize and is not always easy to translate into daily business practices. As pointed out in Chapter 1, businesses are playing a more prominent role in society, given their dominant economic position. But addition to economic factors there are ecological and social factors to be considered. One could say that CSR is all about satisfying the needs and expectations of a growing range of stakeholders with diverse interests. Chapter 2 traces the development of the debate over the decades and concludes that we are now witnessing a new episode in which issues such as citizenship, power and (social) ideologies have to be reevaluated, given today's turbulent and complex environment. In Chapter 3 it is noted that the discussions on corporate citizenship, despite their emancipatory rhetoric, all too often result in social responsibility and sustainability being defined on the basis of narrow business interests. CSR should not become a one-dimensional ideology in itself. There is a danger that the current discourses on sustainability, with their focus on what is sustainable and how it should be measured, could lose their radical political edge. Perhaps sustainable development will come to share the fate of the environmental movement, which is being increasingly depoliticized by environmental policies that translate environmental choices into market preferences.

Context management

Much of the CSR debate is about stakeholder dialogue, and sometimes seems as though stakeholder dialogue is viewed as the panacea for all organizational problems. However, it is noted in Chapter 7 that, 'As the explicit communication technique behind many newly minted statements of corporate social responsibility, the latest practice of social dialogue appears too weak to maintain the questioning attitude that dialogue implies'. Because stakeholder dialogue seems to be disconnected from actual organizational practices, Chapter 8 proposes that a stakeholder theory of the firm be developed, a theory in which firms are viewed as the product of social interactions and not as the cause. It is argued that an organization's activities are necessarily based on the interactions of its participants, and that benefits are generated by their collective action.

The ability to engage with stakeholders implies that particular competences have to be developed in this regard. In Chapter 10 it is pointed out that working on CSR requires competences that can make organizational decisions and behaviour broader, deeper, richer and easier to defend. A distinction is made between individual and collective competences for CSR. In order to develop collective competences for CSR must be anchored in organizational identity; in cooperation, so that individual actions constitute organizational actions; and in accountability which is required to act responsibility. The development of these collective competences requires a strategic process of capability building, of learning to be responsible. Chapter 9 implicitly draws on these ideas but turns them into a 'cocreative engagement model'. Good stakeholder relationships are built up during an ongoing process of interaction and engagement among the members of a network. As the network develops social capital increases and the members become more willing to take risks and act for the benefit of the network as a whole.

Organizational management

Chapter 5 elaborates on the notion of social capital and its significances for organizations. Social capital is described as the number of active connections between the members of a community. More importantly, these networks involve a degree of trust that makes it easier for the members to act. The capacity for trust is grounded in a broader social, political and economic setting than simply the organization itself. Chapter 4 looks at networks in terms of communities of work; in which social capital and organizational design play a crucial part. Talent-centred organizations create a social glue by introducing recognized values quintessential to the strengths of a social network. Networks are talent-centred organizational designs based on first- and second-order value systems. Two-layered organizational value systems offer a particularly fertile ground for reconsidering present organizational designs. Social capital reflects and reinforces relationships of trust and produces individual and collective business benefits. Such organizational identity makes clear what the second-order values of the organization are. When there is a bridge between the first and the second-order values, and the latter are used to guide the operations of the organization, the second-order values can be made useful in the marketplace. Not surprisingly, what still needs to be discovered is the 'design' of communities of work.

Implementation

The notion of CSR is still rather abstract and detached from actual business practices. Most organizations focus on internal change and are not able to handle external and internal change simultaneously. We believe that the key to implementing CSR lies in the values and norms developed in the community of work. This is in contrast to the predominantly used rational linear planned-change approach. Chapter 12 discusses the trend away from 'directive' change towards a more 'emergent' approach. This requires less centralization and the creation of an environment in which the emergent can approach function. In this regard leaders to have lead less, engage with a wider range of communities and accept that they are not heroic champions with all the answers.

Of course there is no single formula for success. When CSR is approached as a 'sensitizing' concept the approach adopted will have to be based on an informed understanding of the business and the dynamics of what is required. Chapter 13 addresses this process of sense making. The first step is to appoint change agents to coordinate the process of sense making in the company. These agents translate generic concepts of CSR into specific local actions and develop a language that fits the vocabulary of the organization. As the process evolves the people involved move towards a common understanding by means of arguing, commitment and manipulation.

Organizing the business proposition

Chapter 6 discusses a number of factors that have combined to prompt the introduction of CSR policies and practices, and examines the drivers and facilitators of the process of implementing CSR. The drivers and facilitators are identified as the individual actors who drive change and innovation, organizational factors such as new management systems and practices, institutional factors such as rules and organizational belief systems, and internal and external stimuli. The Chapter also addresses companies' motives for adopting CSR. The authors conclude that there is no superior route to the implementation of CSR.

In a similar vein, the focus in Chapter 14 is on factors that drive change and innovation, and on means of integrating CSR into business practices. This chapter is based on a case study of frontrunners in the field of CSR across Europe. The companies in question had been confronted with a growing array of issues that required them to reformulate their relationships with other groups in society. They had chosen to address this by developing a new vision based on social innovation. Key ingredients in the companies' success were the encouragement of new ideas from all employees, of the establishment of champions to foster the CRS process, and the introduction of a knowledge development network. The result was a true integration of CSR into the companies' everyday activies, and this was reflected in their business performance. There is much to be learnt from this chapter in terms of involving employees and other stakeholders in the CRS process.

A more common business practice is to base CSR on existing new standards. As Chapter 11 shows, there has been a rapid emergence of standards for CSR-related issues. However, it is questionable whether CSR can be standardized. This also accounts for the attention to the question of measurability. The empirical evidence suggests that CSR standards provide limited guidance to organizations in their effort to organize and implement CSR. Moreover, standards can be counterproductive in an emergent change process where sense making is a key issue. The main conclusion of Chapter 11 is that CSR standards come in many shapes and sizes and provide different degrees of benefit to organizations that are being urged to incorporate them into their daily business practices. It remains to be seen what the true added value of this may be.

An emerging CSR business model

Most businesses are still in the process of discovering CSR and tend to be preoccupied with doing things right rather than doing the right things. This might be due to the rather fuzzy definition CSR or to the fact that no organizational model is yet available to support the implementation of CSR in a business context. For this reason we propose a management model based on the views put forward in this book. Classical management theory mainly concentrates on the company itself and the management of its business context, while CSR requires businesses to extend their horizons to the wider social context. To this end a new organizational theory is needed, one in which widely accepted but internally focused, one-dimensional managerial concepts could become obsolete. In a way this could be seen as the re-emergence of the classical contingency problem of the fit between a business and its context.

For managers it requires the development of a vision of the role and position of the business in its multidimensional context. This vision has to be crafted through interaction and dialogue, and should be based on values such as inclusion and respect for diversity. It should be driven by a strong conviction about the contribution the business can make to society. Next this vision has to be translated into strategies, plans and activations. This requires managers to think beyond their one-dimensional economic perspective and combine the two contexts in which they operate: social and business. Furthermore, the functional perspective has to be replaced by a complex management agenda. The items shown in Figure 15.2 appear on this agenda and make up the CSR business model.

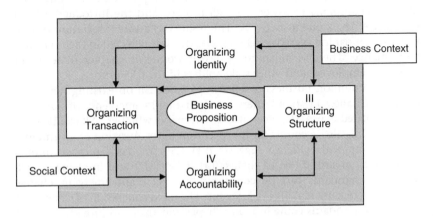

Figure 15.2   The CSR business model

At the heart of the model is the business proposition. This reflects the company's reason for being and should encompass the CSR imperative. Each of the four components of the model focuses on one specific aspect of CSR: organizing identity focuses on internal direction and external visibility: organizing transactions focuses on the way in which the business interacts with actors in its external environment; organizing structure focuses on the organization of internal affairs; and organizing accountability focuses on accounting for the business's external and internal activities. These will be discussed in turn below. Although the model is grounded in the literature and the contributions in this volume, it is a synthesis of such wide-ranging ideas that concrete references cannot be provided.

The business proposition

The business proposition, or *raison d'être* of the company, should reflect the fact that CSR plays a central role in the business and should be linked to the process of value creation. While the purpose of the business is to make a profit (otherwise it would cease to exist), thinking has to extend beyond this horizon. Making money is important, but based on what principles? To what extent and for what purpose should new core values play a role in the business?

Organizing identity

An business's foremost duty to society is to provide goods or services and thereby create wealth, generate jobs and pay taxes. All these factors determine the identity of the business. Organizing identity is a fundamental dimension of organizing CSR as it places the business in its individual context, defines what it is and gives direction to organizational processes. Identity is dynamic and changes during the lifetime of the business in a world where stakeholder relationships are complicated and important to a business's success, organizational identity car provide value to customers, business partners, investors, employees and other stakeholders. Response to stakeholder issues is shaped by the business's identity.

The contents of the business's mission statement and vision reveal the importance placed on CSR. The underlying philosophy of the mission statement provides an indication of the direction the business intends to take in respect of its social, economic and environmental contributions. The vision provides clear guidance when determining the business's strategy. It expresses the challenges the business experts to in order to fulfil its stated mission. The business's values reflect the issues that are considered important in the larger scheme of things, including the relative worth, utility or importance of certain ideas. They are part of the business's culture and attached to its mission and vision.

Organizing transactions

CSR involves increased interaction with stakeholders in a complex environment, and it is essential to take account of the wishes and needs of the various groups and individuals who can affect or will be affected by the business's pursuit of its objectives. Over the past decades organizational strategies *vis-à-vis* stakeholders have changed, and the influence that customers, employees and citizens have on the business's policies, practices and actions has grown. As the interaction with stakeholders increases, so too does its importance. For most of the twentieth century, businesses in the UK and USA that were run with a view to the long-term interests of their stakeholders were more likely to prosper than those which took a short-term, stakeholder first approach. Economic globalization and developments in technology will make stakeholder inclusion an increasingly essential component of corporate strategy in the twenty-first century.

A dialogue-driven approach is needed to nurture stakeholder relationships. This not only increases communication and interaction but also leads to a nexus of transactions. The business's sphere of influence thus becomes a dynamic space in which new transactions develop and change with the entry of new partners. Stakeholder engagement enables the business to identify the views and requirements of the key stakeholders, and thus improve its performance and accountability.

The business needs to develop and manage the organization of transitivity in such a way as to facilitate:

- The identification of stakeholders with a legitimate interest in its activities, and to prioritize them according to their relative importance with regard to its objectives and performance.
- Commitment to foster relationships with different stakeholder groups. The more interaction and involvement there is with stakeholders, the more solid and sustainable the relationship and the stronger the mutual commitment. Building trust between the business and its stakeholders is of prime importance in this regard and this depends crucially on the degree of openness and commitment exhibited by the business.
- Stakeholder dialogue, is much more that a one-way information transfer; it must include feedback on stakeholders' comments and consideration of their views. This demands both a different attitude and new skills on the part of the business.

Stakeholder engagement is essential to the implementation of CSR, and it is important for the business to consider all the wishes and needs of groups or individuals who are in a position to affect its ability to attain goals, or will themselves be affected by the business's activities. Of course, it will be impossible to satisfy all their needs and expectations, so achieving a balance is of utmost importance.

Organizing structure

Being a good corporate citizen entails more than paying attention to external affairs; it must be intrinsic to every facet of the business. Holistic CSR requires the external activities of the business to be guided by its internal structures, but all too often those structures and the business' patterns of behaviour are insufficiently examined. CSR is therefore best viewed not as a programme of activities but as a holistic organizational system. This requires the distribution of CSR-related responsibilities throughout the business, plus rules and procedures for making decisions on corporate affairs, a structure for corporate objectives and the means to attain these objectives and monitor performance.

Embedding CSR in the business cannot be done unless the employees are convinced of its necessity. To this end leaders have to act as formulators, communicators and custodians of the corporate values. The introduction of CSR results in many changes to the business's operating culture, including increased employee interaction and new roles, responsibilities and communication flows. The formulation of a mission statement and a strategy to encourage common values must take account of the specific working practices in the various units and avoid causing any conflict between them. A culture of commitment to enhance the integration of CSR then has to be developed.

An business that continuously interacts with stakeholders in its value chain and the society of which it is part needs to have a balanced range of CSR activities in place. This requires an organizational structure, internal coordination and means of communication between people and departments that may not have existed before. There is no one right way of organizing an internal structure for CSR, as this depends on the particular environment in which the business operates and its own identity.

Organizing accountability

The final factor in the development of a socially responsible business is accountability: all aspects of the business, including procedures, rules and processes, must be examined to determine whether they help or hinder the business's ability to account for its activities and improve its performance. Accountability is a way of showing the extent to which the business is meeting its declared CSR goals and taking account of the social, environmental and financial consequences of its operations. A wide range of initiatives have emerged to regulate performance, ensure compliance with standards and establish a system of accountability and comparability in the field in CSR. For example, the Global Reporting Initiative offers a common reporting tool that facilitates comparability and transparency among the participating companies and institutions. The SA 8000, the AA 1000 series and related ISO principles on the environment are aimed at ensuring that businesses adhere to higher standards than is usual in the global arena.

Monitoring and reporting systems are necessary to track how businesses are progressing with CSR. They are expected to inform all their stakeholders about their CSR performance by regularly issuing honest and detailed reports. This also stimulates stakeholder engagement and ultimately creates support for and commitment to CSR initiatives.

The implementation of CSR

As we have consistently stressed it is essential to embed CSR in all aspects of the organization. This should be directed by its specific business strategy. CSR can only be viewed as properly embedded if it is resulting in all-round added value. Based on this perspective we have developed an integrated management model to help managers to shape CSR in their businesses. The associated concepts, indicators and content are shown in Table 15.1.

Table 15.1 Organizing corporate social responsibility

	Indicators	*Content*
Organizing identity	Mission	Statement of the business's mission with regard to its contribution to CSR
	Vision	Statement of the business's vision and strategy in respect of CSR
	Values	Statement of the business's values that relate to CSR
Organizing transactions	Stakeholder engagement	Description of basis for identifying and selecting major stakeholders; description of measures to increase commitment and build trust between the business and its stakeholders; description of stakeholder dialogue and feedback processes
Organizing structure	Corporate governance	Specification of the distribution of rights and responsibilities among the various participants in the corporation, and the rules and procedures for making decisions on CSR matters
	Leadership	Description of the drivers of CSR and the role of its leaders
	Culture	Description of the commitment to CSR-related issues throughout the business
Organizing accountability	External and internal	Description of aspects of the governance system that help or hinder the business's ability to account for its CSR activities

A key issue that remains is the integration of CSR into the business proposition and overall strategy of the business, and then extending it to day-to-day operations. In the words of Sir Geoffrey Chandler (*The Economist*, 2005):

> The responsibility of the company to society is not about benevolence, philanthropy or solving the problems of the world, but about conducting its business profitably in a way which matches the values of contemporary society in its treatment of its employees and the physical and social environment wherever it operates. Certainly, a company whose practices are based on 'ordinary decency' will thrive, but this attractively naïve concept is unlikely to be helpful to those who actually have to manage in the many countries today characterized by unrepresentative government, corruption, discrimination, violence and human rights violations. Companies are learning the hard way that their hugely increased scope and influence require ... recognition that without forethought and principles they can and do exacerbate problems.

Conclusions

This book has juggled with a diversity of issues, themes, notions and sometimes rather vague theories. It is clear that the core issue in the present debate is the role, function and responsibilities of the business enterprise. CSR is a truly sensitizing concept, both in itself and in its implementation. Theories and practice are in the midst of a process of discovery. Repositioning the business enterprise in contemporary society is not a task that can be accomplished overnight, and we are witnessing a multitude of attempts to grasp the true meaning of CSR. What the real impact of these efforts will be remains to be seen. In the end, true implementation means translating the contextual meaning of CSR into the business proposition. This means reconsidering present business strategies and practices, but for many modern businesses addressing the newly imposed responsibilities involves venturing into unknown territory. We consider it to be a rewarding trip. When 'the talk starts to walk' then corporate social responsibility will reveal its long-term value to the business and society as a whole.

Index